SOMERLED

AND THE EMERGENCE OF GAELIC SCOTLAND

For M.J.H.R.
with gratitude

SOMERLED

AND THE EMERGENCE OF GAELIC SCOTLAND

John Marsden

TUCKWELL PRESS

First published in Great Britain in 2000 by
Tuckwell Press
The Mill House
Phantassie
East Linton
East Lothian EH40 3DG
Scotland

ISBN 1 86232 101 9

British Library Cataloguing in Publication Data

A catalogue record for this book is available
on request from the British Library

Typeset by Hewer Text Ltd, Edinburgh
Printed and bound by Creative Print & Design, Ebbw Vale, Wales

CONTENTS

List of Illustrations vi

Acknowledgements vii

Preface viii

Abbreviations xi

Map xii

1 *Gall-Gaedhil*

CELTIC SCOTLAND & THE NORSE IMPACT 1

2 *'Gillebride's son'*

THE EMERGENCE OF SOMERLED 23

3 *'In wicked rebellion against his natural lord'*

GAELDOM'S CHALLENGE TO THE CANMORE KINGS 47

4 *'The ruin of the kingdom of the Isles'*

SOMERLED'S WAR ON THE KINGDOM OF MAN 69

5 *'As good a right to the lands . . .'*

INVASION OF THE CLYDE & DEATH AT RENFREW 93

6 *'Icollumkill'*

THE HOUSE OF SOMERLED & THE CHURCH ON IONA 115

7 *Gàidhealtachd*

THE LONG SHADOWS OF SOMHAIRLE MOR 135

Notes & References 145

Genealogies 161

Bibliography 167

Index 173

ILLUSTRATIONS

1. The 'Lewis Chessmen'
2. Page from the *Chronicle of Man*
3. Page from the *History of the MacDonalds*
4. Reconstruction of a sixteen-oar West Highland galley
5. The seal of Somerled's great-grandson Angus Mor
6. Drawing of the galley motif on the Great Seal of the Isle of Islay
7. Malcolm IV with his grandfather David I
8. St Oran's Chapel on Iona
9. Saddell Abbey, Kintyre
10. Ruins on the islets in the loch at Finlaggan

ACKNOWLEDGEMENTS

No book such as this would be possible without access to the work of generations of other writers, from the chroniclers and annalists who set down its raw material of documentary record to the modern historians who have applied themselves to its interpretation. My debt of gratitude to them all is acknowledged either in the main text or in accompanying notes and references. Access to that great wealth of scholarship, however, is quite another matter for an author working so far distant from the resources of national libraries and I am enormously grateful to the staff at the Stornoway headquarters of Western Isles Libraries for their unfailing assistance with my research.

A note of gratitude is also due to John Gregory, a friend and colleague of long-standing who came to my aid once again in seeking out and translating the more obscure Durham sources. Finally the customary, but nonetheless sincere, word of thanks to my publisher, John Tuckwell, not only for his reassuring interest in this project but also for his forbearance with its author beset by various tribulations.

JM

PREFACE

If only in deference to the time-honoured concern of the Gael with kinship and lineage, I feel obliged to explain at the outset why a northern English author with no claim to Clan Donald ancestry, nor indeed to any trace of Scots descent, should take it upon himself to write a book about Somerled, the twelfth-century forebear of the later medieval Lords of the Isles and the warlord traditionally accredited with having first reclaimed the west Highlands and Hebrides from Norse domination.

I'm sure that I must have known Somerled's name, and at least something of his stature, for the most part of the four decades I've had any sort of interest in Scotland's past, but it was only six or seven years ago that some time spent on Islay prompted a more serious curiosity about the man, which led me to seek out a book on the historical Somerled and eventually to the discovery that there wasn't one. Other than an unashamedly fictional treatment by Nigel Tranter, I have failed to find a reference to any book-length account of Somerled in or out of print and it seemed that no such volume had seen the light of a publication day. Which is not to say that there hasn't been a great deal written about him because Somerled has been held in the highest honour by all historians of the Clan Donald and the Lordship of the Isles, just as he has been afforded varying weights of consideration, or at the very least some mention, by almost every other writer, lay and learned alike, who has had occasion to touch on the medieval history of Argyll and the Hebrides. Yet not one of those authors has extended an account of Somerled's life and times beyond the length of a single chapter.

The reason for what does seem a somewhat surprising gap in the literature is usually said to be the shortage of material and, while I have never been fully persuaded by that explanation, it is certainly true that Somerled is mentioned by barely a dozen entries in the closely contemporary chronicles and annals which make up the historian's 'primary sources'. Nonetheless, it is also true that the same sources bear full testimony to his impressive political stature – styling him '*regulus* [usually translated as "kinglet"] of Argyll' and, in one case, 'king of the Hebrides and Kintyre' – in their notices of his rebellion of 1153 in support of the Mac Heth claim to the kingship of Scots, his war on the kingdom of Man in the later 1150s and his death in 1164 at the head of an invasion of the Clyde. Because none of those entries bears directly on Somerled's activities prior to the last eleven years of his life, the principal source of information as to his background, earlier career and rise to power is that preserved in Clan Donald tradition whose evidence, while sometimes offered up without question as genuine history by writers for a popular readership, is usually discounted as unreliable by all but a few academic historians. In so predominantly oral a culture as that of Gaelic Scotland, however, the recollection of the past preserved in tradition cannot be discarded without some investigation as to its provenance and antiquity, and especially in the case of Somerled where evidence of any kind is in such short supply and where the Clan Donald historians' sympathy for an esteemed ancestor can supply a measure of counter-weight to the almost universal hostility shown by the more formal historical record.

It still cannot be denied that a 'cradle-to-grave' biography of Somerled lies entirely beyond the bounds of possibility – if only because his date of birth is nowhere recorded and his place of burial is claimed for two quite separate locations by different sources of Clan Donald tradition – but to assemble and evaluate the full spectrum of evidence for his life and times would certainly overreach the bounds of even the longest single chapter, while to place that material into its cultural, as well as historical, context might well extend to a book of at least moderate length. Just such a volume, attempting the fullest possible portrait of Somerled as an historical personality in his own right rather than as a prologue to the subsequent history of the Lordship, was what I had been looking for and if I really did want a copy, then perhaps I should attempt to research and write it myself.

Hence *Somerled and the emergence of Gaelic Scotland* – and that choice of title might need its own word of explanation because it points quite intentionally to the perspective on the subject running throughout the following pages.

It is a perspective which must have been influenced, in at least some degree, by having made my home in recent years on the Isle of Lewis, the location of most concentrated Norse settlement in the Hebrides a thousand years ago and today the capital stronghold of Scotland's *Gàidhealtachd.* Working on this book in this place – where I look out from my desk towards hills whose old Norse names are only thinly veiled by their more recent Gaelic spelling – can only have encouraged the recognition of how virtually everything that is known of or has been claimed for Somerled, even the most obviously apocryphal anecdotes found in the most doubtful sources, reflects some aspect of the characteristic fusion of Norse and Celt which binds the cultural roots of Gaeldom.

That same fusion, occurring at every turn in the search for Somerled, underwrites the proposal of what I have come to appreciate as his wider importance – beyond that of the founding dynast of the Lordship of the Isles or the forebear of the Clan Donald and its related kindreds – as the one figure who, more than any other, represents the first fully-fledged emergence of the medieval Celtic-Scandinavian cultural province from which modern Gaelic Scotland is ultimately descended.

Just a concluding note of definition as regards the naming of names. I have tried wherever possible to indicate regions of Scotland in terms of modern administrative districts, but it should be said that the medieval province of Argyll extended much further north on the western mainland, even into what is now Wester Ross, than does the modern county of Argyll.

The Hebrides indicates the whole archipelago from Lewis to Islay (and, in medieval times, including Rathlin) as also does 'the Isles', a term I have used in especially political, as distinct from purely geographical, contexts. The Inner Hebrides refers to those islands from Mull southward, while those to the north of Skye, sometimes called the 'Outer Hebrides', I have referred to by their modern administrative name of the Western Isles. Skye fits conveniently into neither group and so is usually referred to by its individual island name.

Personal names I have rendered in forms corresponding as closely as possible to their Norse or Gaelic originals but using spellings which will not demand of the reader any great familiarity with the original languages. Finally, I should mention that the term 'viking' is applied here, in the strict sense of the Old Norse *vikingr*, to mean 'sea-raider'.

JM 1999

ABBREVIATIONS

ed.	edited by
ESSH	A. O. Anderson, *Early Sources of Scottish History*
PSAS	*Proceedings of the Society of Antiquaries of Scotland*
RCAHMS	Royal Commission on the Ancient and Historical Monuments of Scotland
rep.	reprinted edition
rev.	revised edition
SAEC	A. O. Anderson, *Scottish Annals from English Chroniclers*
SHR	*Scottish Historical Review*
TGSI	*Transactions of the Gaelic Society of Inverness*
trs.	translated by

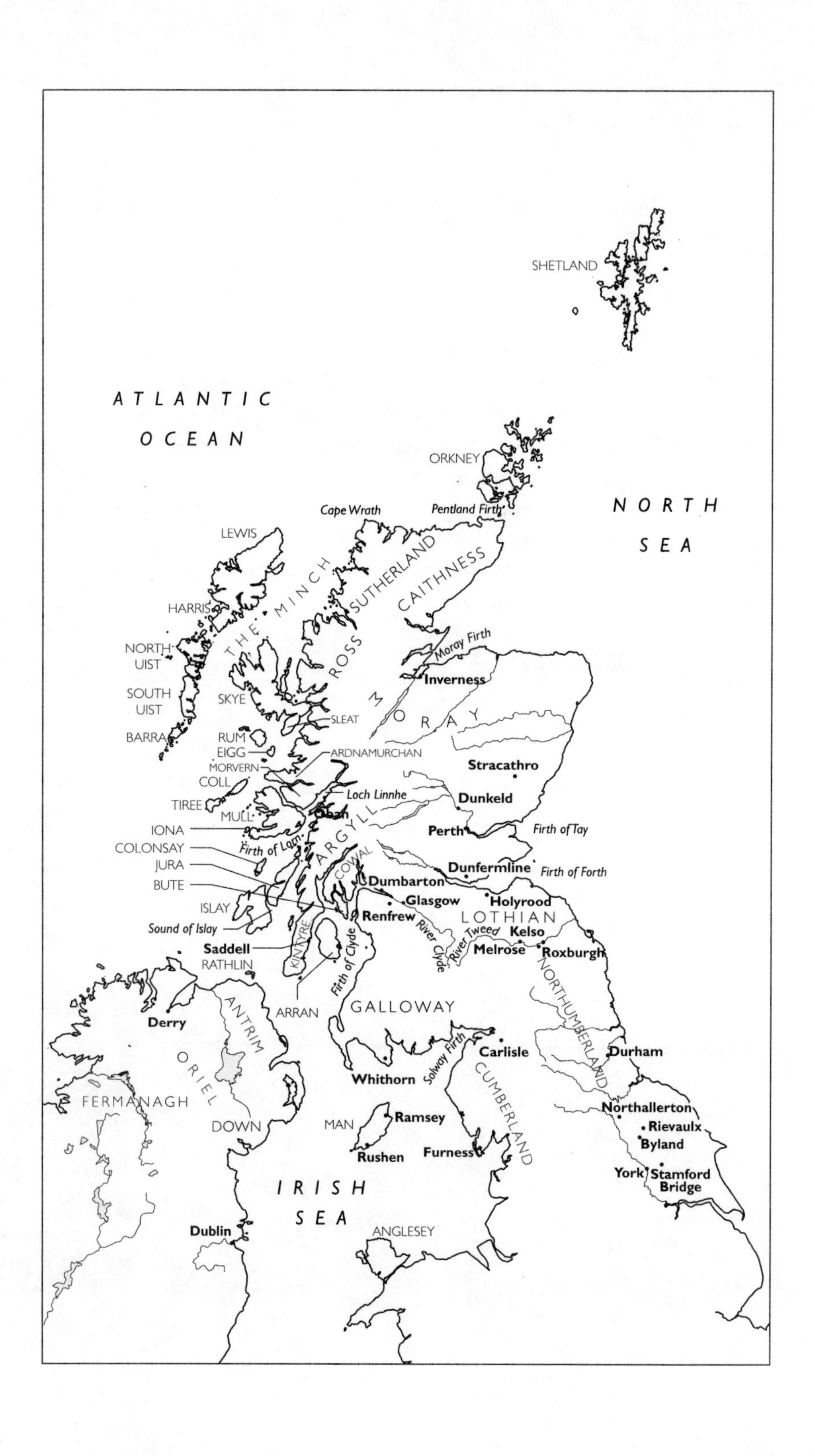
SHETLAND
ATLANTIC
OCEAN
ORKNEY
Cape Wrath
Pentland Firth
NORTH
SEA
LEWIS
HARRIS
NORTH
UIST
SOUTH
UIST
BARRA
THE MINCH
SUTHERLAND
CAITHNESS
ROSS
Moray Firth
Inverness
SKYE
SLEAT
MORAY
RUM
EIGG
ARDNAMURCHAN
MORVERN
COLL
Stracathro
Loch Linnhe
Dunkeld
TIREE
MULL
Oban
ARGYLL
Perth
Firth of Tay
IONA
COLONSAY
Firth of Lorn
JURA
COWAL
Dunfermline
Firth of Forth
BUTE
Dumbarton
Glasgow
Holyrood
ISLAY
Renfrew
LOTHIAN
Sound of Islay
KINTYRE
River Clyde
River Tweed
Kelso
Saddell
Melrose
Roxburgh
RATHLIN
Firth of Clyde
NORTHUMBERLAND
ARRAN
GALLOWAY
Derry
ANTRIM
Carlisle
Durham
ORIEL
Solway Firth
Whithorn
CUMBERLAND
FERMANAGH
Northallerton
MAN
Ramsey
Rievaulx
DOWN
Byland
Rushen
Furness
York
Stamford
Bridge
IRISH
SEA
Dublin
ANGLESEY

1

GALL-GAEDHIL

CELTIC SCOTLAND & THE NORSE IMPACT

Vastatio omnium insularum Britanniae a gentilibus. 'The devastation of all the isles of Britain by the heathens' was the form of words chosen by a monastic scribe, writing in the last years of the eighth century and almost certainly on Iona, to describe the most significant occurrence of the year AD 794.[1]

The events indicated by that annal entry – occurring as it does in the year after the first-recorded viking raid on the British Isles fell upon the Northumbrian monastery of Lindisfarne – are understood to have been a similar onslaught by a fleet of Norse sea-raiders operating out of a forward base in Orkney or Shetland and rounding Cape Wrath to break loose among the Outer Hebrides. In the light of that interpretation, those half-dozen words of Latin assume a strategic significance as the earliest record of the Scandinavian impact on the Celtic west of the British Isles, an impact which was to play a decisive role in the passage of Scotland's peoples through the following centuries.

The text of the annal entry can also be shown to contain its own fragment of intrinsic evidence for the disposition of those peoples and their cultures in what can still be recognised at the end of the eighth century as 'Celtic Scotland', and it lies in the phrase *insularum Britanniae* where the annalist's *Britannia* represents his Latin equivalent of the Irish proper noun *Alba.* Although later applied specifically to the territory of what is now Scotland – as indeed it still is in its modern Scottish Gaelic usage – *Alba* was originally the Irish name for the British mainland together with its island fringe as distinct from the island of Ireland itself. Since the end of the fifth century AD, however, when the royal house of Dalriada in Antrim moved across the North Channel to establish itself in the west of Scotland, Argyll and the Inner Hebrides had been considered as an extension of Ireland. Consequently the annalist's reference to the 'isles of Britain' can be taken to indicate those of the Hebridean archipelago to the north of Skye – effectively those now known as the Western Isles – which lay beyond the bounds of Irish settlement and would thus have been considered as islands pertaining to mainland Britain.

While the historical record places the beginning of this Irish presence in Scotland at a date around 498, Fergus Mor mac Erc of Dalriada in Ireland having crossed to Scotland with his royal kindred some three years before his death entered in the annals at 501,[2] there is no shortage of credibly historical evidence from Irish tradition to indicate a sequence of similar migrations from Ireland to Alba having taken place from at least as early as the third century AD. Perhaps the foremost example is that of Cairbre Riada, who is said to have been driven out of Munster by famine in the late third century and to have claimed for his people a new territory in the north of Ireland, named for him as *Dalriada* or 'Riada's share'. An extension of the legend has Cairbre moving on yet again, this time over the Irish Sea to establish a further dominion in the Cowal peninsula on the north bank of the Clyde, and while that story is preserved in no Irish manuscript older than the late fourteenth century, it was evidently current at least six hundred years earlier when it was known to the northern English historian Bede writing sometime before the year 731.[3]

Another similar legend – and one which will merit further attention here – is set in the early fourth century and preserved in its most ancient form in two important Irish manuscript collections dating from the eleventh and twelfth centuries.[4] It tells the story of the 'Three Collas', sons of an Irish king and the daughter of a nobleman of *Hí* (one form of the Middle Irish name for Iona), who fled Ireland to escape vengeance for having slain a king in battle and found sanctuary with their mother's people in the west of Scotland. After some years of exile they were invited back to their homeland by the son of the king they had slain and fought as his allies to conquer great tracts of Ulster. Two of the three were afterwards content to settle in the north of Ireland, but the eldest brother, Colla Uais ('Colla the Noble'), chose otherwise and returned to his 'great lands on the mainland and in the isles of Alba'. There are numerous other stories on similar themes found in Irish tradition and so many of them as to indicate some extent of Irish settlement having been long established in Scotland by the time Fergus Mor crossed over from Antrim to Argyll.

An especially informative source of evidence for the earlier centuries of Dalriada in Scotland, the tract known as the *Senchus fer nAlban* ('History of the Men of Alba') and preserving a tenth-century text which has been shown to derive from an original of the mid-seventh century, identifies the principal kindreds of the kingdom as the *Cenél Oengusa, Cenél Loairn,* and *Cenél Gabrain.* The last named of these three *cenéla* – directly descended from Fergus Mor but named for his grandson Gabran – represented the ruling house of Dalriada throughout the sixth and seventh centuries, while the other two kindreds are said by the *Senchus* to have been descended from Fergus' brothers, Oengus and Loarn. Such a relationship certainly owes much more to the 'three brothers' formula occurring so often in Irish tradition than to the historical reality of sixth-century Scotland and is most plausibly interpreted as the kindreds of Oengus and Loarn representing earlier Irish settlements in Argyll who accepted Fergus and his successors as their over-kings by right of their royal status in Ireland.

Over a period of some two or more centuries, then, these Irish – in fact, of course, the original 'Scots', a name deriving from the Latin *Scoti* identifying the Irish – had established themselves alongside the Britons and the Picts as the latest-arriving of the Celtic peoples occupying north Britain.

At which point it might be appropriate to attempt a definition of the term 'Celtic' as it is applied here, especially in view of the casually extravagant use – and misuse – of the word in recent times. It is a term which is strictly meaningful only as a cultural or, still more specifically, a linguistic identity and a Celt is to be properly defined as a person who spoke a Celtic tongue. Such languages emerged out of the great Indo-European cultural influx which crossed continental Europe in the course of, or possibly even before, the first millennium BC, so that all parts of the British Isles are thought to have been occupied by Celtic-speaking peoples when the Romans arrived. By which time the prehistoric Celtic mother tongue had already diversified into two descendant forms: the 'P-Celtic' or *Brythonic* of mainland Britain which is, of course, the ancestral form of the Welsh language and the 'Q-Celtic' or *Goidelic* of Celtic Ireland from which Irish, Manx and Scottish Gaelic are descended.[5]

Both forms of Celtic tongue had been long established in north Britain by the end of the eighth century since the *Goidelic* had penetrated the western seaboard with the Irish settlement of Argyll, a place-name from the Middle Irish *Airer Gáidel* (later *Oirer Ghàidheal*) translated as 'coastland of the Gael'.[6] *Brythonic* was the language of those tribes collectively known as the 'North Britons' whose culture cannot have been unaffected by their close proximity to the northern frontier of Roman Britain but appears to have reverted to something of its older tribal form after the leaving of the legions. Their territories, extending in the fifth century from the Clyde and Forth down through the Lothians and over what are now the northernmost counties of England, fell early victim to the expansion of the Northumbrian Angles who overran all the land as far north as the Forth and the Solway from the sixth and into the eighth century, leaving just the kingdom of Strathclyde centred on its capital fortress of Dumbarton Rock as the last enclave of the North Britons.

Just about everything that is known of the people remembered as the 'Picts' derives from evidence set down by others who came into contact with them, because there is no Pictish documentary record of their own making. Even the name 'Pict' was of Latin devising, first appearing as *Picti* at the end of the third century AD, and assuredly not the name by which they called themselves. What is known of their language relies almost entirely on place-name elements and personal names preserved in king-lists set down centuries after the Picts disappeared from history, but it has been recognised as a form of P-Celtic which may also have incorporated elements surviving from the pre-Celtic tongues of Scotland. It might then be reasonable to suggest Pictish culture as that of a Celtic warrior aristocracy fused with survivals from prehistoric antiquity, a proposal which would well correspond to the vast and often remote extent of north Britain which they occupied in the historical period, a territory extending over the greater part of the Scottish mainland east of Argyll and north of the Forth, including the islands of Orkney and probably also those of the Outer Hebrides. By the last quarter of the seventh century, when they threw off Northumbrian overlordship at the battle of Nechtansmere, their centre of power had evidently settled around what is now the region of Tayside where it was to emerge in the eighth century as the pre-eminent Pictish kingdom of

Fortriu, whose kings were effectively high-kings of Picts but whose royal house was already showing signs of influence and infiltration from the Scotic west before 790.

If the foregoing paragraphs have been able to supply a summary sketch-map of the disposition of peoples and cultures in north Britain in the last decade of the eighth century, then they will have shown how, despite the short-lived intrusion of Roman and Northumbrian Angle ambitions, the mainland and islands beyond the Forth-Clyde line could still justify description as 'Celtic Scotland'. Three hundred years later no such description would be really meaningful and, indeed, all three of those Celtic peoples were to be dramatically affected, either directly or at an extension, in the course of the following century by the Scandinavian impact first noticed by the annalist at 794.

The stronghold of the North Britons on Dumbarton Rock fell to a long siege by the northmen in 871, leaving it ripe for annexation by the newly ascendant kingdom of the Scots when its old Britonic aristocracy were driven out to find their last sanctuary in Wales. Some thirty years earlier the royal house of Fortriu had been cut down in battle by a viking warband, the Picts soon afterwards disappearing from the historical record and the man recognised by the annalist as 'king of the Picts' now remembered as the first of the mac Alpin dynasty of kings of Scots.[7] But it was in the island groups around Scotland's northern and western edge where the Scandinavian – or, more specifically, Norse – impact was first delivered that it was to leave its most transforming and enduring impression.

What is known of the northern isles of Orkney and Shetland before the coming of the northmen relies almost entirely upon the evidence of archaeology, by reason of their having been noticed with such extreme rarity in the historical record of earlier centuries, but when they do enter more fully into the light of history by the tenth century it is in the form of the Norse *jarldom* of *Orkneyjar* comprising a wholly Scandinavian province. When the findings of the archaeologist are taken together with the evidence of tradition preserved in the *Orkneyinga Saga* set down in Iceland sometime around the year 1200, it would seem that the northern isles were already known to the Norse some time before the end of the eighth century when they were used by them as forward bases for viking expeditions thrusting southward through the Hebrides towards Ireland.

Such, then, would have been the course taken by the sea-raiders in the year following their onslaught on the Western Isles when they were first recorded off the coast of Ireland and the Irish annals notice their attacks on the islands of Skye and Iona in the Hebrides, Rathlin off the coast of Antrim, Inishmurray in Donegal Bay and Inishbofin off the south-west coast of Mayo. The specific annal references to pillaging, burning and 'shrines . . . broken and plundered' correspond to all the islands named being sites of monasteries, although the important foundation at Applecross on the mainland facing Skye was probably the place to which the annalist refers.[8] Monasteries were central to the organisation of the ancient Irish church, many of them richly endowed, all of them entirely undefended, and those on islands or coastal locations offering natural prey placed directly in the path of pagan sea-raiders.

The Irish annal record is dominated through most of the next century by notices of the great monasteries of Ireland plundered time and again by the northmen moving in from the coast to penetrate the Irish mainland, and yet those same annals fall far short of their former value as a record of Scottish history within little more than a decade of the first viking onslaught. Before the second quarter of the ninth century, such annal entries as do bear on events in Scotland – and in the west Highlands and the Hebrides especially – are written exclusively from the viewpoint of the Irish mainland, thus drastically diminishing the value of Irish annals as sources of Scottish history. This sudden shortfall in the documentary record is quite certainly bound up with the impact of the viking raids on the Irish church in Scotland and specifically with events overtaking the monastery on Iona.

The Hebridean archipelago offered a profusion of islands ideally suited to the offshore monastic foundations so characteristic of the ancient Irish church, and of first eminence amongst them was the monastery founded by Columba on Iona shortly after his arrival in Scotland in 563. Although it had suffered some loss of the influence it had enjoyed in Pictland and Northumbria through the century following Columba's death in 597, Iona – or *Í-Columcille* as it is called by the Irish and Gaelic sources – still stood in the eighth century at the head of the Columban *paruchia* (or confederation of monasteries) extending down to Durrow in the Irish midlands and served also as the principal port for the monastic seafaring in search of island retreats out into the North Atlantic at least as far as Iceland. Thus informed by contacts throughout and beyond the Celtic west and recognised as a major centre of learning with a great library and accomplished scriptorium, Iona was the natural source of Scottish historical record. The monastery is believed to have been compiling such a record by the middle of the eighth century and it must have been from some surviving form or fragment of this long since lost 'Iona Chronicle' that the later medieval Irish annalists derived their richly informed account of events in Scotland from the early period of the kingdom of Dalriada in Argyll up to the time of the first viking raids three hundred years later. Further continuation of that chronicle might be counted, then, as one of the earliest and most important casualties of the Norse impact – as indeed was the eminent monastic foundation that produced it.

After the first 'devastation' of 795, the annals record Iona having been attacked again and again by the northmen when they enter its being burned in 802 and suffering the slaughter of sixty-eight of its community four years later. By which time it would appear that preparations were already underway for the evacuation of the island, and at the year 807 the annalist enters: 'Cellach, abbot of Ia-Columcille, came to Ireland after the slaying of his people by the *lochlannaibh* [Norse]; and the monastery of Columcille was constructed by him at Kells of Meath'.[9] Some monastic presence is known to have been maintained on Iona, almost certainly to guard the shrine of its founding saint which remained on the island for another forty years, and Cellach himself retired there to die after resigning his abbacy, but his successors in that office were all to be abbots of the new monastery at Kells which thenceforth assumed Iona's former status as principal church of the Columban *paruchia*. So it must have been that the Irish annals were cut off from their principal Scottish-based source of record and future generations of historians consequently deprived of its contemporary chronicle of events from the earliest and most significant region of the Norse impact on Celtic Scotland.

Which is not to say that the Irish annals are no longer of any value for Scottish history after 807, because they can still throw valuable sidelights from an Irish perspective on what is known from other sources to have been extensive Scandinavian penetration and settlement of Scotland's western seaboard through the ninth and tenth centuries. Indeed, there are occasions when the annal record of events in Ireland provides invaluable correspondences to references found in the medieval Icelandic saga histories of Norse kindreds with Hebridean connections, but the overwhelming weight of evidence for the establishment of the northmen in the isles is preserved in the multitude of place-names of Norse origin peppered all the way down the map of the Hebrides and bearing full testimony to their recognition by the Irish sources as the *Innsegall* or 'islands of the foreigners'.

The Scandinavian origin of so many names of mountains, isles and headlands, immediately recognisable by the Gaelicised forms of the Norse endings *-fjall*, *-ey* and *-nes* respectively, indicates topographical features of vital importance for navigation having been named for just that reason by seafarers and corresponding to the location of the Hebrides along the viking sea-route to Ireland. It is that location which suggests the initial Norse foothold in the Western Isles having been in the form of forward bases for sea-raiding further south, very much as the saga evidence claims to have been the case in Orkney. The historian Barbara Crawford has suggested that 'the existence of headland dykes in some of the Orkney islands can be interpreted as indicating that a process of 'ness-taking' (Old Norse: *nes-nám*) was a necessary preliminary to permanent conquest',[10] and the same was surely the case soon afterwards in the northernmost Hebrides. Indeed, their jagged Atlantic shorelines swathed with curving beaches and indented with deep sea lochs were so well suited to landing, launching and sheltering longships as to offer a natural pirate coast to the northmen.

Raiding bases were also the initial form of Norse land-taking in Ireland, where longship havens on the coast and in the estuaries became established as permanent bases for regular plundering expeditions into the hinterland, afterwards evolving into defended trading towns such as Waterford, Limerick and, the most important of them all by reason of its far-reaching political influence, Dublin. While these secular urban centres represented a revolutionary innovation in what had formerly been an exclusively rural society, even as effectively independent 'kingdoms' they still occupied only a tiny fraction of the Irish land-mass and yet contained within it the entire Scandinavian settlement of Ireland. For all the apparent similarity of its earliest phase, the Norse presence in the Hebrides developed along quite different lines as is indicated by so very many place-names with endings derived from original Norse suffixes *-stadr* and *-bolstadr* – both terms meaning 'farm' or 'homestead' and taken to indicate the two earliest phases of Scandinavian settlement – which confirm a much larger population permanently established as farmers, and certainly also as fishermen, throughout all the islands.[11]

So the forward bases seized by the sea-raiders can be said to have opened the way into the Western Isles and further south through the Hebrides for their land-seeking compatriots attracted by terrain bearing so familiar a resemblance to much of their homeland's western coast-line, surrounded by similarly rich fishing grounds and yet offering a greater agricultural potential, not least because livestock could be outwintered as was very rarely possible in Norway. Which is not, by any means, to suggest that settled agriculture and sea-raiding were mutually exclusive activities, especially in the Western Isles where viking plunder would have supplied a useful, even necessary, supplement to what must have been little better than subsistence farming. The *Orkneyinga Saga* account of the latter-day viking Svein Asleifsson tells how his annual round of activities included two raiding expeditions to the Hebrides, Ireland and Man, the first launched in the spring after the seed had been sown and the second in the autumn after the harvest was in. Even though Svein flourished in the mid-twelfth century, his custom was probably much the same as that followed by the Hebridean Norse some three hundred years earlier and, because a viking expedition required the assembly of a capable fighting crew, sea-raiding would have formed an early, if not the first, basis of social organisation in the *Innsegall* if the humbler peasant farming families supplied the crewmen – either as willing recruits or under some form of military obligation – aboard longships owned and commanded by the wealthier warrior nobility.

While all the islands in the Hebridean chain have some examples of Norse place-names and name-forms,[12] the pattern of distribution shows their steady decrease from north to south in proportion to names of more ancient Gaelic origin which has been taken to reflect a corresponding pattern in the concentration of Scandinavian settlement. On the most northerly Hebridean island of Lewis, recognised by one authority as 'more Norse than any other part of the *Gàidhealtachd* [and] perhaps completely Norse-speaking for a limited period',[13] 79% of settlement names have been identified as wholly Norse in origin and a further 9% as containing Norse elements, while no purely Gaelic place-name has been proven to be earlier in origin than its Scandinavian neighbours. At the southern extremity of the Hebrides, however, just some 30% of settlement names on Islay are thought to be of Norse origin, and this on an island known from the documentary sources to have been especially favoured by the Norse of Man and of Dublin.

While the evidence for the past supplied by interpretation of surviving place-names cannot be considered very much better than skeletal – and a much eroded and encrusted skeleton at that – its testimony to an impressive Norse presence throughout the Hebrides lies entirely beyond doubt. The sheer volume of originally Scandinavian settlement names found not only in the northern and western isles but scattered also on to the coastal mainland would correspond to a Norse population numbered in thousands before the end of the tenth century and raises the question of its relationship with the native communities settled there so long before the arrival of the northmen.

The repeated annal references to 'devastation' must be taken as evidence for the first raids in the Hebrides having been accompanied by the same extremes of violence associated with the viking onslaught elsewhere. Even if those raids were exclusively directed at monastic rather than secular targets, it is hardly possible to imagine the land-taking which followed in their wake having been accomplished without at least some instances of conflict, yet it still need not have involved the wholesale extermination, expulsion or enslavement of the native population and there is certainly no evidence that it did so. Even in the Western Isles where the place-name evidence suggests the most concentrated Norse settlement having entirely overwhelmed the host culture, such a process would have taken at least one, and probably more than one, generation. In the course of that time, over a period perhaps as long as fifty or sixty years, the location of the Hebrides along an increasingly important Norse sea-road linking Ireland with Norway by way of Scapa Flow would have brought their islanders into regular contact with the traffic of an expanding Scandinavian world. The Isle of Lewis, most especially, appears to have been drawn into the orbit of Orkney and is, in fact, the only Hebridean island mentioned by name in the *Orkneyinga Saga* where the others are known collectively as the *Sudreyjar* or the 'southern isles'. Over the same period of time it would be reasonable to suggest the native Celtic aristocracy of the Western Isles, cut off from the influence of the church on Iona and whatever remained of the overlordship of high-kings of Picts, adopting the language and custom associated with the wealth and prestige of Scandinavian sea-kings to thus become assimilated into the culture – and assuredly also by intermarriage into the kinship – of the Norse settlement.

Such a relationship would not have been so very different from that which had been developing since the later eighth century between the Pictish royal house of Fortriu and the Scotic kings of Dalriada. The political history of Dalriada is shown by the dislocated record preserved in the Irish annals to have been in successive states of turmoil since the end of the seventh century when the Cenel Loairn appears to have seized the kingship from the formerly ruling house of the Cenel Gabrain and held it through four decades until a high-king of Picts launched a devastating invasion of the west and inflicted a series of crushing defeats to force Dalriada into submission to the kingship of Fortriu. The Pictish ascendancy was only short-lived and in its wake a new generation of the Cenel Gabrain reclaimed sovereignty in Dalriada before striking eastward into Pictland. By the end of the eighth century and into the first decades of the ninth, Cenel Gabrain kings of Dalriada had re-emerged, by a combination of military conquest and marriage to Pictish queens, as the ruling dynasty in Fortriu surrounded by a thoroughly Gaelicised Picto-Scottish courtly culture. Thus the original Scots kingdom of Dalriada was reduced to the westernmost province of the Picto-Scottish kingdom of Fortriu and at just the time when the Norse impact was being felt along the 'coastland of the Gael'.

While it would not be true to say that the relocation of the Cenel Gabrain to Tayside had initially been a reaction to the viking onslaught in the west, the advancing pressure of the northmen can only have made life along the western seaboard increasingly uncomfortable and the prospect of greater security in the more fertile landscape of Tayside all the more attractive. So, too, the removal of the abbacy and community of Iona to Ireland after the raid of 806 must have been seen as the abandonment of the royal church of Dalriada's kings to the fury of the northmen and an omen of the darkest significance for the tide of the times in the west. For their rival kindred of the Cenel Loairn, however, whose territory is thought to have extended north of Oban over Morvern and even as far as Ardnamurchan, the Norse pressure would have been greater and so much so as to force their migration up the Great Glen into Moray where their descendants were to reappear by the beginning of the eleventh century as provincial rulers of formidable power.

Even so, when the *-bolstadr* forms of place-name, key indicators of Scandinavian settlement found on almost all the islands of the Inner Hebrides, are conspicuously absent from mid-Argyll and Lorn on the immediately adjacent western mainland, there is no decisive evidence for the old territorial power-base of the Dalriadic kings having been relinquished to the Norse land-taking. Indeed, and as has been suggested by an important study of Argyll's capital hillforts,[14] it would appear that 'Norse settlers were effectively repulsed from the heartland of Dalriada' and very probably also 'that a major role in the defence was played by the two strongholds of Dunadd [in mid-Argyll] and Dunollie [in Lorn]', especially when viking warbands generally avoided set-piece battlefield and siege warfare.

Relations between Norse and Gael in the orbit of the Inner Hebrides offshore from the mainland of Argyll would have developed, then, from a rather different starting point and thereafter along quite different lines from those further to the north, where a native Celtic population and its culture was effectively overwhelmed by the Scandinavian impact.

Such of Dalriada's Gaelic Scots nobility who remained in the west, while apparently successfully resisting settlement on their mainland territories, would still have been facing an escalating Norse presence in passage along the seaway and establishing itself on the islands lying, in almost every case, clearly visible just across the sound. Instances of conflict there surely must have been, even if on no greater scale than that of defence against a raiding band ready and able to devastate an island monastery but with little expectation of success or profit from an attack on a capital hillfort. The military organisation of Dalriada in the seventh century – when the levies set out in the *Senchus* would have enabled its king to muster a war-host of some two thousand fighting men – can only have been greatly decayed by the political disruption of the eighth century and, by the first decades of the ninth, the king of Dalriada was more likely to be found in residence at the court of Fortriu than at the edge of the western sea. Defence of the lands in the west, even as soon as the first quarter of the ninth century, would have been left in the hands of individual chieftains, ready to fight if needs be but finding themselves more often drawn into a cautious co-existence with not so greatly dissimilar warrior cultures in such close proximity.

Soon enough, then, the Gael of Dalriada would have found themselves not only in closer contact with the northmen in the isles but even sharing more common ground with them than with their kindred Celtic Scots on the banks of the Tay. Nor would difference in language appear to have presented any insuperable barrier between peoples speaking tongues of Indo-European origin and at roughly equivalent stages of development from ancient to modern forms. 'Norse and Gaelic cannot have seemed totally and incomprehensibly alien' – in the view of Kenneth H. Jackson, the eminent authority on Celtic languages and early history – when, for all the dissimilarities between vocabularies confirmed by the exchange of loanwords, 'they *thought* along the same lines'.[15] There would thus have been more than adequate foundation for a relationship developing over one or two generations which led naturally, if not inevitably, to the cultural exchanges already clearly discernible in the evidence of both Irish and Icelandic sources for the second half of the ninth century.

The first records of Norse converts to Christianity are found in the twelfth-century Icelandic sources where they can be identified among the kindreds migrating to Iceland in the 860s and the decades following. All of these converts had come to Iceland – as indeed had virtually all its early colonists – from, or by way of, the Norse settlements in the Hebrides where their new faith had been encountered and adopted; sailing aboard oceangoing craft built along the same innovative principles of design as those used on viking voyages and as would be the later medieval West Highland galleys; and accompanied on their migration by freed slaves or bond-servants of Celtic stock who very probably acted also as pilots along North Atlantic seaways first explored by Irish monks in hide-hulled curraghs some three hundred years earlier.

If the early Icelandic migration can thus be said to supply some of the first evidence of social and cultural exchanges between Norse and Gael in the western Highlands and islands, the principal channel of that interchange must have lain in intermarriage, formal or otherwise, which was bearing offspring of mixed blood a generation before the time of the first voyages to Iceland. Marriage of Scandinavian men, settled however permanently at so great a distance from their homeland, with women of native Celtic stock would suggest itself as the most likely early form of such arrangements, and sons of just such unions were undoubtedly numbered among the warriors identified as *gall-gaedhil* (or 'foreign [i.e. Scandinavian] Gaels') in the Irish annal record of the 850s, where they are found fighting in Munster against a Norse king of Dublin and in Tyrone against Irish kings of Ailech and Ossory. The mid-ninth century would not have been too soon for at least one generation of Norse-Gaelic parentage to have come of age for active military service, and indeed the first individually named example of such descent – a man worthy of consideration in some detail by reason of his further significance here – is placed into the historical record two decades earlier by the entry in the *Annals of the Four Masters* at 836:

> *Gofraidh mac Fearghus* [Gothfrith, son of Fergus], *toíseach Oirgiall*, went over to Alba to strengthen Dalriada at the bidding of Kenneth mac Alpin.

That name-form itself – combining the Scandinavian given name *Gothfrith* with a Gaelic patronymic – must be taken to indicate this son of a Scots or Irish Fergus having been born to a Norse mother. Such a partnership, first of all, represents the reverse of a Norseman settled west-over-sea taking a wife from amongst his Celtic neighbours, but there is archaeological evidence from graves excavated on islands of the Inner Hebrides for Norse women of higher social rank having 'belonged to the first generation of a group or family of settlers'.[16] Gothfrith's title, on the other hand, usually translated as 'chieftain [or lord] of Oriel' in the north of Ireland, calls for some closer investigation because the year 836 would represent an almost implausibly early date for a son of mixed parentage on the Irish mainland to have reached the maturity indicated by the annal entry, but when *tóiseach Oirgiall* is more exactly translated as 'a chieftain of the Airgialla' it can be shown to point more helpfully to Gothfrith's region of origin.

The *Airgialla* were a confederation of tribes who first appear in the fifth century as allies of the Ui Neill conquest of much of the ancient territory of Ulster and afterwards established through to the ninth century as the over-kingdom of Oriel extending from south-west of Lough Neagh northwards into Derry. There are two items of reliable evidence, however, to suggest some of the Airgialla having migrated from northern Ireland to Argyll and to have settled there in the region of Lorn before the mid-seventh century. The survey of military levies in Dalriada at that time, as set down in the *Senchus*, assesses the fighting strength of the Cenel Loairn at 'seven hundred men; but the seventh hundred is from the Airgialla', which would well correspond to the annal entry at 727 which specifies 'men of the Airgialla' having been slain in a battle fought between the Cenel Loairn and Cenel Gabrain. Gothfrith's grandfather is named in the king-lists of Oriel, but his father is not, which suggests the possibility of Fergus having been a younger son who did not succeed to the kingship in Ireland but may have been compensated with some lesser rank, even as a sub-king or chieftain over the settlement of Airgialla in Lorn. If the departure of the Cenel Loairn from Argyll to Moray was indeed prompted by the encroaching Norse presence, then their subordinate aristocracy, probably including among them a chieftain of the Airgialla, would have been left to come to some accommodation with the northmen. A political marriage would have been fully typical of just such an arrangement in ninth-century Scotland and would well explain both why and where a prince of the royal house of Oriel came to take a Norse wife who bore him a son recognised as a *tóiseach Oirgiall* by the year 836.

In which year, then, on the evidence of the Four Masters,[17] 'Gothfrith mac Fergus went over to Alba [presumably, but not necessarily, from Ireland] . . . at the bidding of Kenneth mac Alpin'. The advent and ascendancy of Kenneth mac Alpin is a subject of great complexity, heavily hung with question marks and lying largely outwith the scope of these pages, but there are fragments of evidence implicating the northmen in his rise to power which do have some especial bearing here. Whatever the truth of Kenneth's claim to descent from the royal line of the Cenel Gabrain, it was sufficiently impressive to allow his succession to the kingship of Dalriada around 840. Two years later his name is entered in the Pictish king-lists, and by 848 he had somehow eliminated all rival claimants to establish himself and his successors over the following centuries in effective high-kingship of Picts and Scots and as the founding dynasty of the medieval Scottish nation.

Nowhere in the sources, however, is there further detail of whatever political relationship might have underwritten the apparent alliance between Kenneth and Gothfrith mac Fergus, although it has been suggested, in view of the seventh-century fighting strengths set out in the *Senchus*, that the king of Dalriada might still have been owed some military obligation by the Airgialla in Argyll or in northern Ireland where their north-eastern frontier bordered closely upon the original Irish territory of Dalriada. The difficulty encountered by such a suggestion is the fact that Gothfrith 'went over to Alba . . . at the bidding of Kenneth' some four years (assuming the Four Masters' date is correct) before that same Kenneth became king of Dalriada. Of greater bearing, perhaps, is the clear indication by later medieval sources – principally the Gaelic *Prophecy of Berchan* set down after the end of the eleventh century but preserving much older material – of Kenneth's region of origin having lain in the old western heartland of Argyll where he would have grown to maturity through the earlier decades of the ninth century when the Norse presence was moving from sea-raiding into its land-taking phase. Set against that background, there is more than one item of evidence to suggest his own and his family's contact with the northmen, and especially with the *Gall-Gaedhil*, having been quite the reverse of hostile. The *Prophecy of Berchan* describes Kenneth's brother and successor Domnall mac Alpin as 'the wanton son of the *Gaill* wife', which can be taken to mean his having being born, probably out of formal wedlock, to a Norse mother, while a genealogy preserved in a late source of Clan Donald tradition claims a daughter of Gothfrith mac Fergus to have been 'the wife of Kenneth mac Alpin'.[18] Neither of those fragments can be confidently offered as the most impeccable historical evidence, but their common direction is still entirely consistent with the pattern of political marriages by which native rulers of the ninth century and afterwards secured terms of accommodation with the power structure of the Scandinavian settlement.

Rather more impressive, in terms of authority of sources, is the strategic coincidence of two events, the first of them a conflict entered in the *Annals of Ulster* at the year 839 as 'a battle [i.e. victory] of the heathens over the men of Fortriu; in which fell Eoganan mac Oengus [king of Fortriu] and Bran mac Oengus [his brother and expected successor] and Aed mac Boant [king of Dalriada]; and others beyond counting were slain'. Even though the location of the battlefield and the origin of the victorious northmen remain uncertain, the annalist leaves not the slightest doubt as to the outcome of what can only have been a devastating massacre of the Picto-Scottish royal house and nobility of the kingdom of Fortriu, and prominent among them the king of Dalriada. The second of the two events is placed in the very next year by the most reliable medieval king-lists when they confirm Kenneth mac Alpin having succeeded to the kingship of Dalriada in 840. 'The evidence may not be conclusive,' writes Alfred Smyth in his trenchant history of the period, 'but the fragments of information which survive point to the conclusion that the house of Kenneth mac Alpin rose to power in Scotland, if not openly allied with Viking rulers from the Hebrides and Dublin, then certainly profiting from their attacks on the Picts and Britons.'[19]

As regards Gothfrith mac Fergus, the sources can supply no further detail, other than the reference entered at 836, of whatever might have been his contribution to Kenneth's ascendancy. He is, in fact, noticed on just one more occasion, and once again by the *Annals of the Four Masters* with the summary entry of his obituary placed at the year 853:

> *Gofraidh mac Fearghus, tóiseach Innsi Gall*, died.

For all its extreme brevity, that obituary does at least place on record the new status Gothfrith had attained since his first notice in the annals. Whereas seventeen years earlier he had been styled 'chieftain of the Airgialla', at the time of his death he is afforded the more impressive title of 'chieftain of the Hebrides', which does read very alike to a ninth-century equivalent of 'Lord of the Isles' and might even be taken to indicate his having been appointed in some wise as Kenneth mac

Alpin's sub-king over the *Innsegall*. Such a suggestion does, of course, assume the sovereignty of a king of Scots having still prevailed over some extent of the Hebrides by 853, and if it was so then it was to be only very short-lived, because in that same year – according to the *Annals of Ulster* – Olaf 'the son of the king of Lochlann came to Ireland and the *gaill* of Ireland submitted to him'. So, too, in the course of his eighteen-year reign as Norse king of Dublin, did the '*gaill* of Alba' submit to the man called by *Eyrbyggja Saga* 'the greatest warrior king of the western sea'.

Olaf's arrival can be recognised as the Norwegian response to attacks made on Dublin by Irish kings in 849 and by Danish vikings in 851, with the first intention of regaining control of the foremost centre of Scandinavian power in Ireland, but with the further purpose of securing the submission – and, of course, the tribute – of all the northmen west-over-sea. Whether or not the arrival of Olaf in the same year as the death of Gothfrith was a pure coincidence, the man who apparently followed him as chieftain of the *Innsegall* is called '*Caitil Find* with his *gall-gaedhil*' in the Irish annals. He has been convincingly identified by Professor Smyth as the Norseman known in the Icelandic sources as Ketil Bjornsson called 'flatnose', and his daughter Aud, the first-recorded Norse convert to Christianity and called 'the deep-minded' by the Icelandic sources telling of her migration to Iceland around 875, had been for a time married to Olaf of Dublin. 'Ketil either accompanied Olaf on an expedition of conquest to the Isles, at which time the Orkney earldom was also established, or, alternatively, Ketil conquered the Hebrides independently of the Norwegian king and was later forced to submit to him.'[20] Whether one of alliance or of submission, their relationship had evidently turned to hostility by 857 when Ketil suffered a defeat by Olaf in Munster and thereafter disappears from the historical record, but when Olaf crossed the Irish Sea to plunder Pictland nine years later his forces are said by the annalist to have included the '*gaill* of Alba', quite surely meaning the Hebridean Norse, who had by then apparently been brought under direct rule of the king of Dublin.

In 902, some thirty years after Olaf's presumed return to Norway, the Irish managed to expel the Norse from Dublin. A new viking dynasty was to reclaim the town and establish a more permanent settlement there in 914, but in the meantime some numbers of the Dublin Norse had resettled around the Irish Sea in Cumbria, Galloway and, most significantly of all for the Hebrides, on the Isle of Man, because it was in the orbit of Man that there appear in the sources for the later tenth century two generations of a warrior kindred bearing Scandinavian personal names and accredited with kingship over the Isles.

A 'Maccus' (assuredly a corruption of the Scandinavian *Magnus*), son of Harald, is called 'king of very many islands' by the *Chronicle of Melrose* which numbers him among the kings who rowed Edgar of England on the Dee as an act of homage in 973. His brother is known as 'Gudrod, king of the Isle of Man' in *Njal's Saga* where he appears in contention with Jarl Sigurd of Orkney, and styled *ri' Innsegall* ('king of the Hebrides') by the *Annals of Ulster* at 989, in which year he was slain by 'the men of Dalriada'. While his son Ragnall is still recognised as 'king of the islands' by the same annalist entering his obituary at 1005, lordship over the Isles must have passed very soon afterwards to the Orkney jarls. Later chapters of *Njal's Saga* tell of a 'Jarl Gilli', Sigurd's brother-in-law based on Coll (or possibly Colonsay), collecting tribute from the Hebrides, and when Sigurd brought his fleet to Ireland to fight his last battle at Clontarf in 1014 the Irish sources record his war-host including warriors 'from Man, and from Skye, and from Lewis; from Kintyre and from Argyll' as well as from Orkney and Shetland.[21] A similar, even greater, dominion in Scotland, including 'Caithness . . . and all the Hebrides as well', is claimed by the *Orkneyinga Saga* for Sigurd's son and eventual successor, Jarl Thorfinn, but soon after his death around 1065 control of the *Innsegall* was reclaimed by power centres around the Irish Sea.

The Leinster king Diarmait mac Máelnambó who expelled and personally supplanted a Norse king of Dublin in 1052 is given the title *ri' Innsegall* by his obituary entered in the *Annals of Tigernach* at 1072, but just seven years later the kingship of Man was seized by the extraordinary Godred Crovan,[22] who is perhaps to be most justly recognised as the founding dynast of the Kingdom of Man and the Isles. Godred was the son of Harald the Black of Islay,[23] according to the thirteenth-century *Chronicle of Man* which supplies the fullest available account of his reign and those of his successor kings. He fought in Harald Hardradi's army at Stamford Bridge in 1066 and escaped the slaughter to find his way to Man where he was accepted into the court of the reigning king Godred Sitricsson, possibly a cousin of his father. When the king died in 1075 and was succeeded by his son Fingal, Godred Crovan raised an invasion force in the Hebrides and won possession of Man and kingship of the Isles by his famous victory at the battle of Sky Hill in 1079. He later seized the kingship of Dublin and held it for three years until driven out by an alliance of Irish kings in 1094, but in the following year, struck down by plague, he died on Islay.

The history of the kingship of Man through the decade following the death of Godred Crovan – from the succession of Lagmann, the eldest of his three sons, who blinded and emasculated his brother Harald to eliminate a rival, through to the accession of the youngest, Olaf, nominally placed in 1103 – is less than clear by reason of the confused account in the Manx chronicle, but supporting evidence from Irish and Icelandic sources does confirm episodes of intervention from Norway and from Ireland. The brief reigns of the rapacious Norseman Ingemund and the tyrannical Munsterman Domnall mac Tagd, the first assassinated and the second driven out by island chieftains, are of little importance here, but the dramatic involvement in the kingdom of Man and the Isles by Magnus Olafsson, called 'bareleg',[24] king of Norway, was of such crucial significance for subsequent Hebridean history as to demand at least summary consideration.

The various sources offer their own explanations as to how Magnus Bareleg was prompted to his extraordinary 'royal cruise' of 1098, but if he was not sufficiently provoked by the fate of his nominated sub-king Ingemund there was more than enough internicene contention in Orkney as well as on Man to arouse his concern and cause him to bring a fleet of a hundred and sixty ships on a fearsome demonstration of his sovereignty west-over-sea. He came first to Orkney, there despatching its two jarls back to Norway and installing his own son in their place, then set his course down through the Hebrides. However highly coloured and so often quoted, the verses set down by the king's *skald* (or court poet) Bjorn Cripplehand and preserved in *Magnus Bareleg's Saga* do supply an immediately contemporary account of King Magnus' subjugation of the *Sudreyjar* when they tell of his descent with fire and sword on Lewis, Uist, Skye, Tiree, Mull and Islay, plundering the coastland all about and sparing only the holy island of Iona. The

Saga tells of his putting Lagmann, king of Man, in chains and defeating two Norman earls to claim Anglesey, then turning north to Kintyre where his men carried a skiff overland across the mile-wide isthmus at Tarbert with the king aboard and his hand on the steering-oar, concluding his negotiated agreement with the king of Scots 'that Magnus should possess all the islands west of Scotland, between which and the mainland he could go in a ship with the rudder in place'. While there is no evidence for the richly fertile Kintyre peninsula having been subsequently given over to Norway, Magnus' settlement with the Scots king can be taken as the first formalisation of Norse possession of the Hebrides. It is, perhaps, significant that Robert the Bruce is said by the Barbour poem *The Bruce* to have fulfilled an 'ald prophecy' by securing submission of the Islesmen when he made a similar shipboard crossing overland at Tarbert in 1315, a reference which has prompted the interesting suggestion that 'it may have been a feat demanded of the man who would master the Isles'.[25]

While the Hebrides had been under effective, albeit informal, Norse control for more than two hundred years by 1098 and would remain in Norwegian possession until 1266, Magnus' legacy to Scots history was the creation in the west of an extensive sea-kingdom under formal Norwegian sovereignty and so able to assert its own independence from the kingdom of the Scots, yet so far distant from the land of Norway as to be beyond the range of direct rule. However, the culture of that sea-kingdom would seem never to have become dominantly Scandinavian in character as did that of Orkney and Shetland, but neither, on the eve of the twelfth century, could it be described with strict accuracy as 'Celtic'. 'What the evidence really suggests' – in the view of the Islay historian, W. D. Lamont – 'is the rapid fusion of blood and tradition to produce the people known to the Irish annalists as the *Gall-Gaedhil* and it is extremely difficult to distinguish in detail the Celtic and Norse contributions to the subsequent Hebridean way of life.'[26]

Magnus Bareleg was to come west-over-sea just once more, insisting on the submission of the Irish king and ambitious to add the island of Ireland to his dominions, but venturing ashore and cut off from his fleet he was ambushed and slain in Down in 1103. Although no annalist or chronicler has placed the date or location on record, all the other evidence infers that it must have been within the decade following 1098, probably around the year of Magnus' death and quite possibly at a place not so very far to the west of Down, that Somerled, Gillebride's son, was born.

2

'GILLEBRIDE'S SON'

THE EMERGENCE OF SOMERLED

The name Somerled mac Gillebride, comprising a Norse given name with a Gaelic patronymic, is clearly enough recognisable as indicating a son of Celtic-Scandinavian parentage, but when its components are more closely examined and taken together with the evidence of the old genealogies they can be – and, indeed, have been – shown to reveal rather more detail as to the man's ancestry and background. His name, then, offers the obvious starting point for any account of Somerled, but while the patronymic has been fully considered in the context of his descent in the male line, his given name – which supplies the only clue to the background, if not to the actual identity, of his mother – would seem to have received very much less attention. For that reason alone, the origin and history of the personal name Somerled will be given first consideration here.

While it is found in the Gaelic form of *Somerle* by the mid-sixteenth century and as *Somhairle* in its modern Gaelic usage,[1] its origin is unquestionably Norse, deriving from the term *sumarlidi* of which the most convincing literal translation as 'summer voyager' can be taken as a by-word for 'viking' in the sense of 'sea-raider'. It is in that sense, but in the Old English form of *sumorlida*, that it is used by the *Anglo-Saxon Chronicle* reference to a Danish fleet of the year 871, and similarly by a later medieval Scottish source, using the Latinised form *classi[s] somarlidiorum*, to identify a raiding fleet defeated off Buchan in the mid-tenth century.[2]

Its earliest occurrence as a personal name is found most prominently in the orbit of Orkney, where the *Orkneyinga Saga* mentions six individuals by the name of *Sumarlidi* (in addition to a reference to Somerled of Argyll whom it knows as *Sumarlidi holdr*), but the first and most important Orcadian Somerled was the eldest son of the Jarl Sigurd slain at Clontarf in 1014. Further evidence for use of the name is supplied by the Icelandic sources where the sinister Hrapp Sumarlidason, called 'Killer-Hrapp' and active in the tenth century, is said by the *Laxdæla Saga* to have been 'Scottish on his father's side, but all his mother's family came from the Hebrides and Hrapp had been born and brought up there'. His son was also given the name *Sumarlidi* and is mentioned with others of that same name in the *Landnámabók* ('The Book of Settlements'), which also contains a reference to a farm once called *i Sumarlidabœr*, indicating a 'Somerled's farm' in an unusual Icelandic place-name form.

The personal name is found also in the English Danelaw, where the oldest evidence for its use is preserved on coins impressed with their moneyer's name in the anglicised form of *Sumerleda* and dating from the second half of the tenth century. Place-names have been taken to indicate forms of *Sumarlidi* used as a personal name within the Danelaw as early as the later ninth century, and the *Domesday Book* record of tenants called *Sumarlidi* and *Sumarlidr*, some of them located outwith the counties of the former Danelaw, shows that it was still in use in England in the last quarter of the eleventh century. All of which has led to the authoritative conclusion that 'the name *Sumarlidi* had achieved a wide currency . . . long before it came to be bestowed upon the son of an Orkney earl. All that can be said with certainty, however, is that the name arose in one of the colonies and not in the Scandinavian homelands.'[3]

A name found across such a great extent of the Scandinavian expansion – from family histories of Icelandic settlers to an isolated example preserved in a Normandy place-name – would seem to allow a wide range of possible regions of origin for the wife of Gillebride who chose the name Somerled for their son, but the most plausible range is not really so very wide. Orkney, first of all, might be suggested as a strong possibility when the *Orkneyinga Saga* shows the name to have been current there in the eleventh and twelfth centuries and actually mentions Somerled of Argyll. On the other hand, the *Saga* makes no suggestion of Somerled's mother having been of an Orkney kindred, and had she been so then it almost certainly would have done, just as it would assuredly have been rather better informed as to the fate of Somerled himself.[4]

A Hebridean Norse origin for Gillebride's wife might be thought the next most likely alternative, were it not for there being no suggestion of it anywhere in the Clan Donald tradition and for the extreme rarity, if not apparently total absence, of the name in Hebridean history and tradition prior to the advent of Somerled himself. Even though such a possibility still cannot be ruled out, there must be a greater likelihood of Somerled's mother having been of Hiberno-Norse origin, especially because his father is said to have been living as an exile in Ireland when he is first noticed by the Clan Donald historians. While the name Somerled is hardly prominent in the documentary record of the Scandinavian settlements in Ireland, the Celtic specialist Nora Chadwick has pointed to its occurrence in the Irish form of *Somarlidh* among the ruling kindred of the Norse of Limerick and linked it to their 'immediate connection – in the tenth century and probably earlier – with the Outer Hebrides'.[5] A Limerick Norse mother for Somerled, then, must be admitted as a strong possibility, but an even stronger probability, in my view, lies with the Norse of Dublin.

The name Somerled has been shown to have been established in the English Danelaw since the ninth century and to have been in current use in England within twenty years of his birth, so it could hardly have failed to cross the Irish Sea either during the time of the Scandinavian York-Dublin connection or afterwards, when – as Alfred Smyth confirms – 'in spite of the loss of York in the middle of the tenth century, contacts between Dublin and England must have remained close, particularly in the time of Canute [1016–35]'.[6] When Somerled assembled the great fleet for his invasion of the Clyde in 1164, the two most reliable Irish annals confirm its having included a contingent of Dublin Norse, not the most obvious allies for a twelfth-century lord of Argyll but ones who may well have been recruited, at least in part, under some form of kinship obligation inherited from his mother. There is some further bearing in the Dublin Norse of the eleventh century having maintained an interest in Ulster by reason of its coastal proximity to Man and the sea-road to Scandinavia. It was an interest which brought them into conflict with the Ulstermen, where they shared some common ground with Somerled's father's northern Irish kinsmen of the Airgialla whose traditional hostility towards the men of Ulster had its origins in the fifth century. Such common ground would have naturally led to friendly contact, and perhaps even to occasions of alliance which, however informal, might very well have been sealed by a marriage contract. While far from decisive, those few clues have nonetheless led me to suspect the most probable region of origin for Somerled's mother having lain with the Norse of Dublin.

His paternal ancestry, on the other hand, has been the object of rather more attention down the centuries, which has at least been supplied with the names of his father and his grandfather placed on record by a number of genealogical accounts, the oldest of them dating from as early as the end of the fourteenth century, and by two annalists of most impeccable authority, one of them representing an immediately contemporary source. His father's name of Gillebride (*Gilla-Brigte* or 'servant of Brigid') and his grandfather's of Gilledomnan (*Gilla-Adomnáin* or 'servant of Adomnan') are generally recognised as Celtic in origin, and quite reasonably so when each of them prefixes the name of an Irish saint with the Irish term *gilla* (*gille* or *giolla* in modern Gaelic) meaning 'lad' in the sense of 'serving-man'.[7] While the word *gilla* occurs in the Irish language long before the Norse impact, it is not found in use as a prefix for a personal name until the later tenth century, thereafter gaining increasing currency through the eleventh and twelfth centuries. The phonetic similarity of *gilla* to the Old Norse *gildr*, a fairly compatible term for a 'sturdy' or 'brawny' man, would seem to support the suggestion that 'names compounded with *Giolla-* were in the first instance those of Northmen converted to Christianity'.[8] Whether or not that was the true origin of the *Gille-* name-form, of which both Gillebride and Gilledomnan are prime examples, it clearly did first emerge within the orbit of the Celtic-Scandinavian cultural fusion and so might be most accurately considered *Gall-Gaedhil*, as distinct from purely Gaelic, in character. In which case, it would well correspond to the other evidence for the background and descent of Somerled mac Gillebride.

Somerled's ancestry is set out in fifteen ancient accounts, one of them written in Latin and the others in forms of Gaelic, the oldest being that found in the *Book of Ballymote* which was compiled sometime soon after 1384 and the remainder set down between the early fifteenth and eighteenth centuries. While some of those genealogies omit some names included in others,[9] they are nevertheless unanimous not only in recognising Somerled as the forebear of the Clan Donald and related west Highland kindreds but in tracing his own descent back to Colla Uais, one of the 'Three Collas' descended from the legendary *Conn Céadchathach* ('Conn of the Hundred Battles') and remembered in Irish tradition as founders of the fourth-century Airgialla tribal confederation which later became the kingdom of Oriel. Some, although assuredly not all, of these manuscripts had attracted the interest of antiquarians by the first quarter of the nineteenth century on the evidence of an anonymous genealogical account of the Clan Donald published in 1819 at a time when even the most spurious celebration of clan history was becoming the height of fashion.[10] It is this work which seems first to propose an interpretation of Somerled's ancestry derived from the most extraordinary misreading of the traditional genealogies and yet echoed and elaborated by an alarmingly long list of more recent authors. This theory hinges on the occurrence in all the old genealogies of a 'Fergus, son of Erc' nine generations before Somerled and seeks to identify him with the Fergus, son of Erc, who led the royal house of Dalriada out of Antrim to Argyll in the last years of the fifth century. Even if the chronology extending nine generations across six hundred years were not obviously implausible, the traditional descent of the Dalriadic ruling house from Cairbre Riada, and quite unconnected to Colla Uais or any other branch of the Airgialla, has been well known since at least as early as the time of Bede.

By the second half of the nineteenth century, a new school of thought on the subject had entered into print when the proposal of a Scandinavian origin for Somerled was put forward by P. A. Munch in the introduction to his 1860 edition of the *Chronicle of Man.*[11] This theory, which was followed by a number of later writers, disregards the traditional genealogies and instead takes as its starting point the obituary of a 'Somerled mac Gillebride, king of the Innsegall' entered in the *Annals of the Four Masters* at the year 1083. Both the *Annals of Ulster* and the *Annals of Tigernach* are supported by Scottish and Manx chroniclers when they enter the death of Somerled at 1164, which year must represent its true historical date, but the Four Masters show no such obituary at that year and must have already misplaced it more than eighty years earlier. The Scandinavian school of thought, however, takes the obituary at 1083 as evidence for the existence of an earlier Somerled, son of Gillebride, and identifies him as the father of Gilledomnan and thus as the great-grandfather of the Somerled killed in 1164. Assuming precisely the same sequence of names having occurred in the three generations before Gilledomnan, the theory goes on to propose an earlier Gilledomnan in the later tenth century whom it seeks to identify with the 'Jarl Gilli' known to *Njal's Saga* as the Hebridean-based brother-in-law of Jarl Sigurd of Orkney. In fairness to Professor Munch, an eminent Scandinavian scholar working from a predominantly Scandinavian perspective and at a time when all the Gaelic sources were neither easily available nor highly regarded, his proposal might have been reasonably underwritten by another genuinely historical Somerled, Jarl Sigurd's son, being taken as evidence for the use of the personal name having had its exclusive origin within the Orkney jarl's kindred. This has, of course, since been shown not to have been the case, and so the proposal of a purely Scandinavian ancestry for Somerled can be said to depend entirely upon a misplaced annal entry far from uncharacteristic of the Four Masters and two invented individuals quite unknown anywhere in the sources.

It was, in fact, not until the 1960s that the traditional accounts of Somerled's ancestry and their claim for his descent from Colla Uais were subjected to scholarly scrutiny by David Sellar, and his research was published in a paper which represents the outstanding contribution to the study of Somerled in recent times.[12] Sellar separates the traditional genealogy into two sections, setting their dividing line eight generations above Somerled at the *Gofraidh*, son of the aforementioned Fergus, son of Erc, whom he convincingly identifies with the Gothfrith mac Fergus noticed in the *Annals of the Four Masters* at 836 and 853. Those eight generations – three of whose names are independently confirmed by annal sources and the remainder so unusual in character as to eliminate almost any likelihood of forgery – correspond perfectly plausibly to a period extending over some three hundred years, so the direct descent of Somerled from Gothfrith mac Fergus can be reasonably accepted as a full and genuinely historical genealogy. The same obviously cannot be said of the five generations separating Gothfrith in the mid-ninth century from the legendary Colla Uais who is traditionally dated some five hundred years earlier, but it would be hardly reasonable to expect a genealogy preserved in tradition and reaching back as far as the fourth century to supply a fully comprehensive record of lineage, so the evident omissions might even be taken as evidence for its authenticity when the names which are recorded are all independently confirmed by ancient Irish genealogies. Without going any further into the detail of Sellar's investigation of the Irish sources for the Airgialla kindreds, suffice it to quote from his conclusion: 'The remote ancestry of Somerled is seen to be traced from a tribe . . . belonging to the northern branch of the *Ui' Maic Uais* ['the race of the son of Colla Uais'] of Oriel originating in Country Derry'.[13]

The especial significance at this point of Sellar's findings lies with the nearer ancestry of Somerled and in particular with his descent from Gothfrith mac Fergus who is, after all, the first individual of Norse-Gaelic parentage to be identified by name anywhere in the historical record. On the strength of that lineage, Somerled can no longer be claimed for a principally Norse descent or a purely Celtic background, but must be recognised instead as having been born of a long and distinguished *Gall-Gaedhil* ancestry. Of still more immediate importance is the testimony borne by Sellar's researches to the historical value of the sources of tradition because it is they, and they alone, which supply any account of the first emergence and rise to ascendancy of Gillebride's son.

Probably of greatest authority among the sources of Clan Donald tradition is the *History of the MacDonalds* found in the 'Red' and 'Black' *Books of Clanranald*, collections of Gaelic verse and prose set down in the later seventeenth and early eighteenth centuries respectively, which represent the documentary legacy of the MacMhuirich family of hereditary bards and historians (or 'seannachies' from the Gaelic *seanchaidh*, literally 'teller of tales') to the Clan Donald from the thirteenth century.[14] As to the precise authorship of this *History* – which is preserved in its fullest text in the earlier 'Red' *Book of Clanranald* and in edited form in the slightly later 'Black' *Book* – it is the opinion of the editors of the edition used here that while the concluding account of 'the Montrose wars and of the events thereafter is clearly the work of Niall MacVurich [d. c.1726] . . . the early history of the MacDonalds down to about the year 1600 was probably composed by different and successive generations of the family.'[15]

These earlier passages of the MacMhuirich *History* open with an account of the legend of Colla Uais which leads into a genealogy of his descendants down to Gillebride who first enters the story at the point of his exile in the north of Ireland:

> Gillebride, son of Gilledomnan, having been among his kindred in Ireland, that is from the Clan Colla which are the tribes of Macguire and Macmahon, it happened that this tribe held a meeting and conference in Fermanagh, on the estate of Macguire and among matters to be transacted was that Gillebride should get some estate in his own country, whence he had been banished from his inheritance by the power of the Lochlannach and the Finngallach. When Gillebride saw a large host of sturdy young people in the assembly, and that they were favourable to himself, the favour that he asked of his friends was that so many persons as the adjacent fort in that place could hold should be allowed to go to Scotland with him, in the hope that he might obtain possession of his own inheritance and portion of it.

With the possible exception of the use of the capacity of a hillfort to define the size of a warband, a seemingly formulaic device fairly reminiscent of the old Irish tradition, there is no reason to suspect the MacMhuirich account of being anything less than a substantially historical account of an episode from Gillebride's sojourn in Ireland. The Macmahons of Monaghan and the Macguires of Fermanagh could certainly have been considered 'his kindred in Ireland' when they originated as tribes of the Airgialla confederation, but they were not his most immediate tribal kin when – as the MacMhuirich *History* itself admits – they claimed descent not from Colla Uais but from his brother Colla Da crioch ('Colla of the Two Bounds'). There would still have been good reason for Gillebride having sought them as allies in his bid to reclaim his lost patrimony in Scotland, because they are thought to have been more powerful tribes in medieval times than were his closer kin of the Ui Maic Uais.

These earlier passages of the MacMhuirich *History* supply no dates for the events they describe and, indeed, it would be wildly optimistic to expect such properly chronological detail of a source rooted in oral tradition, but such an omission does mean that there is no evidence for when Gillebride decided to reclaim his 'estate in his own country' and neither is there any very clear account of when, how, or by whom his patrimony was lost in the first place. While the MacMhuirich claim that Gillebride had been 'banished from his inheritance by the power of the Lochlannach and the Finngallach' points to Scandinavian involvement when both of those terms are applied to the Norse by the Irish sources, another traditional *History of the MacDonalds*, attributed to a 'Hugh MacDonald of Sleat' and written in English during the reign of Charles II, spreads the blame rather more widely when it claims 'Argyle' to have been 'wrung out of the hands of his [Somerled's] father unjustly by MacBeath, Donald Bain, and the Danes'.

This Sleat *History* survives as an apparently incomplete text in only one manuscript copy which bears no indication of its authorship but is considered to be slanted in favour of the MacDonalds of Sleat, while the attribution to a 'Hugh MacDonald' was made by Donald Gregory who owned the manuscript in the 1830s. How he knew of its author's name is not recorded but it may have been simply by deduction from a reference made by Martin Martin in his *Description of the Western Islands of Scotland* written around 1695 to 'the Genealogist Mack-Vurich and Hugh Mack-Donald in their Manuscripts' as having been among his sources. John Bannerman has occasion to consider the Sleat *History* in his study of the Beatons and explains its occasionally garbled content as the consequence of 'an attempt to write a consecutive narrative in translation from what were probably disparate and disjointed Gaelic originals, [which] nevertheless gives the impression of deriving from the shared corpus of historical and genealogical material available to the learned professional orders of Gaelic society'.[16]

It is strictly in terms of Gaelic tradition as it was preserved in the later seventeenth century, then, that the Sleat historian's account of Somerled and his background can be properly considered. So if by 'MacBeath' he means the famous Macbeth, then the period of his reign as king of Scots from 1040–58 lies before the time of Somerled's father and improbably early for the adult years of his grandfather, but the unlikely date does not necessarily disqualify the claim. Macbeth was an immediate contemporary of Jarl Thorfinn of

Orkney and, while scholarly opinion is far from unanimous as to the nature of their relationship, some historians have proposed that they may have been cousins who came together as allies to bring down Duncan in 1040, afterwards dividing the spoils of victory between them. Thus it might well have been that Macbeth succeeded to the kingship of Scots and Thorfinn greatly extended his dominions, which are said by the *Orkneyinga Saga* to have included 'all the Hebrides', so there is a genuinely historical possibility that Macbeth's dealings with the Orkney jarl could have diminished the authority or reduced the landholdings later passed down to Gilledomnan and Gillebride.

As to the responsibility apportioned to 'Donald Bain' – assuredly meaning Malcolm Canmore's brother *Domnall Bán* whose Gaelic name-form reflects his long years of exile in the Isles during and after the reign of Macbeth – there is a corresponding reference made by Martin Martin who claims 'that Donald Bane intending to secure the Kingdom [of Scotland] to himself, promis'd the Western Isles to Magnus [Bareleg], King of Norway, upon condition that he should support him with a competent Force: which he performed; and by this means became Master of these Isles'. Domnall did succeed to the kingship of Scots on the death of his brother in 1093 and was deposed soon afterwards by Malcolm's eldest son who reigned briefly as Duncan II until Domnall reclaimed the kingship in the following year to reign again until finally driven out in 1097. There was at one time a belief among historians that Magnus Bareleg had been in the Isles five years before his expedition of 1098 from which might be inferred his involvement with Domnall Ban, and while it is now thought to be erroneous and based on unreliable references in the sources, it may well have been maintained in Gaelic traditions of the seventeenth century which informed both Martin Martin and the Sleat historian. It is almost certain, however, that Domnall's seizure of the kingship was accomplished on both occasions with support from the Gaelic west, thus perhaps incurring obligations long remembered in local tradition as having been unfulfilled. He was, moreover, a contemporary of both Gillebride and his father Gilledomnan, so there might just possibly be some significance to be drawn from the *Prophecy of Berchan* passage bearing on Domnall when it says that 'in his time the men of Alba will come hither to Ireland'.

When the Sleat historian finally casts blame on the 'Danes' – by whom can only be meant the Norse – he approaches agreement with the MacMhuirich *History* when it accuses the *Lochlannach* and *Finn-gallach* of having deprived Gillebride of his patrimony. The intended distinction between those terms is less than clear and may simply reflect a garbled usage out of oral tradition, unless it might be otherwise interpreted as distinguishing the Norse kings of Man and the Isles from Norwegian chieftains imposed on the Hebrides by Magnus Bareleg.[17] While the Sleat historian's account can be read to suggest that it was Gillebride who lost his family's lands, the MacMhuirich *History* infers their 'estate' having been lost by Gilledomnan in the previous generation and it would be supported in that by other evidence from Clan Donald tradition.

The monumental three-volume history of *The Clan Donald* set down in the last years of the nineteenth century by the Reverend Angus Macdonald of Killearnan and the Reverend Archibald Macdonald of Kiltarlity, two ministers of parishes around Inverness, recognises Gilledomnan to have been 'a person of consequence . . . [and] a leader of some note' on the evidence of 'his daughter having been the wife of Harold, King of Norway'. 'This cannot be confirmed, but is quite plausible', in the opinion of David Sellar who has traced the claim back to the eighteenth century and cautiously identifies this 'King Harold' with Harald 'Gilli', king of Norway 1130–6, 'born and raised in Ireland or the Sudreys [who] claimed to be the son of Magnus Bareleg by a Gaelic mother'. A further reference in *Harald Gilli's sons' Saga* calls Harald Gilli's wife by 'the name *Biadok* which may be the same as the Gaelic *Bethoc*, the name also of the only recorded daughter of Somerled'.[18]

The inference of this fragmentary evidence would place the loss of Somerled's patrimony into the last quarter of the eleventh century, possibly during the years of Godred Crovan's rise to power in the kingship of Man after 1079 but more probably as an immediate consequence of the 1098 expedition made by Magnus Bareleg, who is actually acclaimed as 'Scots-expeller' by the skaldic verses describing his ferocious descent on the Hebrides.

In distinct contrast with the eminence claimed for Gilledoman, his son Gillebride's greatly reduced circumstances are reflected in his Gaelic soubriquet of *na h-Uamh* ('Gillebride of the Cave'),[19] an allusion to his 'time of trouble' as a fugitive in the caves of Morvern following his return to Argyll with the warband raised in Fermanagh, when the MacMhuirich *History* takes up the story:

> Gillebride proceeded with that party to Scotland, where they landed. They made frequent onsets and attacks on their enemies during this time of trouble, for their enemies were powerful and numerous at that time. All the islands from Man to Orkney, and all the coastland from Dumbarton to Caithness in the north, were in possession of the Lochlannach; and such of the Gael of those lands as remained were protecting themselves in the woods and mountains; and at the end of that time Gillebride had a good son, who had come to maturity and renown.

At which point Somerled's name makes its first appearance in the *History* and, even though there is no form of break in the Gaelic text, there is a discernible shift in quality of content in the MacMhuirich narrative.

> It happened that the small party who were followers of Gillebride and Somerled were in the mountains and woods of Ardgour and of Morvern, and they were surprised there by a great host of the Lochlannach and Finngallach. All Somerled's warriors and raiding bands gathered around him and he arranged them front and rear. Somerled put them in battle orders and made a great display of them to his enemies. He marched them three times before them in one company, so that they supposed there were three companies there. After that he attacked them and they were defeated by Somerled and his party, and he did not halt in the pursuit till he drove them northward across the river Sheil, and a part escaped with their king to the Isles; and he did not cease in that work till he had cleared the western side of Scotland of the Lochlannach, except the islands of the Fionn Lochlann, called the Innsegall; and he gained victory over his enemies in every field of battle.

The MacMhuirich *History* then moves straight into its account of Somerled's last campaign and his death at Renfrew in 1164, so the last line of the passage quoted above must be taken to be all that the MacMhuirich tradition has to offer on his intervening career. Even the Sleat historian has been found to add a valuable fragment to what little is elsewhere recorded of Somerled's uprising of the 1150s on behalf of the MacHeths, but he too pays much more attention to this conflict in Morvern, offering an elaborated account of it in his *History of the MacDonalds* which opens (in its surviving form) with Somerled in Morvern at the low point of his father's fortunes.[20]

> Sommerled, the son of Gilbert, began to muse on the low condition and misfortune to which he and his father were reduced, and kept at first very retired. In the meantime, Allin MacVich Allin, coming with some forces to the land of Morverin for pillage and herships [plunder], intending to retire forthwith to Lochaber, from whence he came. From this Allan descended the family of Lochiel. Sommerled thought now it was high time to make himself known for the defence of his country, if he could, or at least see the same, having no company for the time. There was a young sprout out of a tree near the cave which grew in his age of infancy. He plucked it up by the root, and putting it on his shoulder, came near the people of Morverin, desired them to be of good courage and do as he did, and so by his persuasion, all of them having pulled a branch, and putting the same on their shoulder, went on encouraging each other.
>
> Godfrey Du had possession of the Isles of the north side of Ardnamurchan from the King of Denmark [in fact, of course, the King of Norway]. Olay [Olaf, King of Man] compelled the inhabitants of some of these Isles to infest Morverin by landing some forces there. The principal surnames in the country were MacInnes's and MacGilvrays, who are the same as the MacInnes's. They being in sight of the enemy could act nothing without one to command them. At length they agreed to make the first person that should appear to them their general. Who came in the meantime but Sommerled, with his bow, quiver, and sword? Upon his appearance they raised a great shout of laughter.

> Sommerled enquiring the reason, they answered they were re-joiced at his appearance. They told him that they had agreed to make the first that would appear their general. Sommerlid said he would undertake to head them, or serve as a man otherwise. But if they pitched upon him as their commander, they should swear to be obedient to his commands; so, without any delay, they gave him an oath of obedience. There was a great hill betwixt them and the enemy, and Sommerled ordered his men to put off their coats, and put on their shirts and full armour above their coats. So, making them go three times in a disguised manner about the hill, that they might seem more in number than they really were, at last he ordered them to engage the Danes, saying that some of them were on shore and the rest in their ships; that those on shore would fight but faintly so near to their ships. Withal he exhorted his soldiers to be of good courage, and to do as they would see him do, so they led the charge. The first whom Sommerlid slew he ript up and took out his heart, desiring the rest to do the same, because that the Danes were no Christians. So the Danes were put to the flight; many of them were lost in the sea endeavouring to gain their ships; the lands of Mull and Morverin being freed at that time from their yoke and slavery. After this defeat given to the Danes, Sommerlid thought to recover Argyle from those who, contrary to right, had possessed it, being wrung out of the hands of his father unjustly by MacBeath, Donald Bain, and the Danes.

While there can be little doubt that Sommerled's efforts to reclaim his patrimony in Argyll would have inevitably brought him into conflict with Norse warlords in the Isles subordinate to the king of Man, one such apparently being meant by the Sleat historian's 'Godfrey Du', and also with local Gaelic chieftains, as indeed the same source says he did when it states that 'some of the Argathelians [men of Argyll] made resistance but were defeated', it is hardly possible to accept either of these accounts of the battle in Morvern as a genuinely historical record of any such conflict. Nevertheless, by the mid-nineteenth century when the Reverend John MacLeod of Morvern supplied a description of his parish to the *Statistical Account of Argyleshire* (included in what is now known as the 'New Statistical Account') he set down a description of the battle in his 'Civil History' of the parish. Drawing on what seems to a source similar to that used by the Sleat historian, he embellishes the earlier version of the story with local place-name associations even as he opens his narrative with the Clan MacInnes seeking Somerled's assistance against 'Lochalin galleys moored on their shores . . .'

> Proceeding in the direction of the not very capacious cave occupied by him and his father on the shores of Linnhe Loch, still known as the cave of Gille-Bride, [they] found Somerled angling in the Gear-Abhain . . . At length, he observed that he was enticed by a sportive salmon and, if successful in landing him, he would consider it a good omen. The eager messengers stood by, the salmon was hooked and, after some bold plunges and struggles, was at length safely landed on the bank.

Agreeing to take command of the MacInnes' defence against the outnumbering northmen, Somerled orders cattle to be slaughtered and their hides used to cloak his forces who are then thrice displayed to the enemy but appearing differently on each occasion, dressed with the two facings of the hides and in their original wargear, thus giving the impression of greater numbers and throwing the enemy into alarm. 'Availing themselves of this sudden panic', Somerled leads the MacInnes warriors to attack the enemy 'with great slaughter . . .'

> Two of their leaders, Borradill and Lundy, were slain in the adjoining corries, which still bear their names, and another, Stangadill, was so closely pursued that to escape the sword he leaped into a boiling linn, which, in commemoration of the event, is still known as *Eass Stangadill* . . . Somerled in a short time succeeded in expelling the marauding Norsemen from Morvern, and thus at length the humble occupant of the cave became the powerful Thane of Argyle.
>
> Morvern, thus recovered by Somerled, continued to form part of his wide dominions down till the period of his death in 1164, and remained afterwards, with occasional interruptions attendant on the troubles of the times, in possession of his lineal descendants, the Lords of the Isles.

There are good grounds for believing Morvern to have been included in Somerled's lost patrimony if it formed part of the lands of Lorn which passed on his death to his son Dugall, thought to have been his eldest legitimate male offspring and, of course, the forebear of the MacDougall lords of Lorn. Even given the inevitability of Somerled having come into conflict with rival chieftains in his struggle to win back his family's estate and the likelihood of at least some of those conflicts having been fought in Morvern, it is still hardly possible to accept the foregoing accounts as an authentic record of any genuinely historical incident. Nonetheless, it is still true that the sources of tradition supply more detail of this legendary battle in Morvern than is found in the historical record of the real conflicts fought by Somerled and, for that reason alone, the tale must be traced as nearly as is possible back to source. To do so may not add anything to what is known of the true events of his rise to power but will, I think, throw its own sidelight on the Norse-Gaelic interchange so characteristic of Somerled in history and in legend.

While it is just possible that the Reverend MacLeod might have had access to the MacMhuirich and Sleat histories from which to draw his account of the Morvern battle, it is more likely that he accepted the story as genuine local history having learned it from local seannachies. There is evidence of an almost identical story still current in oral tradition as recently as 1963 when it was recorded from Alasdair Cameron, 'the great tradition-bearer and self-taught scholar', who told of Somerled's taking refuge with the MacInnes on Morvern and leading them to victory against the vikings near Lochuisge, the defeated Norse fleeing along Loch Sunart where their leader Torcull was killed crossing a ford, from which the Gaelic place-name *Ath Tharacaill* ('Torcull's Ford') now anglicised as Acharacle. 'Though Alasdair Cameron was a highly literate and indeed scholarly man . . . I believe that his account probably represents a genuine story in oral tradition', wrote Donald A. MacDonald of the School of Scottish Studies,[21] when he linked it to the wealth of stories and verse centred on *Fionn mac Cumhaill* (or 'Finn MacCool'). This 'Fenian' tradition was developed in Ireland through the eleventh and twelfth centuries just as the Celtic west was recovering from the Norse impact, which is assuredly the reason for so many of its tales setting Finn and his warband in contention with the *Lochlannach* quite regardless of the extraordinary anachronism of Finn's adventures being traditionally placed in the third century AD and thus almost six hundred years before the first viking raids.

While the tradition reached its widest popularity in the 1760s with the publication of James Macpherson's spurious 'Ossian' epics – which recast the Irish hero as a Scotsman, renamed him 'Fingal' and called his mythical Scottish realm by the name 'Morven' – the authentic originals had by then been long established in Gaelic Scotland. So popular were they at the time of the Reformation that Bishop John Carswell of Argyll and the Isles, writing the dedicatory preface to his Gaelic prayer book of 1567, found cause to complain of his parishioners' preference for the 'idle, turbulent, lying, worldly stories of Fionn Mac Cumhaill and his heroes rather than write and teach and maintain the faithful words of God'. There is, then, some gentle irony in an Argyll clergyman of some three centuries later including in the 'Civil History' of his parish an account of Somerled's battle in Morvern which contains unmistakable evidence for the influence of Fenian folklore. That evidence lies in the anecdote linking Somerled with the salmon, a creature associated with the otherworld throughout ancient Celtic tradition and especially in the tale of Finn's acquiring his magical wisdom by sucking the thumb he had burned in touching a cooking salmon. It is curious also that one of John MacLeod's predecessors in the same parish, a Reverend Norman MacLeod, did not even mention Somerled when writing of Morvern in the 1790s for the earlier *Statistical Account of Scotland* (now known as the 'Old Statistical Account'), but did betray an acquaintance with Macpherson's 'Ossian' in the list of local place-names for which he claimed associations with 'Fingal'. Somehow, then, in the course of the sixty years separating the two Statistical Accounts, the Finn of Gaelic legend, newly fashionable as the Ossianic 'Fingal', had become entangled with the historical Somerled and both of them accredited with expelling the 'Lochlann' from Morvern.

Set down at least a hundred years before the publication of Macpherson's 'Ossian', the Sleat historian's version of the Morvern battle reveals no obvious influence of the Fenian tradition but, as elsewhere in his passages on Somerled, he does embellish the tale with clan associations which are hardly meaningful and even anachronistic in terms of Somerled's historical period. While it is true, for example, that the Clan MacInnes are associated with Morvern and especially with lands around Loch Aline in the later medieval centuries, neither they nor any other Highland clans can be recognised as such in Somerled's time. Clan identities and traditions did not emerge until rather later in the medieval period and after, when clan historians sought to associate their forebears, wherever possible and however accurately, with prominent figures from history and tradition. Such a process would have forged a natural link between the MacInnes association with Morvern and the Clan Donald tradition locating Somerled and his father in the same region, thus creating one of a number of later clan traditions incorporated by the Sleat historian into his *History of the MacDonalds.*

There is one element in the Sleat *History*, however, which may point more helpfully to the source of the Morvern battle story and it lies in the grisly fate meted out by Somerled to the first of the enemy that he slew, when 'he ript up and took out his heart, desiring the rest to do the same'. Such an unsavoury action is entirely out of character with behaviour elsewhere attributed to Somerled, but it is to some extent reminiscent of the Norse ritual sacrifice called the 'blood-eagle', described in greatest detail by the *Orkneyinga Saga* account of a killing inflicted by the jarl Torf-Einar in the later ninth century. In fact, there is little if anything about the Morvern battle itself reminiscent of any Fenian adventure or Celtic contention and very much more that is Scandinavian in character, leading to the likelihood of a Norse origin for the whole episode and raising the question of how it found its way into the MacMhuirich *History of the MacDonalds* which can be taken to represent the oldest known form of the story.

To attempt to answer that question calls first for some brief account of how the MacMhuirich family found its way to becoming the hereditary bardic dynasty in the service of the Clan Donald and it must begin with a Muireadhach of the *Ó Dálaigh* (or 'O'Daly') bardic family of Westmeath origin and his flight to Scotland in the second decade of the thirteenth century. Muireadhach fled Ireland after killing a tax collector, in 1213 according to the *Annals of the Four Masters,* and found his way to Scotland from where he set out – perhaps as a penance – on the Fifth Crusade which began in 1217. The evidence of his own surviving poetry indicates his return to Scotland, where he married and fathered children before going home at last to Ireland around 1228, after which no more is known of him. From this Muireadhach *Albanach* (or 'the Scotsman') were descended the MacMhuirichs and while there are few records of the family until the fifteenth century – by which time they had been long established as hereditary bards to the Clan Donald – a reference by the Sleat historian to a MacMhuirich on Jura in the late thirteenth century has led the Gaelic authority Derick Thomson to venture that 'we are probably justified in assuming that one or more representatives of the family held bardic office with Somerled's descendants before 1300.'[22]

If the forebear of the MacMhuirichs did not find his way to Scotland until after 1213 and there is no evidence to indicate any association of his descendants with the Clan Donald before the later thirteenth century, then their evidence for the history of the house of Somerled is hardly valid until some four generations after his death in 1164 and it is significant that the narrative – as distinct from the strictly genealogical passages – of the MacMhuirich *History of the MacDonalds* becomes very much richer in detail around the time of Somerled's great-great-grandson Angus Og. Having said that, Muireadhach *Albanach* himself was descended from the prominent Irish bardic family of O'Daly from whom he or his descendants may very possibly have gleaned genuinely historical traditions bearing on Somerled's father's exile in Ireland, a possibility which would lend further credibility to the already very plausible account preserved in the MacMhuirich *History* of Gillebride among the Macguires and Macmahons in Fermanagh.

The appearance of Somerled, however, marks a discernible change in the character of the narrative which would correspond to a quite different source having informed the story of the battle in Morvern and that source can only have lain in local west Highland tradition already at least a century old when it entered into the collective memory of the MacMhuirich bardic family. The origin of that local tradition might just as probably have lain in a Scandinavian as in a Celtic cultural milieu, and the character of the battle in Morvern does incline towards a Norse origin, most especially in its distinct similarity to the victory at Sky Hill by which the *Chronicle of Man* claims Godred Crovan to have won the kingship of the Isle of Man. Both battles reversed a sequence of earlier defeats, both were won by a ruse, and both claimed possession of the land as the fruit of victory. In his editorial introduction to the *Chronicle of Man* account of Godred's victory at Sky Hill, P. A. Munch points to the same tale being told of the Norwegian king Harald Finehair who appropriated to himself all the *udal* (or hereditary lands) of the kingdom and to similar stories told of Jarl Torf-Einar of Orkney in the ninth century and of the conqueror kings of Denmark at much the same time. Professor Munch's comment on Sky Hill could, in fact, just as accurately describe Somerled's victory in Morvern, when he finds that 'a legendary character pervades the whole narrative . . . No doubt the same or similar legends only with local variations existed all over the German[ic] world where kingdoms or lordships had been founded by conquest, in which case property of the soil was always or generally allotted to the conqueror.'[23]

Just such a right of possession by Somerled and his descendant Lords of the Isles is the clear inference of the Sleat historian – who was, of course, writing some two hundred years after the forfeiture of the Lordship to the king of Scots – in the paragraph immediately following his account of the battle in Morvern:

> In a short time he [Somerled] mastered Lorn, Argyle, Kintyre, and Knapdale; most of the inhabitants, knowing these lands were his by right, as formerly belonging to and possessed by his predecessors.

Those lands would indeed have comprised Somerled's domains at the time of his entry into the formal historical record as '*regulus* of Argyll' in 1153, but the date at which he established himself as their overlord remains unknown because the sources of tradition preserving the only account of his rise to power concern themselves hardly at all with details of chronology. Consequently, any chronology for the emergence of Somerled can never be considered better than speculative when it can only be constructed in terms of the reliable dating of other related contemporary events, but might still be worth attempting here.

When Somerled rose in rebellion in 1153, he is said by the *Chronicle of Holyrood* to have done so on behalf of his nephews, the sons of Malcolm mac Heth. The enigmatic Malcolm and his claim to the kingship of Scots will be considered in greater detail in the following chapter, but suffice it to say here that the house of Mac Heth represented the Moray claim to the kingship once held by Macbeth. The marriage of Somerled's sister to Malcolm, who began an imprisonment of more than twenty years in 1134, must have taken place before that date and so it is reasonable to recognise Somerled's family having already achieved some stature by the 1130s. A still greater prominence is implied by Somerled's own marriage to Ragnhild, daughter of Olaf of Man, which has been placed by more recent Clan Donald historians in the year 1140, a plausible date but supported by no real evidence and possibly inferred from the assumption that their eldest son Dugall would have been in his mid-teens when he was offered the kingship of the Isles in 1155.

The dating of Olaf's succession as king of Man and the Isles might offer the most helpful framework for a speculative chronology of Somerled's rise to power, because Olaf, the youngest of Godred Crovan's sons nicknamed *bitling* or 'morsel' by the *Orkneyinga Saga*, is remembered by the *Chronicle of Man* as 'a peaceful man, and had all the kings of Ireland and Scotland so in alliance with him that none dared to disturb the kingdom of the Isles during all his days'. Olaf does seem to have been a monarch more inclined to diplomacy than to warfare, taking as his own wife a daughter of Fergus, lord of Galloway, and giving his daughter by another liaison in marriage to Somerled of Argyll, both unions most realistically understood as sealing alliances with neighbouring rulers. The Sleat historian includes an anecdotal account of Somerled's persuasion of Olaf, whom he calls 'Olay the Red', by having holes drilled into the hull of the king's ship and filled with tallow which dissolved when the vessel put to sea, then demanding the promise of the king's daughter as his bride before supplying plugs to fill the boreholes and save the ship from sinking. The story assuredly owes more to a formula occurring elsewhere in Hebridean folk tradition than to anything in Somerled's authentic marital history, but there might be some genuinely historical implication to be found in its context of a sea expedition launched by Olaf of Man with Somerled as his ally against rebellious Isles chieftains to the north of Ardnamurchan.

The date of Olaf's accession to the kingship of Man is left unclear by the *Chronicle*, which places it at 1103 yet credits him with a reign of forty years when his obituary is reliably dated to 1153. The probability is that he was brought back to Man from his childhood fosterage at the English court of Henry I following the death of Magnus Bareleg in 1103, but did not assume full kingship of Man and the Isles until ten years later, so most historians reasonably consider his effective reign to have begun in 1113. It might well have been the accession of Olaf and its promise of a more pacific kingship of Man and the Isles which encouraged Gillebride's return to Argyll shortly after the year 1113, because had Somerled been born (presumably in the north of Ireland) around 1103, he would have been entering adolescence through the period of his father's low fortunes in the legendary cave and reaching manhood around 1120. Had his rise to power been accomplished through the following decade, his political stature as lord of Argyll by 1130 would have raised his family to the eminence implied by his sister's marriage to Malcolm mac Heth which cannot have taken place more than a very few years after that date. So too and soon afterwards, would Somerled himself have been recognised by Olaf as a formidable ally well worth securing by the customary and convenient device of a marriageable daughter.

When Henry I died in 1135 and his crown was seized by his nephew Stephen to the exclusion of Henry's daughter and favoured successor Matilda, Norman England was thrown into civil war. David I of Scotland was not slow to cross the Tweed in arms, officially in support of his niece Matilda but assuredly also with the intention of pushing his own frontier further to the south. He invaded first in 1136, only to withdraw on the approach of Stephen's army, and again in 1138 when he managed to salvage remarkably generous peace terms from the defeat of his army at the Battle of the Standard.

The name given to the battle commemorates the English army's bringing the standards of three great northern saints to Cowton Moor near Northallerton in Yorkshire, there to confront David's extraordinarily various battle array in which wild warriors out of Galloway fought beside the mailed Norman knights who made up the royal bodyguard. The Cistercian abbot Ailred of Rievaulx, who had known David since boyhood and been in his service before entering the church, set down an account of the Battle of the Standard which preserves careful detail of the deployment of the Scots forces and notes their third line having included 'the men of the Isles and the men of Lorn'. It would seem to have been that specific reference which led the eminent historian A. A. M. Duncan to his persuasive suggestion that 'Somerled, Lord of Argyll,

. . . was doubtless the leader of the West Highland contingent in King David's army in 1138'.[24] If indeed he was and if his presence there can be taken as evidence of loyal submission to the kingship of Scots, then that loyalty was not to outlast David's reign by more than a few months.

3

'IN WICKED REBELLION AGAINST HIS NATURAL LORD'

GAELDOM'S CHALLENGE TO THE CANMORE KINGS

While the authentic detail and precise chronology of events marking out Somerled's rise to power must be considered almost entirely lost to history, those events clearly lay far behind him by the time of his first appearance in the formal historical record, because the Somerled who is noticed by the *Chronicle of Holyrood* in its entry under the year 1153 is already a man of full maturity and firmly established as *regulus* of Argyll.

This term *regulus* – literally translating as 'ruler' – has been variously rendered into English, at one time in the Anglo-Saxon form of 'thane', more often by modern historians as 'kinglet' and most simply by others as 'lord'. It was probably used by the chronicler as the Latin word best corresponding to the Irish *rí* (a provincial king subject to a *rí ruirech* or over-king), but the precise political stature which such a title signified in twelfth-century Scotland remains less than certain. Under the terms of the agreement secured by Magnus Bareleg in 1098, there is every reason to consider Argyll as a part of the mainland confirmed under Scottish sovereignty, but so too would have been the former Norse territories of Caithness and Sutherland whose submission to the king of Scots was neither urgent nor eager. There is good evidence, however, for David I having been due revenues from Argyll and Kintyre and it is preserved in charters from his reign endowing the abbeys of Dunfermline and Holyrood with portions of royal income from those specifically-named territories.[1]

So, too, the presence of 'the men of Lorn' among David's forces at the Battle of the Standard could be taken as evidence for Somerled's domain having owed a military obligation to the king of Scots, unless it might be otherwise explained by their having been recruited to the Scottish muster in some mercenary capacity reminiscent of the activities of the *Gall-Gaedhil* warbands of the ninth century and foreshadowing the service of west Highland and Hebridean 'galloglass' companies in later medieval Ireland. Whether as subject levies or hired soldiery, the arrangement which brought Somerled's warriors to David's banner was in all probability the same as that under which the men of Galloway served in the front line of the same battle-host, because the political status of Somerled is thought to have been very alike to that of his contemporary Fergus of Galloway.

Fergus' origins and ancestry are much more obscure than those of Somerled, although it is highly probable that he was of some similar Celtic-Scandinavian stock,[2] and, while their patterns of alliance do appear to have been differently oriented, the two were certainly related by marriage. Like Somerled, Fergus is recognised as *regulus* by some sources, but as 'lord' (*dominus*) or 'prince' (*princeps*) by others, while the record of a land-grant styling him *Rex Galwitensium* has been recognised by the Galloway historian Daphne Brooke as 'apparently quoting Fergus' own charter and this was the style he applied to himself . . . while he was consistently styled in other men's charters as ruler of Galloway, it was as the King of the Gallovidians that he saw himself.'[3] Although drawing on the evidence of a different range of sources, there is every reason to imagine that the same could just as well be said of Somerled of Argyll. Indeed, the close correspondence between the two in terms of political status was underlined in the influential study by A. A. M. Duncan and A. L. Brown which found 'much to suggest that Somerled held in Argyll a position like that of Fergus in Galloway, and that David I was willing to allow those two to govern their provinces in near independence. The king had thereby two advantages: he had from Galloway and Argyll military contingents when he needed them; and he had two powerful marcher lords protecting the kingdom from the attacks of the Islesmen. Fergus and Somerled were in fact though not in name "mormaers" . . . although their provinces were not those traditionally associated with this office.'[4]

In the minds of contemporary Scottish chroniclers, however, there was no question of Somerled's legitimate subjection to the king of Scots nor of his failure to fulfil that obligation because on those very few occasions when they notice him at all he is recognised as a rebel: specifically in the *Chronicle of Holyrood*, where his rising in alliance with the Mac Heth claim to the kingship is entered under the year 1153, and the *Chronicle of Melrose* entry of his invasion of the Clyde in 1164, on which occasion he is described as having been 'in a state of wicked rebellion for twelve years against his natural lord'. It is a view of Somerled in striking contrast to the unswerving admiration shown him by the Clan Donald seannachies, and yet one which set the mould for the still more hostile accounts of him set down by subsequent generations of Scottish historians of the later medieval period and after. For that reason as much as for their close contemporaneity to Somerled's own lifetime, the origin and perspective of those two twelfth-century chronicles might usefully bear some consideration here.

Both are believed to have had their origin in the monasteries for which they are named: the *Chronicle of Holyrood* in the church of the Holy Rood at Edinburgh, a foundation begun in 1128, and the longer and more expansive *Chronicle of Melrose* in the abbey of St Mary at Melrose which was completed in 1136. In view of those dates, their chronicle entries bearing on Somerled can be accepted as an immediately contemporary record of events, yet of more strategic importance for the chroniclers' perspective is the fact of the Augustinians of Holyrood and Cistercians of Melrose representing two of the religious orders who followed in the wake of the Norman aristocracy imported into Scotland by the Canmore kings and most firmly established there by David I. The monasteries of Holyrood and Melrose might even be said to have enjoyed something of the status of a royal church in David's kingdom, and there can be little doubt of their churchmen being creatures of the same Anglo-Norman cultural milieu as the mailed knights who formed David's bodyguard at the Battle of the Standard or – ironically enough – the northern barons who commanded the opposing forces on that same field. It was a cultural milieu shared also by David himself, and yet at the same time utterly alien to that of Fergus' Galloway and Somerled's Argyll. The chronicles of Holyrood and Melrose must be recognised as the work of total strangers to the language, culture and society of which Somerled was representative, and yet the chroniclers' antipathy towards him sprang from something more pragmatic than that cultural divide, when it is most realistically read as a reflection of the hostility borne by Scotland's new feudal order to the Gaelic-Norse outlands of the west, and also those of the north, which it had come to recognise as breeding-grounds for dynastic challenge to the Canmore kings.

Something more than three hundred years separate Somerled's first recorded 'rebellion against his natural lord' from Kenneth mac Alpin's finally decisive transplantation of the kingship and culture of Scotic Dalriada on to the Pictish royal centre on Tayside where he was to establish in embryo the medieval kingdom of the Scots. Each successive tide of history in the course of those three centuries appears now to have further eroded virtually all that remained of the cultural and political common ground linking the royal house of Mac Alpin to its former western heartland.

The Norse impact, already manifest in Kenneth's own time, was to draw the western coastland and the Hebrides ever further into the orbit of the Scandinavian world while at the same time creating the Norse-Gaelic fusion of blood and culture represented by the *Gall-Gaedhil* aristocracy into which Somerled was born. So too in the north – although perhaps less often emphasised – the immediate proximity of Moray to the southern extent of the Norse mainland territories, comprising Caithness and Sutherland, brought about a cultural fusion in the northern Highlands bearing some similarity to, and kinship with, that of the *Gall-Gaedhil* in the west.

The Mac Alpin kings of Scots, for all their various points of contact with the Scandinavian presence, looked almost always to the southward. Kenneth himself is said by the later medieval Scottish *Chronicle of the Kings* to have 'invaded Saxonland [in fact the northernmost extent of Northumbria] six times . . . and seized Dunbar and burned Melrose'. It was a direction of ambition followed by most of his successors down to Malcolm II, the last king of Scots in direct male line of descent from Kenneth mac Alpin, who inaugurated his reign by laying unsuccessful siege to Durham in 1006 and twelve years later finally confirmed the river Tweed as Scotland's southern frontier with his victory at the battle of Carham.

With no son to follow him into the kingship, Malcolm went to some violent lengths to secure the succession for his grandson Duncan mac Crinan, the son of his daughter and the secular abbot of Dunkeld. Duncan did indeed succeed his grandfather on Malcolm's death in

1034 and would appear to have had his view focussed also to the southward, besieging Durham in 1039 and taking as his queen a kinswoman, possibly a sister, of Siward, the Anglo-Danish earl of Northumbria. Yet the fatal threat to Duncan's kingship was to come from the north and was not long in so doing in the person of Macbeth mac Findlaech, mormaer of Moray. The claim of Macbeth, who seized for himself the kingship when he slew Duncan near Elgin in 1040, may have derived from the right of matrilinear descent if his mother had indeed been a daughter of Malcolm II. It might, also or otherwise, have been rooted in the more distant past and harked back to the eighth-century contention over the kingship of Dalriada between the kindreds of the Cenel Loairn, from which the house of Moray believed itself descended, and the Cenel Gabrain, claimed by the genealogies to have included the ancestors of the Mac Alpin kings. If so, then that ancient dynastic rivalry was to cast its long shadow over the history of the kingship of Scots through the most part of the two centuries following Macbeth's downfall in 1057.

The sons of Duncan apparently sought the security of exile soon after the death of their father, Domnall said to have taken flight to the Isles while his elder brother Malcolm found sanctuary with his mother's people in Northumbria and also a formidable ally in Earl Siward with whom he returned to Scotland to challenge Macbeth in 1054. It took another three years for Malcolm to bring down Macbeth at Lumphanan at the southernmost extent of Moray, and even then it was not until the following year of 1058, after his further northward advance to slay Macbeth's stepson and immediate successor Lulach in Strathbogie, that Malcolm mac Duncan, more usually remembered as Malcolm Canmore,[5] began his thirty-five year reign in the kingship of Scots.

If the feudalisation of Scotland – which was to be most fully accomplished by David I and his Anglo-Norman aristocracy established on Scottish estates in exchange for their knightly service – can be recognised as a 'Norman Conquest' then its beginnings are surely to be found in the reign of his father Malcolm Canmore.

It has been said of Malcolm that it was his 'destiny to be confronted by Normans all his life'.[6] He would, indeed, have been barely into his teens when he was introduced and, in all probability, for a time fostered at the court of Edward the Confessor, himself half Norman by birth and raised in Normandy. Thirty years later Malcolm was to confront the more imposing Norman presence of the Conqueror himself when he made formal submission, and gave over his son as hostage, to William at Abernethy in 1072, but the last of those confrontations came in the form of the ambush near Alnwick in November 1093 when he met his death at the hands of a Norman knight in the service of a Norman earl of Northumbria.

Malcolm's most significant contact with Anglo-continental, if not strictly Norman, influence must be placed around the year 1070 when he married his second wife, the famously pious and later sanctified queen Margaret. The daughter of the West Saxon prince Edward, son of Edmund Ironside, and a German princess thought to have been related to the Holy Roman Emperor, Margaret fled with her family when Cnut the Dane seized the English throne in 1016 and spent most of her early life in central Europe, where she was raised in, and undeniably influenced by, the fiercely evangelistic climate of a Hungary only recently converted to Christianity. While the extent of Margaret's influence on Scottish church and culture is considered by some modern historians to have been overstated, her arrival at the Scottish court, accompanied by her brother and their following of English nobility, inevitably brought with it a transforming infusion of Anglo-continental custom and culture which is clearly reflected in the names bestowed on the six sons she bore to the king. Malcolm (Gael. *Mael Coluim*) and his brother Domnall had been given unmistakably Gaelic names, each of which had been earlier borne by two Mac Alpin kings of Scots, as also had Malcolm's own eldest son, born to his first queen Ingibjorg (said to have been the former wife or widow, but more probably the daughter, of the Orkney jarl Thorfinn), who was named Duncan (Gael. *Dúnchad*) presumably in memory of his grandfather. In sudden contrast, then, the names given to the sons of Malcolm and Margaret – Edward, Edmund, Etheldred, Edgar, Alexander and David (the three last-named all eventually following their father into the kingship) – must bear their own testimony to the queen's cultural influence on the Scottish court and, inevitably also, on the succeeding generation of kings of the house of Canmore.

For all that influence and despite the efforts of earlier kings of Scots to secure succession by primogeniture, Malcolm was to be followed into the kingship – as in the old Celtic custom – by his brother. Very shortly after Malcolm's death, and that of Margaret who outlived her husband by just four days, Domnall Ban appears to have emerged out of his long exile to claim the kingship of Scots and if his claim was supported, as it surely must have been, by a warband recruited in the Gaelic west then the entry under the year 1093 in the *Anglo-Saxon Chronicle* supplies the first recorded evidence of Gaeldom's hostility to the character of the Canmore court:

> The Scots elected Donald, brother of Malcolm, as their king and drove out all the English who had been with King Malcolm.

Domnall was to reign for just six months before he faced the first challenge to his kingship, and it came in the person of Malcolm Canmore's eldest son, the Duncan born to him by his first queen. Having been given over as a hostage under the terms of the submission of 1072, Duncan had spent some twenty years of his youth and young manhood in Norman England, many of those years held as a prisoner whenever his father proved troublesome. On the death of William the Conqueror and the succession of William Rufus in 1089, Duncan was released from captivity by personal command of the new king and soon afterwards knighted by Duke Robert of Normandy. The son of a Scots king, grandson of an Orkney jarl, and yet appearing in every aspect as a Norman knight, he would have presented the ideal candidate to a Norman king of England looking to put in place his own client king of Scots, and such was evidently the policy behind the events of 1094 as described in the closely contemporary chronicle of Florent of Worcester:

> Duncan, son of King Malcolm, besought and entreated King William, under whom he then served, to grant him his father's kingdom and swore allegiance to him; so he hastened into Scotland with a multitude of English and Normans, and expelled his uncle Donald from the kingdom, and then reigned in his stead. Then some of the Scots assembled and murdered nearly all his men, and he himself with difficulty escaped with a few. But after

> this day they suffered him to reign, on condition that he would introduce no more English or Normans into Scotland . . .

But not for very long on the evidence of the Scottish *Chronicle of the Kings* when it records 'Duncan, son of Malcolm, reigned for six months [and] was killed in Mondynes by Maelpetair, earl of the Mearns, and again Domnall, son of Duncan, reigned for three years'.

Domnall Ban's second reign was brought to its end when Edgar, the eldest surviving of the sons of Malcolm and Margaret,[7] brought to Scotland another army provided by William Rufus and reclaimed the kingdom for the house of Canmore in 1097. Driven from the kingship for the second and final time, Domnall was deliberately blinded – a retribution reminiscent of the old Irish custom whereby a mutilated claimant was disqualified from kingship – and reduced to an elderly, sightless captive at the disposal of the new royal family. It is of some significance, however, that he was not immediately deprived of his life and, indeed, the only closely contemporary source specifying any date for Domnall's death is the chronicle compiled in Normandy by the English-born Orderic Vitalis which records his having been killed by Alexander when he followed his brother Edgar into the kingship in 1107.

Pitiful creature as he must have been at the last, Domnall was at least afforded the dignity of burial at Dunkeld, the royal church of the Mac Alpin dynasty, until some unspecified later date when – according to the *Chronicle of the Kings* – his remains were removed for the greater honour of interment on Iona, a gesture which will bear some further consideration in a later chapter here. The sources of history preserve little enough detail of the life of Domnall Ban, but such evidence as they do supply points quite clearly to his association with Gaelic Scotland at the close of the eleventh century and it is that association which is of particular importance at this point.

While sanctuary amongst his mother's family must have directed Malcolm's flight to Northumbria after Macbeth's seizure of the kingship in 1040, there is no such obvious explanation of his younger brother Domnall having fled to the Isles, but there is a clue to be found in the claim made by John of Fordun's fourteenth-century *Chronicle of the Scottish Nation* for his grandfather Crinan, abbot of Dunkeld, having also held the office of 'seneschal of the islands'. Fordun would seem to be the earliest source of information for Domnall's having 'betook himself to the isles' and his evidence could be taken to infer Crinan's having had kinfolk, or at least trustworthy friends, in the west willing to provide the security of an offshore refuge for the boy prince.

Unless he can be identified with the unnamed 'king of Scots' whose daughter is said by a sixteenth-century genealogy to have married an Irish prince settled in Argyll in the second half of the eleventh century and from whom the MacSweens claim descent, history knows nothing further of Domnall until his reappearance in 1093. He can only be assumed to have spend the greater part of his adult life, a period perhaps as long as half a century, in the orbit of the Hebrides and, in all probability also, of the coastland of Argyll. Domnall would thus have grown to manhood and into later middle age within the cultural province of the *Gall-Gaedhil*, and so – as the eminent historian Gordon Donaldson observed – 'he has been characterised as "an incorrigible old Celt" but he was as likely to have learned Norse as Celtic ways in the west'.[8] When he does at last reappear in the historical record, it is hardly possible to recognise Domnall Ban as other than the Gaelic-Norse claimant to the kingship of Scots and, even as a mutilated captive, he might still have provided Gaeldom with a figurehead for a renewed challenge to the house of Canmore. The succession of a new king had so often occasioned similar challenges in the past that such a dangerous possibility might very well have prompted Alexander to have had his otherwise apparently harmless old uncle put to death around the time of his own succession to the kingship.

Alexander himself died in 1124, and the kingship had passed to his brother David, the youngest of the sons of Malcolm and Margaret, before Gaeldom once again challenged the Canmore dynasty. Through the intervening decades, however, the source of that challenge appears to have shifted its location from Argyll and the Isles to the northern Highlands where it had found a new focus in the long shadow of Macbeth and his political heirs of the house of Moray. It was in the year 1130 that Angus, grandson of Macbeth's successor Lulach, came out of Moray with an impressive war-host advancing southward until brought to battle – at Stracathro in Forfarshire according to Fordun – and routed by an army mustered in David's defence. The uprising was evidently considered of great moment and noticed across a wide range of closely contemporary sources, whose accounts vary in abundance of detail as much as in terms of reference and, perhaps also, in reliability. Angus' forces are numbered at four thousand strong by the *Annals of Ulster* or at five thousand by the Norman chronicler Robert de Torigni,[9] as by Orderic Vitalis who also identifies the commander of David's forces as 'his cousin' Edward, son of Earl Siward of Northumbria. The *Chronicle of Melrose* and the *Anglo-Saxon Chronicle* both recognise Angus as 'earl' of Moray, while the *Annals of Ulster* style him 'king', but no source denies his having been one of the many men of Moray slain in the battle.

Angus should perhaps be properly styled in the old form of *mormaer* (sometimes translated as 'great steward') of Moray because he was, in fact, the last of a long line of hereditary mormaers of that province, including his uncle Maelsnechtai, his great-grandfather Gillecomgain and, of course, his great-grandmother's second husband Macbeth, later king of Scots. His mother was the daughter of Gillecomgain's son Lulach, adopted or fostered by Macbeth and proclaimed his successor in the kingship, so Angus' claim to the kingship of Scots could hardly be said to lack legitimacy when it was based on his descent not only from Lulach but also from the Cenel Loairn kings of eighth-century Dalriada.[10] In the absence of any reliably recorded offspring, his death amidst the slaughter at Stracathro might have been thought to mark the end of the house of Moray and of its ancient claim on the kingship of Scots; as, indeed, is indicated by Orderic Vitalis' description of David's forces having 'pursued the fugitives and entered Moray, which lacked a defender and lord, and . . . obtained the entire control of that extensive district'. Thus, says Orderic, 'David increased his power', and it is true that he did establish royal burghs at Elgin, Forres and Inverness, but his advance into Moray appears not to have extended beyond the Great Glen and the reason for that restraint may well have been Angus' cause having already been taken up by a successor claimant in the person of the mysterious Malcolm mac Heth.

Malcolm mac Heth's earliest-dated appearance in the historical record is also found in the chronicle of Orderic Vitalis and placed under the year 1124 when he is said to have attempted to 'snatch the kingdom' from

David – who succeeded Alexander in that year – and to have 'fought against him in two sufficiently fierce battles. But David, who was loftier in understanding and in power and wealth, conquered him and his followers'. The historical value of that entry cannot be considered better than doubtful, not just by reason of Orderic's reputation as one of the least reliable authorities for the period but because nowhere else in the sources is there any supporting notice of Malcolm's activity in 1124, so it is possible that Orderic might have conflated the evidence for Malcolm's involvement in two conflicts with David and placed it under the date of David's accession, or that he might simply have misplaced a notice of Malcolm's rebellion of 1134 ten years too early.

The next dated notice of Malcolm is more reliably entered in Orderic's chronicle – as it is almost identically in that of Robert de Torigni and placed by both sources under the year 1130 – where he is identified by name as the ally of Angus of Moray in his widely noticed revolt of that year. Malcolm evidently escaped the fate of Angus in the rout of the men of Moray and, four years later, was able to take up the challenge to David I on his own account, apparently with his own new allies, but with no greater success – on the evidence of the *Chronicle of Melrose* at 1134:

> Malcolm was taken and placed in close custody in the town of Roxburgh.

The truncated evidence of the Melrose *Chronicle* is helpfully elaborated by Ailred of Rievaulx in his account of the Battle of the Standard where he supplies greater detail of the circumstances surrounding Malcolm's capture in a speech he attributes to Robert de Brus – one of the knights at the head of King Stephen's forces and, of course, forebear of a future king of Scots – who reminds David I of his debt of gratitude to the same Anglo-Norman nobility upon whom he had now chosen to make war.

> 'Remember when in a past year thou didst beseech for the aid of the English against Malcolm, the heir of his father's hatred and persecution, how joyful, how eager, how willing to help, how ready for danger came Walter Espec and very many other nobles of the English to meet thee at Carlisle: how many ships they prepared, how they made war, with what forces they made

> defence; until they took Malcolm himself, surrendered to them; taken, they bound him; and delivered him over bound. So did the fear of us while binding his limbs bind still more the courage of the Scots, and by quenching all hope of success remove the presumption to rebel . . .'

As would seem to have been the case when Angus of Moray invaded four years earlier, David had turned once more to the military might of Norman England when threatened with the rebellion of Malcolm mac Heth, and the indications of the character and location of the forces mustered in his support by Walter Espec (who was himself also a principal commander of Stephen's army on the field of the Standard) will bear some further consideration here, but it is the apparent size of those forces and its implication for the strength of Malcolm's rebellion which is of first importance now.

The serious urgency of the response to Malcolm's rebellion and the apparently substantial war-host which had attached itself to his cause bear testimony to his political stature, which must have been founded, in at least some measure, upon his lineage; raising the still unresolved question as to the real ancestry and origins of this Malcolm, son of Heth. The earliest authorities to pronounce upon his parentage are the chronicles of Orderic Vitalis and Robert de Torigni, both of whom describe him, in their entries at 1124 and 1130 respectively, as 'the base-born [presumably meaning "illegitimate"] son of Alexander [I]'. Ailred of Rievaulx, who as a long-standing friend of David was better placed than most to know the truth of the matter, is unhelpfully vague when the speech he attributes to de Brus refers only to 'Malcolm, the heir of his father's hatred and persecution'. Such a description could apply to a son of Alexander because there certainly is evidence for hostility between Alexander and David, but it could be just as well applied to any son of at least one member of the house of Moray and such a candidate might be thought better able to raise a rebellion in the Gaelic outlands than even the most disaffected illegitimate offspring of one of the Canmore kings.

The distinctly Gaelic character of Malcolm's patronymic – 'mac Heth' being usually understood to mean 'son of Aedh' – points to Gaeldom, and specifically to Moray in view of the evidence for his involvement in Angus' rebellion, as his region of origin, but still need not entirely disallow the claim for Alexander having been his natural father. It is quite possible, for example, that 'Heth' might represent the name of his mother or, rather more probably, of his foster-father; and one candidate for such a foster-father – or, indeed, for his real father if Alexander's paternity is rejected – has been suggested as the earl Aed or Heth, who may well have been of Moray and whose name is found among witnesses to charters from the early reign of David I.

Perhaps the most ambitious possibility is that proposed by the clan history of the Mackays – assuming the name Mackay to have evolved from 'MacHeth' which is found in the sources as a family surname, as distinct from a strict patronymic, by the second decade of the thirteenth century. The proposal hinges upon the entry placed under the year 1163 in the *Chronicle of Holyrood* stating that 'King Malcolm [IV, David's grandson and successor] transported the men of Moray', which was elaborated by Fordun into the king having 'transferred all the rebel nation of Moray and scattered them . . . so that not even one native of that land abode there and he installed therein his own peaceful people.' Edward Cowan's study of the historical Macbeth points to Fordun's account being cited by Mackay historians 'to explain the arrival of their supposed ancestors, the MacHeths in Sutherland. The eponymous of the MacHeths is alleged to be Aed, husband of Lulach's daughter, which if true would neatly link the MacHeths into Macbeth's kindred, but the matter is contentious.'[11]

If academic historians have yet to reach conclusive agreement as to who Malcolm mac Heth was, at least they do know now who he was not, because he clearly cannot have been the same person as the extraordinary rebel bishop Wimund (with whom he seems to have been first confused by Fordun and since by an alarming number of historians following in his wake). Wimund's career is remarkably well recorded by virtue of the account of him included by the Yorkshireman William of Newburgh in his *Historia* set down in the later 1190s. Wimund is also noticed by Robert de Torigni, but it is William who must represent the best-placed authority when his own monastery lay just a few miles from Wimund's place of retirement at Byland where he recalled having 'often seen him and heard of his most audacious actions'.

Wimund first enters William's history as one of the company of monks from Furness in Cumbria brought over to the Isle of Man in 1134 to form the community of the monastery at Rushen following its foundation by the Manx king Olaf, youngest son of Godred Crovan and, of course, also Somerled's father-in-law. Once established on Man, says William of Newburgh, Wimund 'so pleased the barbarous natives with the sweetness of his address and openness of his countenance, being also of a tall and athletic build, that they requested him to become their bishop, and obtained their desire'. Almost as soon as he was raised to the episcopacy, however, he gathered around him the beginnings of a personal warband and announced that 'he was the son of the earl of Moray [presumably the late Angus], and that he was deprived of the inheritance of his fathers by the king of Scotland . . . and that it was his intention not merely to assert his rights, but to avenge his wrongs . . .'

> All the people being incited and having taken an oath to him he began his mad career throughout the neighbouring islands. Every day he was joined by troops of adherents . . . and, like some mighty commander, he inflamed their desires. He then made a descent on the provinces of Scotland, wasting all before him with rapine and slaughter; but whenever a royal army was despatched against him he eluded the whole warlike preparation, either by retreating to distant forests or by taking to the sea; and when the troops had retired, he again issued from his hiding-places to ravage the provinces.

He had become 'an object of terror', says William, 'even to the king' so that eventually David 'was compelled to soothe the plunderer . . . yielding a certain province to him, together with the monastery of Furness, he soothed his incursions for a while'. Now in possession of his own estates, Wimund turned from terrorism to tyranny and vented his especial oppression on his former monastic community at Furness until sometime around 1148 when he was ambushed 'by some of his people, with the consent of the nobles', blinded and emasculated 'for the sake of the kingdom of Scotland, not for that of Heaven'. 'Afterwards', concludes William, 'he came to us [i.e. the Cistercian order] at Byland and quietly continued there many years until his death.'

Wimund's dates, first of all, entirely disallow his having been the same person as Malcolm mac Heth, who is known to have begun his twenty-three years' captivity at Roxburgh in the same year as Wimund first came to Man as a monk, only afterwards launching his career of rebellion. So too, the sightless, mutilated Wimund had been almost ten years in enforced retirement at Byland when Malcolm was finally released from imprisonment in 1157. Of greater interest here, though, is Wimund's significance in the wider context – which he does share with Malcolm, as also with Somerled – of Gaelic Scotland in rebellion against the house of Canmore. It is in that context that Wimund's claim to descent from the house of Moray demands some consideration, and perhaps a little more generosity than is afforded him by William of Newburgh who was, after all, a monk of the same Cistercian order and monastic *paruchia* as King David's friend Ailred, evidently subscribing also to closely similar political sympathies. Thus William's allegation that Wimund 'not fearing the judgement of truth, feigned himself to be the son of the Earl of Moray' perfectly concurs with Ailred's own reference (in his *Eulogy to David*) to 'a certain pseudo-bishop who lied and said he was the Earl of Moray's son', and neither can be assumed free from bias.

Whilst not necessarily accepting that Wimund was who he claimed to be, the lavish settlement bestowed on him by David and the striking similarity of his ultimate fate to that of Domnall Ban do raise the possibility of his professed cause having not been – or, at least, not at the time thought to have been – totally fraudulent. Even if William was correct in his dismissal of Wimund's claim, he cannot have been correct in his opening statement that 'this person was born in England'. For Wimund's eloquence to have made so great an impression as William describes on the people of Man, and presumably also those of the Isles, would have demanded of him a fluency in the Gaelic–Norse dialect of the region such as would have been entirely beyond the capacity of a twelfth-century Englishman. There are, in fact, two fragments of evidence, one of them suggesting and the other even confirming Wimund to have been native to the Isles. The first of these is preserved in the letter with which Olaf of Man invested authority of episcopal appointment in the monastery at Furness and lies in his express concern that the Christian faith in his kingdom be not 'rendered desolate under outsiders'; the second in a list of bishops consecrated by Archbishop

Thomas of York which includes a reference to Wimund's ordination as Bishop of the Isles and quotes his 'profession in writing which thus begins: "I, Wimund, of the holy church on Skye . . ."'

His name, on the other hand and assuming it to be his true given name rather than one adopted on his entry into the monastic life, would not indicate any Hebridean or Gaelic origin, because *Wimund* was a name Old English in character and current in Anglo-Saxon England before the end of the eighth century. It would, however, have borne a close phonetic similarity to the Old Norse personal name *Vémundr*, which could well be taken to indicate a man of Hebridean Norse background, and which would have been quite naturally rendered as the Anglo-Saxon *Wimund* among a northern English monastic community.

All of which would support the conclusion reached by Andrew McDonald's investigation of this strange character which finds that 'the evidence strongly suggests that Wimund was drawn from within the ambit of the mixed Norse and Gaelic world of Man, the Western Isles and the Irish Sea in the twelfth century. If this is true, his origins would have lain with the same cultural milieu that produced Somerled, Fergus of Galloway and Malcolm mac Heth – all of them linked by the common thread of challenge they mounted to the MacMalcolm [Canmore] dynasty.'[12]

Such little detail as is known of the two Moray-connected rebellions raised in the years following 1130 does at least confirm their region of origin and activity to have shifted away from the Highlands beyond the Mounth and into the islands and coastland of the west.

The reference to Malcolm mac Heth's revolt made by Robert de Brus, at least in the form of text preserved by Ailred, is quite specific as to the Anglo-Norman nobles who came to David's aid having joined him 'at Carlisle', a place of muster which points to a theatre of operations in the south-west of Scotland and so close to Fergus of Galloway's territory as to implicate his involvement, at least in some wise, with Malcolm's cause. So too, the reference to the 'many ships' which David's allies brought to his defence must infer some naval or seaborne component in the rebellion, which in turn implicates one of the western sea-kings or his fleet in support of the rebel forces, and such an ally can hardly have been anyone other than Somerled, whose sister Malcolm had, by that time, already taken to wife.

Wimund arrived on Man in the year of Malcolm's capture, so his rising must be dated to the years following 1134, but its geographical context prompted Andrew McDonald to recognise implications similar to those of the Mac Heth rebellion: 'Wimund's activities in raiding the mainland would have taken him through the domains of not only the Manx kings of the Isles but also Somerled of Argyll and Fergus of Galloway . . . There is, however, no evidence that they resisted or opposed his activities – indeed we might well imagine that they condoned them'.[13]

There is, of course, no question as to Somerled's direct involvement when the house of Mac Heth next rose in rebellion, because it is in the notice of that rising entered in the *Chronicle of Holyrood* under the year 1153 that he makes his first entry into the formal historical record.

> David, king of the Scots, of pious memory, died upon the ninth of the kalends of June [24th May], upon the Sunday before Ascension Day. His successor in the kingdom was his grandson Malcolm, the son of Henry, the earl of Northumberland: he was twelve years old . . . Stephen, king of England, entered into a treaty of perpetual peace and friendship with Henry, the most noble earl of Anjou, upon the feast-day of St Leonard the Abbot [6th November]. Upon that same day, Somerled and his nephews, that is to say, the sons of Malcolm [mac Heth], having taken to themselves many associates, rebelled against king Malcolm and caused grievous disturbances over the greater part of Scotland.

It would have been more than likely – and, indeed, only natural – for the wife of Malcolm mac Heth, and her sons with her, to have sought refuge with her brother following her husband's capture and imprisonment in 1134 and it would follow that the sons of Malcolm, having grown to manhood under Somerled's protection, should turn to him as their closest and most powerful ally when the opportunity arose for them to renew their father's challenge to the house of Canmore.

Just such an opportunity offered itself in 1153, following the death at Carlisle of the elderly king David, 'oppressed by sickness' according to a contemporary Hexham chronicler,[14] and the succession of his grandson

Malcolm. David's only son Henry – whose name reflects his mother's kinship to the Anglo-Norman royal house – had died in the previous year, leaving his eldest son Malcolm, then just some twelve years old, as heir apparent to the Canmore kingship. Thus came about the succession of the boy-king Malcolm IV,[15] and it must have been the high probability of just such a situation occurring in earlier centuries – when warrior kings rarely survived to any great age and a brother was more likely than a son to offer a credible successor – which had become institutionalised as the 'kinship' system of royal succession (whereby kingship passed alternately between two related lineages within a kindred), especially characteristic of the Celtic kingdom of the Scots. The same situation, however, presented an obvious difficulty for an emergent feudal monarchy seeking to follow the 'primogeniture' system of succession (under which the father was followed into the kingship by his eldest son) when the successor was so young as was Malcolm and dangerously vulnerable to challenge from any rival claimant.

Nonetheless, the boy Malcolm was inaugurated into the kingship of Scots following the death of his grandfather, but 'hardly had the plaudits died away on the Moot Hill at Scone' – writes the historian of Norman Scotland, R. L. Graeme Ritchie – 'when the smouldering hostility to the sons of Margaret broke out again'.[16] That smouldering hostility would have been fanned into a wider conflagration by the 'very great famine and pestilence among livestock' entered by the Holyrood chronicler under the following year, because the uprising dated to the November of 1153 almost certainly achieved greater momentum through the spring and summer of 1154.

Other than the identification by the same source of Somerled as its leader and its claim for his causing 'grievous disturbance over the greater part of Scotland', the formal historical record preserves no further detail of the course of events of the 1153 rebellion.[17] Neither do the sources of Clan Donald tradition contain any specific reference to the Mac Heth rebellion, although there is an episode found in the Sleat *History of the MacDonalds*, apparently placed in the years following the succession of Malcolm IV, which has been shown on closer investigation to contain at least one feature of plausibly historical bearing on Somerled's rebellion of that period.

> Now, Sommerled being envied by the rest of the nobility of Scotland for his fortune and valour, king Malcolm being young, thought by all means his kingdom would suffer by the faction, ambition, and envy of his leading men, if Sommerled's power would not be crushed. Therefore, they convened and sent an army to Argyle under the command of Gilchrist, Thane of Angus, who, harassing and ravaging the country wherever he came, desired Sommerled to give up his right to Argyle or abandon the Isles. But Sommerled, making all speed he could in raising his vassals and followers, went after them; and, joining battle, they fought fiercely on both sides with great slaughter, till night parted them. Two thousand on Sommerled's side, and seven thousand on Gilchrist's side, were slain in the field. Being wearied, they parted and marched off at the dawn of the day, turning their backs to one another.

There is, of course, no contemporary record of the blood-fray described by the Sleat historian and neither is anything known of the origin, authority or provenance of his original source. There are, moreover, aspects of the story bearing a suspicious similarity to other conflicts fought by Somerled and, indeed, to one from the later history of the Clan Donald,[18] but it would not have been uncharacteristic of the Sleat historian to incorporate such elements to elaborate his account of what might still have originally been a real battle. Neither the circumstances nor the character of the events he describes lie entirely beyond the realm of possibility, especially when his story has been shown to contain one fragment of plausibly historical substance.

This clue lies in the name given to Somerled's opposing commander – identified as 'Gilchrist, Thane of Angus' – which attracted the curiosity of R. Andrew McDonald, who is almost alone among academic historians in his pursuit of genuinely historical evidence from the Sleat historian. While there was a twelfth-century earl of Angus by the name of Gilchrist, his earliest appearance in the historical record is not found until 1198 which would place him rather too late to have been at war with Somerled more than forty years earlier. 'There is, however, another candidate for Somerled's opponent', suggests McDonald, 'who is viable in terms of his name, chronology and geography: Gilchrist, the earl of Menteith first mentioned in about 1164 and dead by 1198, so it is not impossible that he was active in the late 1150s . . .'

> The strategic position of Menteith, which shared a common frontier with Argyll, makes it quite possible that an earl of Menteith might well have fought against Somerled. In this context it is also interesting to note that the rulers of Menteith seemed to have exercised intermittent authority over Cowal and Kintyre, although how they acquired such authority remains unknown.[19]

This identification of a plausible, even likely, opponent does lend a new measure of credibility to the story in the Sleat *History*, which if rooted in an actual event might suggest its outcome having led Somerled to withdraw from the Mac Heth rebellion of the early 1150s.

As to the subsequent course of that uprising, all that can be said is that it appears to have been effectively over by 1156, on the evidence of the entry placed under that year in the *Chronicle of Holyrood* and, similarly but rather more fully, in the *Chronicle of Melrose*:

> Dovenald [Domnall], the son of Malcolm [mac Heth], was captured at Whithorn [on the Solway], and imprisoned in the tower at Roxburgh, along with his father.

Malcolm mac Heth was to be reconciled with the king and released from captivity, presumably with his son, in the following year. The Mac Heth claim, however, was still not extinguished and would continue to bedevil the royal house of Canmore into the thirteenth century when Kenneth MacHeth (another son or, more probably, a grandson of Malcolm) was killed in contention with Alexander II in 1215. By this time, the MacHeths had become allied with another disaffected kindred, the MacWilliams who claimed descent from Duncan II, and Edward Cowan has explained how 'remoteness of location, rebellion and revolt, and possibly even reality, conferred a kinship with Macbeth upon these two kindreds. The last of their line was a young child of MacWilliam descent who in 1230 had her brains dashed out on the mercat cross at Forfar.'[20]

The chronicler's claim for Somerled's having been 'in wicked rebellion for twelve years against his natural lord' has led to the inference that he continued the MacHeth rebellion until his own apparent reconciliation with the king in 1160, if not indeed until his last battle at Renfrew in 1164, but there is no evidence in the historical record to link any aspect of his activities with the MacHeth cause after the entry under 1153 in the *Chronicle of Holyrood*. Indeed, even by the time of his nephew's capture at Whithorn, there is every indication of Somerled's attention having been already drawn away from contending claims to the kingship of the Scots and newly focussed on the kingdom of the Isles.

4

'THE RUIN OF THE KINGDOM OF THE ISLES'

SOMERLED'S WAR ON THE KINGDOM OF MAN

The obituary of David, king of Scots, was entered under the year 1153 across a wide range of closely contemporary sources and framed by almost all of them in terms of the highest honour. The death of Olaf, king of Man and the Isles, occurred just five weeks later and was noticed by only one of those sources, the chronicle set down by monks of the church he himself had founded at Rushen some twenty years before,[1] yet his passing can be seen now, in the light of ensuing events, as the landmark of rather greater prominence from the viewpoint of Gaelic Scotland.

Olaf's death brought to an end a long reign which represented an interlude of tranquillity rare in the history of his vast island kingdom and attributed by the *Chronicle of Man* to his own natural and accomplished diplomacy.

> He was a peaceful man, who had all the kings of Ireland and of Scotland so much in alliance with him that none dared disturb the kingdom of the Isles through all his days. He took a wife, Affrica by name and a daughter of Fergus of Galloway.

It was this 'Affrica' – a name almost certainly representing a latinised form of the Norse *Aufreka* – who bore Olaf his one legitimate son, while his other offspring, including the daughter who was to marry Somerled, are said by the *Chronicle* to have been the children of his 'several concubines'.

The *Orkneyinga Saga*, however, tells of an Ingibjorg, one of the daughters of Jarl Hakon Paulsson, who 'married Olaf *bitling*, king of the Sudreys'. Even though the *Chronicle of Man* makes no mention of Olaf's marriage to any Ingibjorg and neither does the *Saga* record any offspring of that union, the claim has led to the proposal of Ingibjorg having borne the daughter who became Somerled's wife. For all the difficulty of believing an Orkney jarl's daughter considered as just another anonymous concubine, the monastic chronicler's allegation of Olaf's over-indulgence in 'the domestic vice of kings' bears its own testimony to ecclesiastical disapproval of all but the most proper of marital arrangements. Although frowned upon by the church, such irregular marital practices as concubinage and even polygamy were far from uncommon among the royalty and nobility of the Norse-Gaelic world (a convenient example being Jarl Hakon himself all of whose offspring were born to his mistress), so it is fully possible that the omission of Ingibjorg's name by the Manx chronicler simply reflects the informal nature of her relationship with Olaf.[2] Neither is Somerled's wife actually named either by the *Chronicle of Man* or the Clan Donald histories where she is referred to only as Olaf's daughter, leaving the *Orkneyinga Saga* as the only early source to identify her by name as *Ragnhild.* That fact alone does lend considerable weight to the possibility of a noble Orcadian lineage for Somerled's wife, through her for his sons, and, ultimately also, for their descendant Lords of the Isles and prominent west Highland kindreds.

It was Olaf's fully legitimate son Godred, however, who was to follow him into the kingship of Man and the Isles, but not without some intervening violent contention. In the year 1152, Godred had sailed for Norway to do homage to its king Inge, who was, of course, his father's overlord. Possibly tempted by the absence from Man of the heir apparent, the three sons of Olaf's elder brother Harald (Godred Crovan's second son, who had been blinded and emasculated by his elder brother Lagmann almost sixty years earlier) returned from their long exile in Dublin in company with a warband to assert their claim to 'half of the whole kingdom of the Isles'. While the course of events comprising this effective invasion of Man is left indistinct by the *Chronicle*,[3] its finale is recorded in vivid detail of the meeting arranged by Olaf to negotiate with his nephews which one of them chose to conclude by producing an axe and striking off the king's head.

'A few days afterwards,' according to the chronicler, 'they collected a fleet and sailed over to Galloway, wishing to subdue it to themselves.' The men of Galloway were ready for the invasion, assembling so formidably to resist it that the nephews' forces 'fled in great confusion [back] to Man', where they turned on Galwegians settled on the island, of whom 'some they slew and the others they expelled'. All of which, especially in the light of the *Chronicle* account of subsequent events, raises the possibility of the pursuit of a family feud by the Haraldssons – who must have been in later middle age, if not fairly elderly, by 1153 – having supplied the pretext for a Dublin Norse bid to seize kingship of Man and the Isles. Whatever might have been the real background to the invasion, the *Chronicle* confirms its initial success as having been only short-lived.

> In the following autumn [whether of 1153 or, more probably, of 1154 is unclear], his [Olaf's] son Godred came from Norway with five ships; and landed in Orkney. All the chieftains of the Isles rejoiced on hearing that he had come and, meeting together, chose him unanimously as their king. Godred therefore came to Man, seized the three sons of Harald and in vengeance for his father punished them with a fitting death.

After an admission of the 'many things worthy of remembrance [relating to Godred], which we have omitted for sake of brevity', the *Chronicle* continues with an account of events placed 'in the third year of his reign', by which it is generally taken to mean the year 1155.[4]

The first of these is presented as the response to a request by 'the men of Dublin' for Godred to become their king when he crossed to Dublin, with 'a huge fleet and a numerous army'. Within a few days, however, Muirchertach mac Lochlainn, 'the king of Ireland', had assembled a force of 'three thousand horse', entrusted it to the command of his brother and despatched it to Dublin, where it was confronted by Godred 'with his followers and all the people of Dublin'. Driven back by 'a great attack' and demoralised by the death in battle of the king's brother, the survivors of the Irish host were reduced to making their escape on horseback and the campaign was abandoned. 'And after a few days, Godred returned to Man.'

The fact of there being no notice of Godred's seizure of Dublin in any of the Irish annals does cast doubt on the historical authenticity of the whole episode as presented by the Manx chronicler, especially when a suspiciously similar battle against the Dublin Norse fought and lost by the same Muirchertach – although probably in the Boyne valley – is entered in the *Annals of Ulster* at 1162, by which date Godred is known to have been in Norway, having fled Man four years earlier. Nonetheless, the Irish historian Seán Duffy finds it 'impossible to tell if this alleged incident is real or not, but there hardly seems much reason for inventing it and the details, if vague, are at least plausible'.[5] While the shadow of suspicion still hangs over this Dublin episode, its more immediate importance at this point lies in Godred's return to Man, which is presented by the *Chronicle* as a prelude to the entry of Somerled into the history of the kingdom of the Isles.

> Godred returned to Man and gave the chieftains of the Isles leave to return home. When he saw himself firmly established as its king, and that none could oppose him, he began to impose tyranny on the chieftains, disinheriting some of them and dismissing others from their dignities. One of these chieftains, called Thorfinn, son of Ottar, and more powerful than the rest, went to Somerled and requested of him his son Dugall that he should be set in kingship over the Isles.
>
> Somerled rejoiced when he heard this and gave his son Dugall to Thorfinn, who took him and conducted him through all the Isles, making them subject to him and receiving hostages from each island.

This Thorfinn Ottarsson occurs nowhere else in the sources, but was certainly a kinsman and very probably the son of the 'Ottar, son of Ottar's son, one of the men of the Isles' who is noticed in the *Annals of the Four Masters* at the year 1142 when he is said to have assumed the kingship of Dublin. Ottar's grandfather would have also held that kingship if he was the same 'Mac Ottar, prince of the Innse-gall . . . chosen to be prince of the Danes [i.e. Norse] of Dublin' according to the *Annals of Clonmacnois* at 1134, so Thorfinn can be fairly safely recognised as a member of a Hebridean Norse kindred long associated with the Dublin kingship. If, as seems no less likely, he was also the great-grandson of an earlier Ottar identified by the *Chronicle of Man* as leader of what appears to have been the Hebridean Norse element in a battle between contending Manx factions at Santwat in 1098,[6] then 'Thorfinn, son of Ottar' could, indeed, be described with full justice as 'more powerful than the rest' of the island chieftains.

While it has been suggested that Thorfinn's real purpose might have been 'a bid to revive his family's fortunes in Dublin with Somerled's assistance',[7] it seems to me very probable that the initiative came from Somerled himself and – as Hugh Cheape has suggested – that he simply 'took the opportunity of dynastic weakness in the Sudreys to have his eldest son Dugall proclaimed king over the isles'.[8] If the contemporary source noted earlier was correct in identifying a contingent from the Isles among Somerled's forces in the Mac Heth rising,[9] and even if those warriors were recruited on the promise of plunder alone, it would follow that Somerled had become well acquainted with Hebridean Norse chieftains in the orbit of Thorfinn Ottarsson by the end of the year 1153. In view of his political stature at that time, it is unlikely that the '*regulus* of Argyll' would have entertained negotiations with the Islesmen below the highest level, namely Thorfinn himself, and so there is every reason to assume personal contact, or even some form of alliance, still maintained between the two men just a few years afterwards.

Whatever motives other than obligation of kinship by marriage might have prompted Somerled's support for the Mac Heth cause, the natural direction of his ambition must have lain ultimately in the realm of the western sea, a direction temptingly opened up to him by the tides of turbulence following in the wake of Olaf's death. If the first target of such ambition lay in lordship of the islands of the Inner Hebrides lying offshore from his mainland domain of Argyll – as subsequent events would certainly indicate it to have done – then his claim would have been most realistically pursued through a son borne to him by a daughter of the royal house of Man. When Godred's personality would surely have been well known to his younger half-sister, Somerled would thus have been excellently informed as to his brother-in-law's likely behaviour in the kingship. It only remained, then, to wait until Thorfinn Ottarsson and his kind had become so offended by their new king's tyranny as to welcome a rival claimant to the kingship, especially one endowed with a legitimate claim by right of his mother and a powerful ally in the person of his father. So eminent a candidate could then be offered by Thorfinn to sympathetic island chieftains, whose approval would enable his formal 'request' to

Somerled for his son Dugall, 'that he should be set in kingship over the Isles'.

The MacMhuirich *History of the MacDonalds* says of Somerled that he 'had a good family', but all the accounts of that family set down over some five centuries are at such variance as to the identity and seniority of its members that it is necessary to examine their evidence for some context in which to place Dugall mac Somerled.

The more authoritative of the two earliest sources identifying Somerled's sons – or, at least, those considered his legitimate offspring – is the *Chronicle of Man* at the point where it makes reference to Olaf's 'several concubines'.

> By whom . . . he had many daughters, of whom one married Somerled, lord of Argyll; and she was the cause of the ruin of the whole kingdom of the Isles, because he begot by her four sons, Dugall, Ranald, Angus and Olaf.

The *Orkneyinga Saga*, although compiled somewhat earlier than the Manx chronicle, cannot be considered so authoritative a source for Somerled, but is still able to identify three of his sons by their Norse name-forms and, no less usefully, to preserve the only surviving record of their mother's name.

> Somerled [*Sumarlidi*] was married to Ragnhild, daughter of Olaf *bitling*, king of the Sudreys. Their children were king *Dufgall* [Dugall], *Rognvald* [Ranald], and *Engull* [Angus].

The evidence for Somerled's family found in the sources of Clan Donald tradition does fill gaps left by the saga-maker's omissions and the Manx chronicler's exclusive concentration on legitimate male progeny, yet manages to create gaps and confusions all of its own making, as is illustrated by the account set down in the MacMhuirich *History*.

> Somerled had a good family: *Dubhgall* [Dugall] and *Raghnall* [Ranald], and the *Gall mac Sgillin*, this man being so named from whom are descended the Clann Gall of the Glens [of Antrim]. *Beathog* [Bethoc], daughter of Somerled, was a religious woman

> and a Black Nun . . . Dugall, son of Somerled, took the chiefship of Argyll and Lorn. Ranald and his race went to the Hebrides and Kintyre, where his posterity succeeded him.

Whilst omitting two of the sons born to Ragnhild and identified by the *Chronicle of Man*, the MacMhuirich account can at least supply the names of Somerled's daughter and an illegitimate son born to a northern Irish mother, both of whom are confirmed by the corresponding passage from the Sleat *History*, which offers intriguing comparison with the MacMhuirich version.

> He [Somerled] had Dugall, a natural son, of whom are descended the Macdugalls of Lorn. He had, by Olay the Red's daughter, Sommerled, Reginald or Ranald, and Olay; he had Gillies by a woman of the Bissets, and had only one daughter called Beatrix, who was a prioress of Icollumkill.

The omissions and confusions immediately apparent in these accounts from the Clan Donald histories derive from the fact that their authors cannot be considered as genealogists or historians in the modern sense of those terms and are better recognised as seannachies, whose role was rooted in that of the 'praise-poet' and whose function was effectively that of 'in-house propagandist' on behalf of the kindred they served. Both of these histories 'of the MacDonalds', then, were written in the service of one or other branch of the Clan Donald,[10] descended from Somerled's son Ranald although named for Ranald's son Donald, which had become firmly established as the ascendant line of the house of Somerled by the time of its formal assumption of Lordship of the Isles in the second quarter of the fourteenth century.

Perhaps it was the damage inflicted on the prestige of the Clan Donald by the forfeiture of the Lordship to James IV in 1493 which made its clan historians in the following centuries so very defensive of their patrons' ancestral history, but the trait is clearly discernible in their accounts of the sons of Somerled where the prestige of the Clan Donald demanded seniority for its forebear Ranald when his brother Dugall was evidently the eldest (or, at least, the first-born legitimate) son. In fact, the MacMhuirich *History* does place Dugall's name before that of Ranald and also clearly acknowledges his succession to 'the chiefship of

Argyll and Lorn', but concentrates exclusively on Ranald's descendants through the three following generations until it reaches the point in the early fourteenth century when 'the tribe of Dugald, son of Somerled, took the [losing] side of the Baliols' in their war with Robert the Bruce, in stark contrast to the Clan Donald whose rise to ascendancy was the reward for their chieftain Angus Og's staunch support of the Bruce. The Sleat historian dealt with the same problem by the simple device of rewriting history, first alleging Dugall to have been 'a natural [i.e. illegitimate] son, of whom are descended the Macdugalls of Lorn'; then placing a 'Sommerled', known to no other source and evidently fictitious, at the head of his list of Somerled's sons 'by Olay the Red's daughter'; and finally claiming that 'after Sommerled, his son Sommerled succeeded him as Thane of Argyle'.

No authority apart from the Sleat historian even hints at Dugall's having been other than a legitimate son, so the allegation can be discounted as a transparent mischief, but one possibly owing some measure of its inspiration to the only documented son borne to Somerled by a woman other than his wife and identified by the MacMhuirich historian as 'the Gall mac Sgillin . . . from whom are descended the Clann Gall of the Glens' and by the Sleat historian as 'Gillies by a woman of the Bissets'. The variant name-forms – characteristically Irish in the MacMhuirich version and anglicised by the Sleat historian – would seem to identify the same son of Somerled known as 'Gillecoluim' (in the Latin form of *Gillecolanus*) to Fordun and as 'Gille-brigte' (apparently a confusion with Somerled's own patronymic) in the *Annals of Tigernach*, those last two sources both recording his having been slain with his father in 1164.[11] There is good evidence, then, for Somerled having fathered a son in his early manhood, evidently out of wedlock and probably whilst still in Ireland, to 'a woman of the Bissets' of Antrim, a son who was given a name (probably Gillecolm) of the same typically *Gall-Gaedhil* form as Somerled's own father and grandfather, and whose death in battle is entered by two authoritative Irish annals.

As to the sons borne to Somerled by Ragnhild, the most comprehensive record must be that set down in the *Chronicle of Man*, especially when each of the four names listed by the Manx chronicler is independently confirmed by other sources. Other than the notice of his name as 'Olay' by the Sleat historian and the inference of his having been named for his grandfather, nothing further is known of Olaf, which would suggest the likelihood of his having died young. Angus, however, appears again in the *Chronicle of Man* where he is noticed at war with his brother Ranald in 1192 and finally with the entry of his obituary under the year 1210. While no such closely contemporary source can offer a date for the death of Ranald,[12] he must still be considered the best-documented of the sons of Somerled by virtue of the fulsome account of him preserved in the Clan Donald histories and the charter evidence for his endowment of monasteries.

It is Dugall, though, who is of first importance here as the only one of Somerled's legitimate sons whose activities form any part of the historical record of his father's lifetime. Despite the mischievous contrivance of the Sleat historian, there can be no doubt as to Dugall's having been the eldest of Somerled's legitimate sons, and not only on the evidence of his name being entered at the head of the lists in the *Chronicle of Man*, the *Orkneyinga Saga* and the MacMhuirich *History*. While there is no closely contemporary record of Somerled's bequest to his heirs, his territories do appear to have been apportioned among his sons according to the traditional custom of *gavelkind*, and the fact of Dugall's descendant lords of Lorn being styled *de Ergadia* ('of Argyll') led the historian of Argyll Colin MacDonald to conclude that 'Dugall succeeded to the territories commonly regarded as the ancestral lands of Somerled'.[13] Such a legacy clearly points to Dugall as the first-born and also as the natural choice, even by age alone, among Ragnhild's sons for the rival claimant to his uncle Godred's kingship of the Isles.

Dugall makes just one further appearance in the historical record – fully twenty years after the events dated to 1155 by the *Chronicle of Man* – when he is noticed by an immediately contemporary Durham annal:[14]

> In the year 1175, in which king Henry the elder [II] received allegiance and fealty from the Scots at York, Dugall, the son of Somerled, and Stephen his chaplain . . . received the brotherhood of our church at the feet of Saint Cuthbert on the Vigil of Saint Bartholomew [23rd August]; and the same Dugall offered two gold rings to Saint Cuthbert and promised that in every year for so

> long as he lived he would give one mark to the convent either in money or in kind.

Scholarly opinion is divided as to whether Dugall was one of the 'earls and barons and knights' who accompanied the Scots king William, brother and successor to Malcolm IV, in his submission to Henry II. Dugall's name certainly does not appear among those of the few Scots notables listed by the chronicler Benedict of Peterborough as in attendance on that occasion and there is doubt as to whether a son of Somerled would have been so close to the Scottish court little more than a decade after his father's last rebellion. On the other hand, there is no very obvious alternative explanation of why a lord of Argyll was paying homage at Cuthbert's shrine barely a fortnight after the royal ceremony at York, especially when Durham lay so directly along the probable route of the Scots' journey home.

Of particular interest here, though, is the entry in the margin of a Durham manuscript which might supply an especially apt footnote to Dugall's pilgrimage.[15] This manuscript, set down around 1174, is an account of Cuthbert's posthumous miracles which includes the story of a Norse cleric travelling far and wide in search of a miraculous cure for his grievous afflictions and failing to find relief at the shrine of any saint until he came to the church of Cuthbert at Durham. In the margin of the passage describing the supplicant's travels along northern coastlines, a contemporary hand has inserted a list of island and regional names, twenty-one in total – ranging from Greenland to Orkney and Caithness – of which no less than thirteen identify islands (or, in the case of Sleat, an island district) along Scotland's western seaboard:

> *Yuiste* [Uist], *Leothus* [Lewis], *Barriem Coll* [Barra and Coll], *Tirieth* [Tiree], *Coluense* [Colonsay], *Achum* [Arran?], *Slete* [Sleat], *Bote* [Bute], *Schy* [Skye], *Hyle* [Islay], *Hii Colmekille* [Iona], *Mulih* [Mull].

The proximity of the date of the manuscript to the date of Dugall's visit to Durham must suggest someone in his entourage, if not Dugall himself, as the source of information for the place-names listed in its margin, especially when the name-forms as written so often suggest their having been transcribed from the spoken Gaelic. While it is impossible to know what the selection of names was originally intended to indicate, it is tempting to wonder if they might not be related, in some wise, to Dugall's voyage through the Hebrides with Thorfinn Ottarsson twenty years before.

Even though the *Chronicle of Man* supplies no detailed itinerary of that proclamatory progress through the Isles, it might be no pure coincidence that the names entered in the margin of the Durham manuscript correspond so well to its likely ports of call. What the *Chronicle* can confirm, however, is that the proposal of Dugall mac Somerled as king of the Isles did not meet with the unanimous support of the island chieftains. Its reference to his (or, more probably, Thorfinn's) having 'received hostages from each island' betrays an anticipation of at least some elements of dissent and the chronicler goes on to show that anticipation having been well-founded.

> But one chieftain, a man named Paul,[16] made his way in secret to Godred and told him of all that had taken place. Godred was alarmed at these tidings, immediately commanding his fleet to be assembled and setting forth at once to encounter the enemy. Meanwhile, Somerled brought together a force of eighty ships and hastened to meet Godred.

The next entry in the *Chronicle of Man* tells of the ensuing conflict and of its outcome, preserving the only remotely contemporary record of an event of key significance not only for the kingdom of the Isles but for the future history of Gaelic Scotland.

> In the year 1156 on the night of the Lord's Epiphany [5th/6th January], a naval battle was fought between Godred and Somerled with great slaughter of men on either side. And when day broke they made peace and they apportioned between them the kingdom of the Isles; and the kingdom has been divided from that day to the present time. And this was the cause of the ruin of the kingdom of the Isles, beginning from the time when the sons of Somerled took their possession of it.

Writers on the subject of this battle 'on the night of the Lord's Epiphany' can be roughly segregated into two lines of approach: the academics paying greater attention to the terms of its peace settlement and very much less, if any at all, to the conduct and location of the conflict itself, while many of the more popular authors are ready to offer, and with confidence, much more detailed accounts of the battle than can be confirmed by the *Chronicle of Man.* Most of them, for example, locate the sea-fight in the waters around Islay and almost all take the vessels of Somerled's fleet to have been of the type recognised as the west Highland 'galley', yet the Manx chronicler – whose entry represents the only early source of history on the subject – supplies not the least indication of where it was fought and no more precise identification of the craft engaged than the Latin noun *navis,* simply 'ship'.

Whilst not suggesting the more popular accounts as utterly fanciful, there is an ever-present danger of conflating the little that is really known of Somerled with the more abundant evidence for his later medieval successors. In view of that situation – and because it represents a landmark of such importance – the 'Epiphany battle' is worthy of some close attention here, and the substance of Somerled's seapower might offer its most useful starting point.

'The significant legacy of the Viking age to the western seaboard was not an infusion of Norse blood and speech', in the view of A. A. M. Duncan, 'but the design of ships',[17] and there is certainly no question as to the direct descent of the west Highland galley – so long established, in history as well as heraldry, as the symbol of lordship of the Isles – from the oceangoing craft similarly symbolic of the northmen.

It is hardly possible to overestimate the significance of seafaring in the Hebrides, and so also on the western coastland where the intractable nature of the terrain left the sea as the natural highway until relatively recent times. The native peoples of the western seaboard, then, could have been no less creatures of a maritime culture than were the Norsemen who came to settle their territory and so it is hardly surprising that the interchange between their two cultures becomes first apparent in the orbit of the sea. The maritime vocabulary of the Gaelic language, for example, is almost entirely made up of words of Norse origin and there is now a growing recognition of Irish monastic voyaging in earlier medieval centuries as a major inspiration for the Norse ventures into the North Atlantic.

If the Norse impact served to re-invigorate the ancient maritime culture of the peoples of the western seaboard, then Professor Duncan is fully justified in pointing to the superiority of Scandinavian ship technology as the dominant feature of that new impetus. From their first point of entry into history, the characteristic craft of the Celts of the west was the hide-hulled curragh, but for all its extraordinary qualities the skin boat was inevitably outclassed by the timber-built vessels which brought the northmen west over sea. The celebrated 'dragonship' – its sleek-lined, oak-planked hull hung with shields along some twenty-five metres of its length, driven by oar and a broad square-sail billowing from its single tall mast – has long represented the 'Viking' phenomenon in the popular imagination, but such longships are thought to have made up very little of the regular traffic of the Norse settlements in the Hebrides or further out into the North Atlantic. Much more typical were vessels built on the same principles but broader in beam, higher in freeboard and deeper in draft, being intended for transport and trade rather than for raiding and war, and it is such *kaupskip* (literally 'trade-ship') types – specifically the big, oceangoing *knarr* and the similar, but smaller, *byrding* – which should be recognised as the true forebears of the west Highland galley.

This term 'galley' – most simply defined as a craft driven by oar and by sail – is from the Middle English *galeie* (ultimately of Old French origin) and would not have been the name used in medieval Gaelic currency, where the names of ship types bear their own undeniable testimony to Scandinavian origins. The *lymphad*, a name found in later medieval references to the larger galleys of the grander chieftains, probably represents a corruption of the Gaelic *long-fada* (literally 'long-ship' and corresponding to the Norse *langskip*), but the most often occurring term would seem to have been *birlinn*, clearly a Gaelicisation of the Norse *byrding*. The craft most usually associated with Somerled, however, (although on no very early historical authority that I have found) is the *nyvaig*, seemingly alike to the *birlinn* and possibly a local name for the same craft. The term itself is sometimes translated as 'little ship', but might be most convincingly recognised as a corrupt transliteration of a Norse-Gaelic fusion: *nyvaig* from *knarr-bheag* or 'little knarr', indicating the largest *kaupskip* type remodelled on smaller lines better suited to operation along the jagged coastlines of the Hebrides and west Highlands.

Other than what are thought to have been galley end-posts found on the Isle of Eigg in the late nineteenth century, archaeology has yet to uncover the remains of any of these craft of any type or period. Consequently, the most abundant evidence for their structure and design is that carved in stone on medieval grave slabs, all of which confirm the galley's incorporating an innovative advance on Scandinavian ship design in the form of a stern rudder in place of the traditional starboard-mounted steering oar. While these, often usefully detailed, carvings certainly bear impressive testimony to the appearance and importance of the galley throughout the period of the Lordship of the Isles, none of them is of a date earlier than the fourteenth century – almost two hundred years after Somerled – so they can hardly be taken as the most conclusive evidence for the ships of his time.

The galley, nonetheless, has been closely associated with Somerled since at least the time of the Sleat historian, so it is perhaps fortunate that there is probably just enough evidence to support that association. First of all, there are two valuable references in the *Orkneyinga Saga* to ships of apparent *nyvaig* or *birlinn* type deployed in fleets recruited from the Hebrides and from Caithness, as early as the mid-1040s in a sea-fight off Roberry in the Pentland Firth, and again in 1136 – only twenty years before Somerled's Epiphany battle – off Mull Head on the north coast of Deerness. Yet the saga evidence for both conflicts leaves no doubt as to these smaller craft having been fighting at a great disadvantage against the larger longships, a factor which well corresponds to other evidence for the character of Scandinavian sea-fighting, and which may also explain a curious reference in the *Chronicle of Man* to Godred Crovan's reign in Man in the last quarter of the eleventh century which claims 'he so tamed the Scots that none who built a ship or a boat dared to put into it more than three iron bolts'. Denis Rixson's recent history of the galley points to evidence for the keels of larger medieval ships being formed of more than one piece of timber 'scarfed' together with bolts and goes on to suggest that, if the 'iron bolts' of the *Chronicle* entry were those needed for keel-scarfs, 'perhaps this restriction prevented the launching of any over-large vessels that might challenge Godred's hegemony'.[18] Whatever might have been the impact of such restriction on ship size in stimulating the development of the smaller vessels as warships, the *Orkneyinga Saga* can clearly confirm ships of a west Highland galley type having made up Hebridean warfleets through more than a hundred years before 1156, which evidence alone makes it more than likely that some, if not all, the 'eighty ships' assembled by Somerled against Godred Crovan's grandson were akin to the type known as the *nyvaig*.

There is one further item of evidence which, although not securely connected either with Somerled or the Epiphany battle, has been suggested as bearing very significantly on both and it is found, in its most tangible form, in the seal of Somerled's great-grandson Angus Mor (d.1292). While one side of this seal shows an armoured knight on horseback, the other – which forms the inspiration for the crest of the Isle of Islay – centres on a galley with a stern rudder and four male figures looking out from amidships. The seal of Angus' grandfather, Ranald mac Somerled, has not survived, but it is described in a fifteenth-century copy of the text of his charter endowing Paisley Abbey:[19] 'In the middle of one side was depicted a ship full of armed men; on the reverse side, the figure of an armed man on horseback with a drawn sword in his hand.' The authority of that description is beyond doubt, when its author states that he had the original document and seal 'impressed in white wax' in his hand, and its correspondence with the extant seal of Angus Mor so impressive as to indicate both having been engraved with the same device. When Ranald's charter has been convincingly dated prior to 1192,[20] the political significance of the galley must have been long enough established in the culture of the Gaelic west by the last quarter of the twelfth century to feature so prominently in its heraldry. Neither might it be too wildly ambitious cautiously to identify the four 'armed men' featured on Angus' (and, presumably also, on Ranald's) seal as Somerled and his three adult legitimate sons, who – as the *Chronicle of Man* acknowledges – 'took their possession' of the island kingdom he had won in the Epiphany battle of 1156.

The image on the seal, then, can be proposed as bearing with some significance on that battle, but still cannot supply any indication as to where it was fought. A culture with so long a memory as that of the Gael would not soon forget the whereabouts of a conflict which had left so many dead, and – in the absence of any more reliably historical evidence – the sources of tradition should offer the best available information on the location of the Epiphany battle. The earliest such reference that I have been able to trace is in a relatively late source, *The Clan Donald* of 1896, which locates the 'long, obstinate and sanguinary conflict . . . off the north coast of Islay'.

Some of the more recent accounts of the battle have proposed (on whatever undisclosed authority) that it was fought off the west coast of Islay, but Wallace Clark – whose opinion on the subject is informed by his practical experience of sailing a replica sixteen-oar galley through the Hebrides – 'cannot think of any reason why Godred or Somerled would expose his fleet to the navigational risks of a passage round the west of Islay in midwinter . . .'

> The tides run up to eight knots off the Rhinns at the south west creating the fiercest tide rips in Scotland, there is a perpetual heavy swell and no shelter on that rockbound shore. So I disregard the statement of some authorities that the battle took place off it. For a superior fleet hunting an enemy, as Godred was, the Sound of Islay would offer the advantages of secure landing and easy access to seaward from either end.[21]

The historical geography of the time would also support the location of the sea-fight in that Sound, lying between Islay and the neighbouring Isle of Jura, because it was evidently recognised as a passage of strategic significance along the Scandinavian sea-road through the Hebrides and into the Irish Sea. Barbara Crawford explains how '*Ilasund* [in its Norse name-form] was a sufficiently important navigational feature to be referred to in the twelfth-century poem *Krákumál*',[22] and so too *Magnus Bareleg's Saga* indicates his expedition of 1098 having followed a course through the Sound of Islay on voyage to Man. The narrows formed at its northern extent and called *Caol Ila* in the Gaelic would so well correspond to the traditional location of the Epiphany battle 'off the north coast of Islay' as to leave the very least reasonable doubt that those waters were precisely where it was fought on that January night in 1156.[23]

If the evidence of the chronicler for Somerled's having assembled a fleet of eighty ships and that of the aforementioned seal for the appearance of those craft are both accepted, then much more is known of his forces

The 'Lewis Chessmen'.
So called by reason of their discovery on the western shore of that island in the early 1830s, these medieval gaming pieces carved from walrus ivory are undeniably Norse in character and probably Norwegian in origin. They have been securely dated to the second half of the twelfth century, and so the examples shown here - a King (below) and two 'Wardens' (the chess piece now known as the 'Rook') - can be taken as closely contemporary evidence for the appearance of a warlord and his warriors in the Norse-Gaelic world of Somerled's time. *(National Museums of Scotland)*

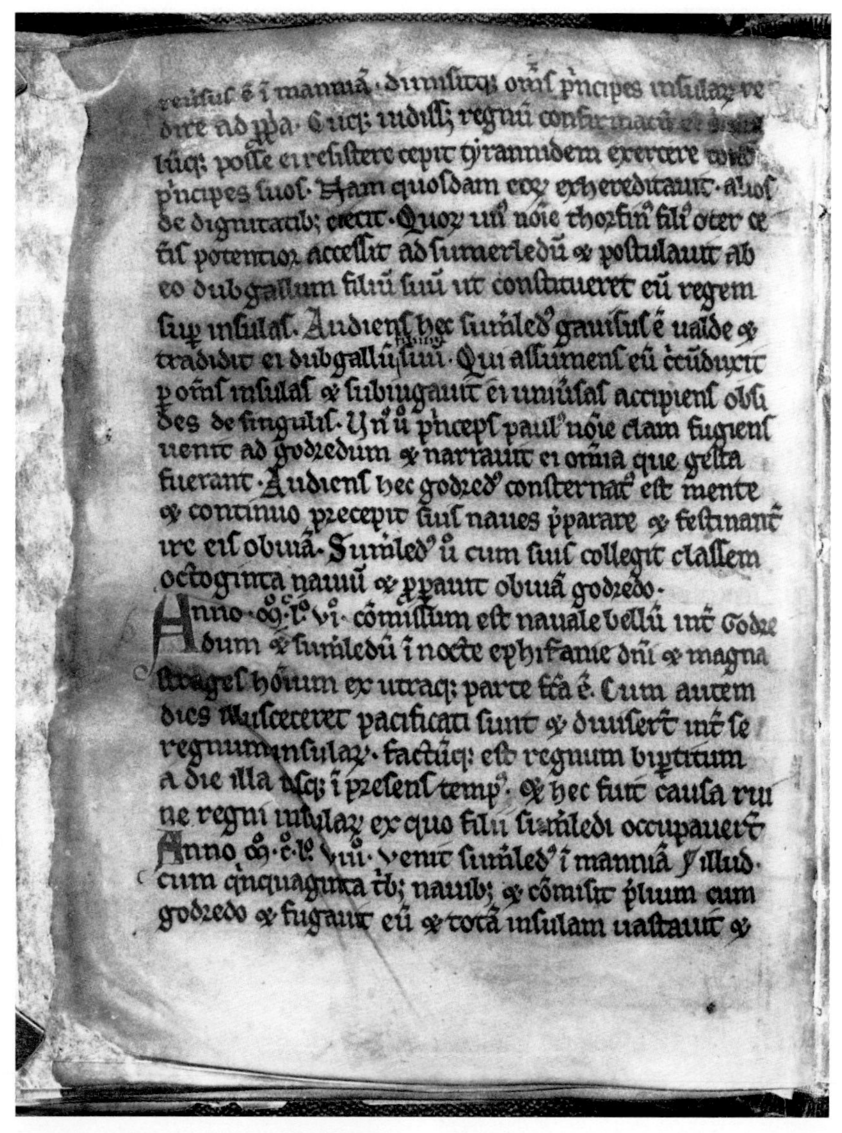
reversus est in manniam. dimisitque omnes principes insularum re-
dire ad propria. Cumque intellexisset regnum confirmatum et nul-
lumque posse ei resistere cepit tyrannidem exercere contra
principes suos. Nam quosdam eorum exhereditavit. alios
de dignitatibus ejecit. Quorum unus nomine thorfinus filius oter ce-
teris potentior accessit ad sumerledum et postulavit ab
eo dubgallum filium suum ut constitueret eum regem
super insulas. Audiens hec sumerledus gavisus est valde et
tradidit ei dubgallum filium suum. Qui assumens eum conduxit
per omnes insulas et subiugavit ei universas accipiens obsi-
des de singulis. Unus vero princeps paulus nomine clam fugiens
venit ad godredum et narravit ei omnia que gesta
fuerant. Audiens hec godredus consternatus est mente
et continuo precepit suis naves preparare et festinanter
ire eis obviam. Sumerledus vero cum suis collegit classem
octoginta navium et properavit obviam godredo.
Anno MCLVI commissum est navale bellum inter Godredum et sumerledum in nocte epiphanie domini et magna
strages hominum ex utraque parte facta est. Cum autem
dies illucesceret pacificati sunt et diviserunt inter se
regnum insularum. factumque est regnum bipartitum
a die illa usque in presens tempus. Et hec fuit causa rui-
ne regni insularum ex quo filii sumerledi occupaverunt
Anno MCLVIII venit sumerledus in manniam et illuc
cum quinquaginta tribus navibus et commisit prelium cum
godredo et fugavit eum et totam insulam vastavit et

Sources of history and tradition. . .
The entry of Dugall mac Somerled's assumption of kingship of the Isles and the ensuing battle between the fleets of his father and Godred of Man fought on the night of Epiphany 1156 as it appears in the manuscript of the *Chronicle of Man*. (*British Library, Cotton Julius A vii, f. 37v*)

Sommerled the son of Gilbert, began to muse on the low condition and misfortune to which he & his father were reduced and kept at first very retired. In the meantime Allin MacVach [illegible] coming with some forces to the Lands of Morvirin for pillage & [illegible] ships, intending to retire forthwith to Lochaber from whence he came — From this Allen descended the Family of Locheil. Sommerled thought — now, it was high time to make himself known for the defence of his Country, if he could or at least see the same having no company for the time. There was a young Sprout, out of a Tree near the cave, which grew in his age of Infancy; he plucked it up by the root, and putting it on his Shoulder came near the people of Morvevin, desired them to be of good courage & do as he did and so by his persuation, all of them having pulled a Branch and putting the same on their Shoulders went on encouraging each other.

Godfrey Du had possession of the Isles of the North side & Ardnamurchan from the King of Denmark — Olay compelled the Inhabitants of some of these Isles to infest Morvern by landing some forces there — The principal surnames in the Country were MacInnes & MacGilvray who are the same as the MacInnes. They being in sight of the Enemy, could act nothing without one to command them. At length they agreed to make the first person that should appear to them, their General, who came in the meantime but Summerled with his Bow, Quiver and Sword; upon his appearance they raised a great shout of laughter. Sommerled enquiring the reason they answered they were rejoiced at his appearance — They told him that they had agreed to make the first that would appear their General — Sommerled said He would undertake to

Please

The account of Somerled's famous victory in Morvern from the manuscript of the *History of the MacDonalds* attributed to 'Hugh MacDonald of Sleat'. (*National Library of Scotland, Adv. 73.1.12/MS cvii*)

Of ships and seals ...

The *Aileach* - Wallace Clark's reconstruction of a sixteen-oar west Highland galley - photographed off Ardmore in the Sound of Islay. (*Photo: Miles Clark*)

The seal of Somerled's great-grandson Angus Mor showing the same or a similar galley motif recorded as appearing on the seal of Ranald mac Somerled. (*Public Record Office*)

The same motif is shown with greater clarity as it appears on the Great Seal of the Isle of Islay.

'His natural lord...'

This closely contemporary portrait of Malcolm IV with his grandfather David I - thus showing the two kings of Scots reigning through Somerled's adult lifetime - is enclosed within the illuminated initial 'M' from the charter of Kelso Abbey dated to the spring of 1159. (*By permission of His Grace the Duke of Roxburghe*)

... and the holy places claiming his tomb:

The Saint Oran Chapel on Iona (facing page above) - commissioned either by Somerled himself or his son Ranald - is the place of burial indicated by the Sleat historian. (*Photo: Geoff Green*)

The ruined chancel of Saddell Abbey, Kintyre (facing page below) is the alternative site claimed by later Clan Donald tradition. It should be mentioned that the plaque shown in the picture and commemorating the names of Somerled and Ranald as founders of the abbey is of a relatively modern date. (*Photo: Jenni Marsden*)

The legacy of the Lordship ...

'Into this Ile of Finlagan the Lords of the Iles had wont to remain oft to their counsel...' Dean Donald Monro. The gaunt ruins preserved on the islets in the loch at Finlaggan, Islay, bear their own evocative testimony to the ascendancy of the Clan Donald Lordship of the Isles and, by extension, to the legacy left by Somerled to his descendant successors. (*Photo: National Museums of Scotland, Scottish Life Archive*) than of those deployed by Godred. There is still good reason, nonetheless, to expect that Godred's fleet would have been made up of warships of Scandinavian type, when he had returned from Norway just a few years earlier and 'with five ships' according to the *Chronicle of Man*. Some of those would surely have been longships, if only for reasons of prestige, but others might well have been of the oceangoing *knarr* type when Godred must have also brought with him a warband large enough to reclaim his kingdom from the Dublin usurpers. There is, in fact, evidence from the *Faereyinga Saga* for *knarr* capable of carrying sixty warriors having been specially built (presumably in some form of warfaring modification) for an invasion fleet of the last quarter of the tenth century.

It would be reasonable, then, to assume the five ships which Godred had brought from Norway supplementing, if not comprising the core of, the Manx warfleet, which has been assessed by one authority at twelve longships.[24] Even allowing for some supplementary vessels, a total of some twenty ships might not be too conservative an estimate for the size of Godred's fleet assembled at short notice, which would seem then to have been greatly outnumbered by that of his enemy if all eighty of Somerled's vessels were actually engaged. The fighting manpower of the contending forces, however, would have been rather more evenly matched if the Manx warships were carrying crews of at least twice the number of those aboard Somerled's galleys, when a *nyvaig* complement would have totalled less than twenty men. It would still be reasonable, though, to recognise the Manx fleet as the superior force in an early medieval Scandinavian sea-fighting context.

Unlike the naval battles of later history, which were actually fought at sea and under sail, the evidence preserved in the saga sources invariably describes battles fought on fjords or in more sheltered coastal waters. The longship clearly did not have the stability needed to engage in battle on the open sea and neither did it fight under sail, because the essential function of the warship was to deliver its warrior crew to the place of combat. As A. W. Brøgger explains in the highly-respected history of the subject, medieval Scandinavian sea-fights 'were simply contests between floating fortresses moved to the scene of the action where . . . the aim was to manouevre in such a way as to afford a chance of grappling ships together for close fighting'.[25]

When the ship effectively served as a fighting platform for contending warbands, the smaller galley suffered obvious disadvantage when engaged against the higher freeboard of the longship, and therein lay the superiority of Godred's warships over Somerled's *nyvaig* fleet. Yet the *Chronicle of Man* evidence for the Epiphany battle's having been fought through the night to a stalemate in the breaking dawn can only be interpreted as Somerled's forces having somehow held their own against the Manxmen. The reconstruction of any battle so poorly served by the historical record depends almost entirely on speculation, but it would not have been unimaginable for Somerled's fleet to have included some longships, perhaps supplied by Hebridean Norse allies. It might otherwise have been that the smaller size of the galley was turned to advantage in the crucial opening phase – especially if its helmsman was operating in familiar waters and equipped with the stern-mounted rudder shown on the Islay seal – against the longship fitted with the more unwieldy traditional steering oar and needing so much wider range to manouevre.

What can be said with confidence of this battle, as of any sea-fight in Somerled's world and time, is that victory was not claimed – as in later naval warfare – by sinking the enemy ship, but by cutting down the warriors defending its deck. The outcome of such a blood-fray fought out with sword and spear and war-axe through a long winter's night, then, would assuredly correspond in the fullest measure to the chronicler's description of 'great slaughter of men on either side'.

'And when day broke they made peace and they apportioned between them the kingdom of the Isles', but the *Chronicle of Man* supplies no detail of that division of the kingdom. It does, however, identify the settlement as 'the cause of the ruin of the kingdom of the Isles, beginning from the time when the sons of Somerled took possession of it'. So too, the *Chronicle of Lanercost*, which shows a particular interest in Manx affairs, preserves a closely contemporary account of Godred's youngest son and eventual successor, Olaf the Black (d. c.1237), who 'reigned in Man and over all the isles of the Hebrides, except for those held by Somerled's sons'. On the strength of those two references, then, the island possessions of Somerled's descendants should offer the best indication of the division of the kingdom of the Isles concluded in 1156.

There is no real evidence to confirm which of his father's territories were inherited by Angus – although suggestions have ranged from Kintyre to the northernmost extent of mainland Argyll – but wherever they were located they would seem to have been taken over by his brothers or their descendants before the mid-thirteenth century. There is no shortage of evidence, however, from the subsequent history of those two principal kindreds of the house of Somerled to indicate Islay (later the heartland of the Clan Donald Lordship of the Isles) bestowed upon Ranald, and Mull with its outliers (lying offshore from the mainland territory of Lorn) upon Dugall. Thus Donald Gregory, the nineteenth-century historian of the west Highlands and the Hebrides, was led to propose Godred's having 'ceded to the sons of Somerled . . . the South Isles, retaining for himself the North Isles and Man . . .'

> The Point of Ardnamurchan formed the division between the North and South Isles, so that, by this treaty, Bute, Arran, Isla, Jura, Mull, and several smaller islands, as well as the district of Kintyre (which, singularly enough, has always been reckoned among the South Isles), although nominally ceded to the sons of Somerled, were, in reality added to the possessions of that warlike chief.[26]

When Gregory's 'North and South Isles' are identified in the more familiar form as the Inner and Outer Hebrides (the latter group to include the Isle of Skye), his proposal of the division of the kingdom of the Isles can still be accepted as substantially accurate, although it is doubtful whether Bute and Arran were ever included in Godred's kingdom of the Isles.

Gregory's perspective on the subject, though, is a distinctly Scottish one, when a Manx viewpoint might represent the more historically realistic approach and would certainly suggest the most straightforward basis for the settlement of 1156. The administration of the Norse kingdom of Man and the Isles was organised in terms of its constituent island groups, a structure reflected in the membership of its legislature still called the *Tynwald* (or 'Thing-field'), one of numerous *thing-* place-names found throughout the Scandinavian world and deriving from the Norse term for an assembly or council, effectively a parliament. Half of the Manx *thing* comprised representatives from the Isle of Man itself, but the other half was made up of members from four Hebridean island groupings, the Lewis group, the Skye group, the Mull group and the Islay group. Just such an administrative arrangement would have naturally led to the division of the Isles in 1156 having passed the Islay and Mull groups to Somerled, while Godred retained those of Lewis and Skye, and with them, of course, the Isle of Man itself. It would have been a very even-handed apportionment, in reflection of the stalemated outcome of the Epiphany battle, and one which would correspond to what is known of the Hebridean territories of the sons of Somerled and of Godred in the thirteenth century. So too, it was a division which might very well have been recognised by the Manx chronicler as 'the ruin of the kingdom of the Isles'.

At that high point of his ascendancy, then, Somerled's territories extended over the mainland of Argyll, centred on what the Clan Donald historians claim to have been his ancient patrimony, and the islands of the Inner Hebrides, although the latter were held formally by right of his son and, of course, still under the ultimate overlordship of the Norwegian crown; which leads on to the question of the location of Somerled's principal power base, perhaps even in the form of an identifiable capital fortress.

It is a question which has been answered by a number of writers, some of them scholarly and all of them seemingly undeterred by there being not a shred of remotely contemporary evidence in the sources of history or tradition for the location, or even the existence, of any such stronghold. For all the profusion of later medieval castles throughout Argyll and the Hebrides, and their historical associations with his descendant successors, none of their surviving remains have been dated as early as the mid-twelfth century by any reliable archaeological account that I have found. The oldest of the castles of Argyll, Castle Sween in Knapdale, is dated to some few decades after Somerled's death, while the only stone fortifications surviving anywhere in Scotland and immediately contemporary with his lifetime would appear to be those on the Orkney island of Wyre, ascribed by their popular name of 'Cubbie Roo's Castle' to the Kolbein Hruga reliably documented (and his stone castle with him) by the *Orkneyinga Saga*.

None of which has been allowed to stand in the way of various speculative identifications of the site of Somerled's castle: Dunstaffnage (another Gaelic-Norse place-name conjoining *dún* with *stafr* and *nes*) by Oban for one example and Ardtornish on Morvern for another, both of them plausibly located within his core territory but no part of either dated earlier than the thirteenth century. Curiously no-one seems yet to have claimed for him the keep of Dunollie, still closer by Oban and known from the Irish annals to have been the site of a hillfort at least as early as the eighth century. Neither is there genuinely historical evidence to link Somerled with any fortification – or, indeed, with any other location – on the Isle of Islay so firmly associated with his descendant Clan Donald Lords of the Isles and where they held court and council at Finlaggan.

It is perhaps particularly unfortunate that Somerled cannot be associated with Dunyveg castle on Islay, not least because of its name which is most convincingly translated as 'fort of the nyvaigs'. The Islay historian W.D. Lamont thought it 'probable that the earliest parts of Dunyveg belong to the end of the eleventh century',[27] but the ultimate authority of the RCAHMS *Inventory of Argyll* cannot confirm his proposal, dating its oldest surviving remains some two centuries later than the period he suggests. Its name does not make its first appearance in the historical record until the last quarter of the fourteenth century when Fordun's list of the 'Islands of Scotia' singles out the 'castle of Dounowak' for mention in its brief entry on Islay. As splendidly evocative as they are drastically eroded, the ruins of the castle do still preserve some remarkable architectural features testifying to its service as a galley base and which may have been the origin of its name, unless it more specifically commemorates the assembly of Angus Og's great fleet of 1314 around Dunyveg in Lagavulin Bay to ship out his warriors who fought for the Bruce at Bannockburn.

The absence of documentary evidence for Somerled having made similar use of that same haven does not, of course, mean that he did not do so, certainly after Islay had become a part of his territory in 1156, and especially when it would have been so ideally situated as the place of muster for the raid entered in the *Chronicle of Man* under the year 1158.

> In the year 1158 Somerled sailed to Man with a fleet of fifty-three ships and, engaging in battle with Godred, drove him to flight;

> and he devastated the whole island before he left. Godred sailed to Norway, there to seek assistance against Somerled.

As so often, the chronicler supplies the least detail of the events he describes; whether or not, for example, this second contest with Godred was fought on land or at sea. Neither does he indicate what might have prompted Somerled's attack on Man, nor specify whether it was politically motivated or merely a raid for plunder, but the long passage immediately following the entry might be taken to suggest its having been in the nature of the latter. This episode is introduced in the *Chronicle* text in a manner which does seem to imply its being somewhat less than historical: 'Here is inserted an account of Saint Machutus, The Lord's confessor . . .'

'Saint Machutus' is one of the Latin name-forms of Maughold, more a creature of legend than of history, who is entered in an eighth-century Irish calendar of saints and believed to have been a bishop of Man in the later fifth century.[28] The *Chronicle* story tells of Somerled's fleet moored at Ramsey where 'one of the more powerful chieftains, called Gilcolm' hears of the riches deposited in Maughold's church, described as 'a place of safe refuge for all in times of danger'. His proposal of an attack on the church is rejected by Somerled who refuses any part in violation of the saint's peace and tells Gilcolm: 'Let this be between you and Saint Maughold. Neither I nor my warriors will be held responsible.' Acting entirely on his own account, Gilcolm plans to lead his personal warband against the church, but news of his intention reaches those sheltering inside and their prayers to the saint prompt Maughold to rise in their defence, appearing to Gilcolm asleep in his tent and driving his bishop's staff three times into his heart. Just hours later and despite a last-minute attempt at repentance, Gilcolm suffers a horrible death from his wounds.

Thereupon 'Somerled and his host were so stricken with fear by his death that, as soon as the tide was in and their ships were afloat, they sailed from the harbour and returned home with all possible speed'. For all its legendary character, there are still aspects of the tale which can be shown to have some historical bearing on Somerled and his expedition of 1158. The fact of his raid on Man having formed the setting for a saintly vengeance story bears testimony to the prominence of that event in local memory. More significant, perhaps, are its striking similarities to legends found in other – particularly northern English – monastic traditions and preserved in sources set down in the eleventh and twelfth centuries, where the villain of the piece is almost always a Scandinavian sea-raider or land-seeker whose disregard for the local saint prompts supernatural retribution akin to that inflicted on Gilcolm. The construction of such a story in connection with Somerled must infer a 'viking' character having been attributed, if not to him personally, then to his Hebridean *Gall-Gaedhil* kind in medieval Manx tradition, while its inclusion in the *Chronicle of Man* under the year 1158 must be interpreted as an attempt to ascribe the same viking character to the events described in the foregoing entry.

The flight of the defeated Godred and his subsequent six-year absence has led to the quite reasonable assumption that Somerled annexed the whole kingdom of the Isles by his action of 1158, but the true nature of the situation is less than clear. The Manx chronicler's statement that Godred fled to Norway 'to seek assistance against Somerled' does imply his having been driven from his kingship and yet, if such had been the case, it is surprising that the *Chronicle of Man* does not take the opportunity to denounce Somerled as a usurper. If he had indeed seized the kingship when Godred took flight, his coup can have had no formal legitimacy when the Scottish and Scandinavian sources, which supply all the available evidence for Godred's whereabouts and activities during his absence from Man, continue to recognise him as king of the Isles.

Godred would appear to have first made his way to Scotland, in fact to the court of Malcolm IV at Roxburgh, where *Godredo rege insularum* is named as one of the witnesses to a charter of Kelso Abbey in the spring of 1159. By the following year, however, he was in Norway, on the evidence of the entries at 1160 in four sets of Icelandic annals styling him 'king of the Sudreys' and indicating his formal submission to the Norwegian king Inge as his overlord. Norway's politics were in some turmoil through most of Godred's stay in the country and he appears to have changed sides more than once, but still to have been accepted by the new king Magnus before his coronation in the autumn of 1164. The entry under that year in the *Chronicle of Man* notices the death of Somerled and goes on to record Godred's return from Norway, but its dating is imprecise and it could be read to place Godred's return to Man in the following year. It is impossible to be sure whether or not Godred knew of Somerled's demise before leaving Norway, but the *Chronicle* does record his having brought with him 'a large army', which might well be recognised as the 'assistance against Somerled' that he had set out to find some six years earlier having been granted to him at last by a new Norwegian king.

In the event, the usurper he confronted on his return was his own brother, who had fought a battle with dissenting Manxmen to win the kingship only four days before Godred arrived with his Norse warband to claim it back – and to mutilate his brother in the brutal manner which seems to have been the customary form of retribution in the royal house of Man. Restored again to the kingship Godred reigned for another twenty-two years until his death – presumably of old age – in 1187, but he reigned only over those of the Isles which he had retained under the terms of the settlement made with Somerled all of three decades before.

Somerled's war on the kingdom of Man had effectively been won by that battle fought through the night of Epiphany in 1156. Whatever might have prompted his raid on Man two years later, there is no firm evidence for his having had any further occasion to defend his offshore possessions. When he went to war again, and for the last time, in 1164, it was said by the Sleat historian to have been in defence of his 'right to the lands' on the mainland of Argyll.

5

'AS GOOD A RIGHT TO THE LANDS . . .'

INVASION OF THE CLYDE & DEATH AT RENFREW

There is no further notice of Somerled in the *Chronicle of Man* through the five years following his raid of 1158, and neither is he found in the Irish annals nor in the Scottish chronicles until he appears again – and across the full range of those sources – in 1164, the year of his death in the course of his extraordinary invasion of the Clyde.

The absence of any record of his renewal of armed hostilities on the Scottish mainland through those years – and had there been such it is almost impossible to imagine its having entirely escaped the notice of at least the Scottish chroniclers – must call into question the claim made by the *Chronicle of Melrose* in its entry under 1164 for his having been 'in a state of wicked rebellion for twelve years against his natural lord, Malcolm, king of Scotland'. Not only is there no reference anywhere in the sources to his involvement in such rebellion through a full decade after 1153/4 – and every indication of his attention having been predominantly, if not entirely, absorbed in the orbit of the Isles through most of that period – but there are two fragments of unmistakable evidence for his having reached some form of reconciliation, or even agreement, with the king in 1160.

Somerled's involvement with his nephews in the uprising entered by the *Chronicle of Holyrood* under the year 1153 would have been reasonably described as 'wicked rebellion against his natural lord' and his great seaborne invasion of the Scottish mainland in 1164 – which forms the principal subject of this chapter – might be thought to answer at least as well to the same description, but those two events are not easily placed on to any very firm common ground. When the historical record of the intervening decade offers no suggestion of Somerled in contention with the Scottish crown, the evidence clearly cannot support the chronicler's 'wicked rebellion' being taken to signify armed insurgence maintained over 'twelve years'. Unless the phrase represents a purely rhetorical flourish, it is perhaps best interpreted as a reference to Somerled's active insistence on his independence from the king of Scots, which he would have been all the better able to maintain after 1156 when he had expanded his territories to include the Inner Hebrides held under the overlordship of the king of Norway. Had he considered himself 'king of Argyll' (in the same sense as Fergus styled himself 'king of Galloway') prior to 1156, the settlement of that year would have given him a real claim – and one further strengthened by the departure of Godred two years later – to recognition as 'king of the Hebrides'.[1]

It might not, then, be so very unrealistic – even if just from Somerled's own viewpoint – to approach his dealings with the king of Scots as having been conducted between men of comparable stature in their own lands, effectively kings in their own right, and such a perspective would certainly throw its own sidelight on the events of 1160 and after.

The year 1160 marked a passage of some significance, and no little turbulence, in the life and reign of this fourth Malcolm, king of Scots. By the time he held his Christmas court at Perth, the boy-king whose coronation at Scone seven years before had provoked Gaeldom's challenge to the ruling Canmore dynasty had entered the twentieth year of his age and demonstrated a new assertiveness in his own realm, even if he had already shown himself more submissive to an English overlord than virtually any king of Scots before him. In 1157 he had met with Henry II at Chester 'and there became his vassal', in the words of the Melrose chronicler, while the corresponding entry in the *Chronicle of Holyrood* records his having 'surrendered Northumberland and Cumbria to the king of England'.

What seems to have become his great ambition through the two years following bears its own testimony to his Anglo-Norman character, when he paid another visit to Henry II early in 1158 – this time at Carlisle, which was by then an English border stronghold – in the hope of being knighted by the king, but the *Chronicle of Melrose* records that 'they parted from each other not upon the best of terms, and therefore the king of the Scots was not made a knight at that time'. They met again in the spring of the next year, when Henry crossed the Channel to besiege Toulouse and Malcolm was summoned to accompany his expedition, which he was to do with an impressive entourage and, almost certainly also, in the hope of being rewarded with knighthood. So, indeed, he was, on the evidence of the Melrose chronicler's entry under the year 1159 which confirms 'Malcolm, king of the Scots, made a knight at Tours by Henry, king of England'.

The same chronicler, however, goes on to indicate Malcolm's new honour in English court circles having not been so greatly appreciated by the native aristocracy in Scotland.

> In the year 1160, Malcolm, king of Scotland, returned from the expedition to Toulouse; and having come to the town of Perth he was besieged therein by Ferteth [earl of Strathearn] and five other earls who were enraged against the king because he had gone to Toulouse, and who sought to take him prisoner, but did not succeed in that presumption.

Their failure 'in that presumption' is most realistically attributed to the military superiority of Malcolm's train of armoured knights on horseback having overwhelmed – even if not necessarily physically so – the more simply equipped fighting-men mustered in support of the rebel earls.

While only one of these 'earls' is identified by the chronicler, and good reason can certainly be found to suspect Ferteth of Strathearn of anti-Norman sentiment,[2] they have been sometimes assumed to represent six of the seven earls of Scotland, two of whom are known to have been in sympathetic and loyal support of the king while other earldoms may not even have been filled at that time. The chronicler's use of the title, then, might be read as only an approximate indication of the rank of the rebels, especially when the entry in the Melrose chronicle goes on to imply the involvement with the dissidents, at least in some wise, of Galloway and its lord Fergus.[3] So too, and in rather greater detail, does the entry under same year in the *Chronicle of Holyrood*:

> The king Malcolm three times conducted an army into Galloway; and having subdued his confederate enemies there, he entered into a treaty of peace with them, and returned without loss. Fergus, prince of Galloway, assumed the habit of a canon in the church of the Holy Rood at Edinburgh.

It is hardly possible to disconnect Malcolm's subjugation of Galloway from the entry of Fergus into monastic retirement, which would imply his removal from power as retribution for rebellious association, although Fergus does appear to have retained at least his title until his death in 1161, when his obituary entered in the *Chronicle of Holyrood* styles him 'prince of Galloway'.

The royal descents on Galloway and their consequences for a fiercely independent ruler in the western outlands might have been recognised as salutary, if not yet ominous, by another in a similar situation. If so, they may even have had some bearing on another event of the same year which passed without notice in any chronicle and is known to history only from one reference preserved in a charter confirming a royal grant of lands in Elgin to Berowald the Fleming and dated 'at Perth on the Christmas following the *concordia* between the king and Somerled'.[4]

While there is nowhere any record of the date of the *concordia* itself (a term translating literally as 'harmony', but in this case rendered sometimes as 'peace' or, even more meaningfully, as 'agreement'), the charter in favour of Berowald has been confidently assigned to the king's Christmas feast which was held at Perth in 1160. The eminent historian of the period Geoffrey Barrow offers the very convincing proposal that 'the peace in question had been made not very long before Christmas 1160, when it was still an event uppermost in the minds of those concerned . . . There was a notable gathering of prelates and magnates at St Andrews at the end of November 1160 and this group may have re-assembled at Perth to keep the Christmas feast. Such an occasion seems to be the most probable setting for a *concordia* to have been made between the king and his powerful and rebellious vassal.'[5]

If the most probable place and date of this *concordia* can be convincingly identified, and even if there is nothing on record as to whatever might have been its terms, there are two factors of at least some likely bearing upon its context. The first of these might well have been the salutary example of Fergus and Galloway, but the other must have been the new direction taken by relations between Malcolm IV and his namesake and one-time rival Malcolm mac Heth. It had, after all, been Somerled's kinship by marriage with the house of Mac Heth which is implied by the chronicle as having prompted his rebellion of 1153, by which time Malcolm mac Heth had been a captive of the

Scottish crown for almost twenty years. His son Domnall – the nephew of Somerled indicated as one of the principals in the 1153 rising – had himself been seized in 1156 and imprisoned with his father at Roxburgh, but the entry under the following year in the *Chronicle of Holyrood* records a sudden and remarkable reconciliation:

> In 1157, peace was established between Malcolm mac Heth and the king of Scots.

With his brother-in-law freed at last after so long a captivity and, presumably, his nephew also released at the same time, the most obvious source of contention between Somerled and the Scottish crown would seem to have been removed. Whatever mutual suspicions might have remained, and such there surely must have been, relations between the king of Scots and the man now in a position to consider himself king of Argyll and of the Isles can only have been greatly eased, and so much so as to enable the *concordia* of 1160. Around which same time there occurs the first example of charter evidence styling Malcolm mac Heth 'earl of Ross',[6] which raises the possibility – even if no more than that – of Malcolm's receipt of the earldom of Ross having formed some part of the terms of agreement reached between the king and Somerled in the November of that year.

There is also an item of evidence which has been recognised as a footnote to Somerled's reconciliation with Malcolm IV preserved in the immediately contemporary *Carmen de Morte Sumerledi* (or 'Poem on the Death of Somerled') when it calls him 'Somerled Sit-by-the-King'.[7] This curious epithet has been taken to be an allusion to Somerled's attendance at the Christmas festivities at Perth, where the presence of a formerly insurgent warlord from the Norse-Gaelic west keeping close company with his new royal friend would have been a very likely cause of satirical amusement for the surrounding courtiers.

The *Carmen de Morte Sumerledi*, written in Latin by a twelfth-century Glasgow churchman, can be ascribed to an Anglo-Norman cultural milieu akin to that of the nobility at Malcolm's court, so there is every reason to suspect its author's having picked up the 'Sit-by-the-King' epithet from its currency in court circles. It could, in that case, be read as very supportive evidence for the jealous hostility towards

Somerled which is insisted upon by the Sleat historian as having been the cause of the dramatic events of the year 1164.

> When the king came to manhood, the nobles were still in his ears, desiring him to suppress the pride of Sommerled, hoping, if he should be crushed, they should or might get his estate to be divided among themselves, or at least get him expelled from the country. Sommerled being informed hereof, resolved to lose all, or possess all, he had in the Highlands; therefore, gathering together all his forces from the Isles and the Continent [i.e. mainland Argyll], and shipping them for Clyde . . .

The Sleat *History of the MacDonalds* supplies just one of at least a dozen accounts, set down between the twelfth and seventeenth centuries, of events surrounding the death of Somerled, and it is the evidence of the earlier of those records which supplies as much genuinely historical detail as is known about what was clearly a formidable invasion targeted on Renfrew.

The *Chronicle of Man*, first of all, offers a concise account of the expedition and of its outcome, but is most especially valuable in preserving the only recorded estimate of the number of ships involved.

> In the year 1164, Somerled collected a fleet of a hundred and sixty ships, and landed at Renfrew with the desire of subduing the whole of Scotland, but by divine revenge he was overwhelmed by a handful of men, and killed there with his son and others beyond counting.

The similarly framed entry in the *Chronicle of Melrose* stresses Somerled's reputation as a rebel and adds some indication of the regions of origin of his forces.

> Somerled, *regulus* of Argyll, who had been in a state of wicked rebellion for twelve years against his natural lord, Malcolm, king of Scotland, landed at Renfrew with a large army which he had collected together in Ireland and various other places; but at length God's vengeance overtook him and he, and his son, and a countless number of his followers were there slain by a few of the people of that district.

The two most reliable Irish annals can confirm Somerled's death in battle, although neither of them discloses its location, but their notices do offer a distinctly different perspective from that of the Scottish and Manx chroniclers. In terms of historical detail alone, the entry at 1164 in the *Annals of Ulster* is singularly helpful in supplying the most comprehensive account of the composition of Somerled's forces.

> Somerled, [son of] Gilledomnan's son, and his son were killed; and with him were slain the men of Argyll, and of Kintyre, and of the Hebrides and of the *Gall* [Norse] of Dublin.

The immediately contemporary continuation of the *Annals of Tigernach* can also confirm the inclusion of a Dublin Norse contingent in Somerled's host, but is perhaps of greatest interest for its impressive testimony to Somerled's political stature when it styles him . . .

> Somerled, Gillebride's son, king of the Hebrides and Kintyre, and Gillebride [?] his son were killed by the men of Scotland, and with them the *Gall* of Dublin were slaughtered.

The Irish annalists' information as to the regions from which Somerled drew his host enables some attempt at speculative reconstruction of his invasion force, especially when set against the evidence supplied by the Manx chronicler for the sizes of his fleets in the previous decade.

He had been able, for instance, to assemble eighty ships before the Epiphany battle in 1156, and yet the fleet launched against the Isle of Man just two years later was estimated (but with convincing precision) at 'fifty-three ships'. The fewer numbers of vessels deployed in the raid on Man are not necessarily explained by the nature of the expedition, which evidently involved an engagement fought and won against Godred, unless they were larger craft intended purely for troop transport as distinct from sea-fighting. It is hardly likely, though, that Somerled would have had such a wide choice of vessel types at his disposal, so another explanation must be sought and there would seem to be two most plausible suggestions.

First of all – and for all that the sinking of enemy craft is untypical of the saga accounts of sea-fighting – there is still the possibility of some number of his craft having been seriously damaged, if not lost, in the course of the Epiphany battle when it was fought at night and in winter along a hazardous coastline. Replacing, or even repairing, galleys would have taken time and placed a strain on shipbuilding resources never greatly abundant on Scotland's western seaboard. Perhaps rather more likely, though, is the possibility of the eighty ships assembled for the Epiphany battle having included even as many as twenty or more brought by allied island chieftains. The same allies need not necessarily, and probably would not, have been recruited for the raid on Man two years later, but by 1164 – and with Godred in Norway for most of six years – Somerled would have had a stronger claim on support from the Western Isles.

There is good reason, then, to assume his having assembled a fleet for the invasion of the Clyde at least as large as the one he had been able to muster against Godred eight years before, but a hundred and sixty ships would still represent twice the number of vessels assembled before the Epiphany battle. Even had Somerled been able to call on a hundred craft and their crews from Argyll, Kintyre and the Hebrides, the Manx chronicler's estimate taken together with the evidence of the Irish annals must infer the other sixty vessels having been those of the Dublin Norse.[8]

By 1164, the Scandinavian enclave around Dublin was at last entered upon its twilight. Two years earlier the Leinster king Diarmait Mac Murchada had plundered the Dublin Norse so effectively – according to the *Annals of Ulster* – that 'a great power was obtained over them, such as was not obtained over them for a very long time'.

Finally and firmly subject to an Irish overlord, 'Dublin still maintained some measure of independence until the Norman Conquest [of 1171]' in the authoritative view of the historian Peter Sawyer,[9] and there is at least one reliably recorded instance of its fleet employed in a freelance mercenary capacity in the mid-1160s.[10] While there is nowhere any indication of Somerled's having hired auxiliary forces, the promise of plunder would have been sufficient encouragement to secure the Dubliners as his allies, especially when he assuredly had personal contacts within the city, if not through his mother's family and with the kinship obligation that would imply, then by way of his old ally Thorfinn Ottarsson whose kindred had been associated with the Dublin kingship for generations past. However it was actually arranged, the involvement of the Dublin Norse in his expedition of 1164 must infer Somerled's fleet on that occasion having included longships,[11] and possibly in some numbers, as well as the smaller west Highland galley usually associated with his naval operations.

Even if the *Chronicle of Man* estimate is considered a mere approximation, a hundred and sixty ships was exactly the same number entered by that same source for the fleet brought west-over-sea by Magnus Bareleg on his royal cruise of 1098. If, on the other hand, the same figure can be taken as an accurate count, then the fleet assembled by Somerled in 1164 compares very impressively with the two hundred ships brought to England – and intending its conquest – by the Norwegian king Harald Hardradi in 1066. There is, unfortunately, no similarly contemporary estimate of the fighting manpower of Somerled's fleet, but the figure of four thousand warriors brought to Ireland aboard a hundred and eighty galleys by Donald Dubh, the rebellious grandson of the last Lord of the Isles, in the mid-sixteenth century might be reasonably taken to suggest that a fleet only slightly smaller in numbers, but including a fair proportion of larger craft, would have accommodated a fighting force of some similar size.

Somerled had clearly brought together a war-host such as would only have been launched in anger to achieve some very ambitious objective or in response to some very great provocation, which raises the question as to what might have prompted him to come in such force of arms upon so extraordinary a venture.

While the *Chronicle of Melrose* indicates no precise motive for the expedition of 1164, the rather shorter entry in the *Chronicle of Holyrood* claims Somerled to have 'landed at Renfrew with a very great fleet for the purpose of plundering', which assuredly led Fordun – in his fourteenth-century account which clearly draws on both of those older chronicles – to his statement that Somerled was 'bent on plunder'. Such may, indeed, have been true of his Dublin allies, but the *Chronicle of Man* ascribes a far greater ambition to Somerled himself when it maintains that he 'landed at Renfrew with the desire of subduing the whole of Scotland', a claim apparently taken seriously by the sixteenth-century historian George Buchanan if it inspired his proposal of Somerled's objective having been the Scottish throne.

None of those explanations has convinced many modern historians, however, and quite reasonably so. A fleet of the size suggested by the Manx chronicler hardly corresponds to a raiding party for plunder. It might be recognised as an invasion force led by an incorrigible rebel determined upon conquest and kingship, but only realistically so if Somerled had been possessed of some arguably legitimate claim – even akin to that of Malcolm mac Heth – on the kingship of Scots, which he quite clearly did not. He did, however, have the most impressive claim – by right of his patrimony, his conquests, and of his wife and sons – to the kingship of Argyll and the Isles, as was so clearly recognised by the immediately contemporary Irish annalist. The modern historian of Argyll Colin MacDonald follows along just such a line with his suggestion that Somerled was 'not aiming at the seizure of Malcolm's kingdom but rather at the establishment of an independent Gaelic kingdom in Scotland, which . . . was far from having been welded at this time into a compact realm with a definite national consciousness'.[12] While there may very well be some substance underlying that proposal, it still does not explain either the timing or the target of the expedition of 1164.

As to modern scholarly opinion on those specific questions, one of the most recent academic writers on the subject, R. Andrew McDonald, sums it up well enough when he acknowledges that 'the motivation behind the 1164 attack has long puzzled historians'. He goes on, however, to offer what is certainly the most cogent attempt at explanation that I have come across, when he fixes upon the target location of Somerled's expedition as the key indication of its having been driven by 'opposition to the rapidly expanding group of Anglo-Norman fiefs pushed westward by David I and Malcolm IV, and especially to the growth of the Stewart lordship around Renfrew'; leading to his very convincing recognition of the invasion as 'a pre-emptive strike against the expanding Stewart lordship in the west of Scotland'.[13]

The kindred which was to become Scotland's royal house in 1371 took its name of Stewart from the office of High Steward to which its founding dynast Walter fitz Alan had been appointed by David I and which Malcolm IV had made hereditary to the family in 1157. Walter was a younger son of an Anglo-Norman family settled in Shropshire after the Conquest of 1066, but whose origins lay in Brittany where they had formerly provided hereditary Senescals, an office similar to that of the Steward, to the counts of Dol.[14] Perhaps even more impressively than the house of Bruce, whose original name-form of *de Brus* derives from that of their ancestral lands of Brix in Normandy, the ascent of the Stewarts represents the outstanding illustration of the feudalisation, even the 'Norman Conquest', of Scotland.

Bretons and Flemings, as well as Normans, coming north with an entourage of vassals and kinsmen in the reign of David I; granted lands by the king, which were further divided between a knightly following and all held in exchange for military obligation; forming estates and assuming offices inheritable on the principle of primogeniture – such was the process which created in Scotland the structure of a feudal society with the bonds between king, his barons and their lesser aristocracy cemented by the infusion of Anglo-Norman culture and its chivalric ethos. Much as the mailed knight on horseback and his characteristic motte-and-bailey castle were superimposed on Scotland's more ancient way of the warrior, so the establishment of the sheriff (from the Old English *scirgerefa*, 'shire reeve') as the king's representative and the chartered burgh (similarly from an old English term: *burg* or 'fortified town') as his power base represented the transforming feudal impact on the administration of the kingdom of Scots.

The rise of the house of Stewart followed that same pattern and by the time Robert, the seventh hereditary Steward of Scotland, became its king Robert II,[15] Professor Barrow estimates that already 'he and his family held land and lordships on a footing not far short of equality with the Crown itself'. 'Already substantial at its inception',[16] the nucleus of that Stewart lordship had been formed more than two hundred years earlier, soon after the arrival of Robert's direct ancestor Walter fitz Alan when he was granted estates in what are now the Border counties, Lothian and elsewhere, but most strategically for this context in the south-west, specifically in the counties of Ayrshire and Renfrewshire. By the mid-twelfth century, the Stewart lordship centred upon Renfrew and its associated fiefs had every aspect of a buffer zone protecting the increasingly feudalised kingdom centred on the central and eastern mainland against whatever recurrence of the threat from the Gaelic west.

'There can be no doubt', in R. Andrew McDonald's analysis, 'that this represented a deliberate act of policy.'[17] It might be further seen as a drastic revision of earlier policy, if David I had allowed substantial independence in the second quarter of the twelfth century to Somerled's Argyll and Fergus' Galloway that they might serve him as sources of military (even mercenary) manpower and bulwarks against the Norse of the Isles. The challenges presented to his grandson and successor – from Argyll in 1153 and, by implication at least, from Galloway in 1160 – must have provided the young king with reason enough to re-draw that political map in recognition of the potential hostility from the western outlands. His natural allies in so doing would have been his most powerful feudal nobility: hence the establishment, with full royal endorsement, of the Stewart presence on the Clyde.

There may have been some real or perceived act of provocation, perhaps a contravention of the terms of his understanding reached with the king in 1160 similarly unnoticed by the sources, but alarming enough to prompt Somerled to his dramatic action four years later. It might, otherwise and perhaps more probably, have been a plan formed over time and in moods of increasing disenchantment with a *concordia* rendered meaningless by emergent royal policy. The focus of hostility to that developing policy, for those who sailed with him as for Somerled himself, would inevitably have been the Stewarts 'whose *force majeure*' – as Hugh Cheape describes it – 'disturbed the balance of power, the distribution of territories and, speculatively and perhaps most significantly, the sense of rightness of the *Gaidheal* and *Gall-Gaedhil* in the Hebrides'.[18]

Set within that wider perspective, it can only have been the threat posed by the westward advance of the Stewart lordship towards his ancestral heartland of Argyll which was of most urgent significance for Somerled, and so much so as to have provoked his expedition of 1164. There are, in fact, two passages found in the Sleat *History of the MacDonalds* which correspond impressively to just that interpretation of events – and perhaps surprisingly so when the Clan Donald historians are so rarely considered to be the most credible sources of such evidence. There is, however, plausibly historical substance in the Sleat historian's reference (quoted in full above) to Somerled's being resolved 'to lose all, or possess all, he had in the

Highlands' by his invasion of the Clyde, as there is also in the account of his exchange with the king who had brought his own forces to Renfrew when the fleet had landed at Greenock.

> Those about him [the king] thought proper to send a message to Sommerled, the contents of which were, that the king would not molest Sommerled for the Isles, which were properly his wife's; but, as for the lands of Argyll and Kintyre, he would have them restored to himself. Sommerled replied that he had as good a right to the lands upon the continent as he had to the Isles; yet these lands were unjustly possessed by the King Macbeath and Donald Bain, and that he thought it did not become his majesty to hinder him from the recovery of his own rights . . .

The Manx, Melrose, and Holyrood chroniclers all confirm Renfrew to have been the target of Somerled's expedition, but it is only the Sleat historian who provides any further account of the geography of events when he tells of the fleet's having landed at Greenock and been left there by Somerled and his warriors when they advanced along the south bank of the Clyde towards Renfrew. His next reference to the rebels' progress finds 'Sommerled . . . encamped at the confluence of the river Pasley into Clyde', which is presumably where the royal emissary delivered the king's demand and from where he brought back Somerled's reply. At which point any attempt at reconstruction of the sequence of events runs aground on the conflict of evidence from the sources of history and tradition because, while all accounts of the expedition agree on the death of Somerled having formed the centrepiece of events culminating in its disastrous failure, those sources which do supply any explanatory detail are at odds as to the circumstances in which he met his death.

One of the earliest records of the death of Somerled is that contained in the *Orkneyinga Saga* and it is certainly also the one of least historical value. The saga account centres upon Svein Asleifsson's pursuit of a Gilla-Odran, a man well-born who was formerly 'with the Scottish king' until his thuggery and killing made him unwelcome in the kingdom and he moved on to Orkney. There he was adopted by the jarls Rognvald and Harald and appointed their steward in Caithness until he slew a friend of Jarl Rognvald and moved on into western

Scotland, 'where a chieftain called Sumarlidi the Hold [who is clearly identified by the saga with Somerled of Argyll] took him in'. Jarl Rognvald suggested to Svein Asleifsson that he should seek out Gilla-Odran and take vengeance upon him when he was next on one of his regular viking expeditions in the Hebrides.

On reaching the west coast, Svein learned of Somerled's having 'taken to sea intending some raiding with seven ships', one of them in command of Gilla-Odran 'who had sailed into the firths looking for those who had not turned up' to join Somerled's fleet.

> When Svein learned the whereabouts of Sumarlidi, he set out to do battle with him. There was hard fighting then; and in that conflict Sumarlidi was killed and many of his men slain with him. Svein was sure that Gilla-Odran was not amongst them, so he went then to look for him and found him in Myrkvafjord [unconvincingly suggested as the Firth of Forth, but otherwise unidentified]; and Svein slew Gilla-Odran there and fifty of his men with him.

None of which bears any correspondence to the overwhelming weight of evidence for Somerled's having been slain, at least in some wise, at Renfrew in the course of his invasion of the Clyde. Nonetheless, the genuinely historical value of so much of what the *Orkneyinga Saga* knows of Somerled (his wife's name identified as Ragnhild, for one example, and confirmation of the names of three of his sons for another) and the fact of Svein Asleifsson's having been his immediate contemporary does not allow its account of his death to be dismissed without some attempt to explain its inaccuracy. The most generous explanation must hinge on the saga's having been set down in Iceland and by an Icelander, even though one informed by sources of Orkney origin; implying the reasonable probability of the saga-maker having confused two men of the same name, entangling what he knew of Somerled of Argyll with, perhaps no less accurate, information relating to a quite different namesake identified as Somerled the Hold (an epithet often translated as 'the Yeoman'), probably an otherwise unrecorded Hebridean chieftain, perhaps with Caithness connections, who would represent a likely ally for Gilla-Odran and victim for Svein Asleifsson. To which must be added a note of the similarity of name-form of the disreputable Gilla-Odran to that of Somerled's natural son Gillecolm (or *Gilla-Coluim*), a factor which could well have compounded the saga-maker's confusion.

There might yet be something of value in the saga account, though, in the light of the perfectly reliable evidence for a Western Isles component in Somerled's fleet of 1164. The reference to his seven ships – quite plausibly placed under his son Gillecolm's command – cruising the sea-lochs of the western Highlands and Hebrides in search of latecomers to the fleet-muster has a ring of credibility to it, just as the reference to Somerled's 'intending raiding' could be taken to suggest at least some of the Hebridean Norse, like the Dubliners, persuaded to join the expedition by the promise of viking plunder.

Whatever the true origin of the confusion in the *Orkneyinga Saga*, it has never cast doubt upon the greater weight of evidence for Somerled's having met with his violent death at Renfrew. The actual form in which he did so, however, is a subject of dispute between the sources of Clan Donald tradition on one hand and those comprising the more contemporary historical record on the other, these latter being quite unanimous in their claim for his having fallen in battle. The obituary entries in the two most reliable Irish sources can only be taken to read to that effect: the *Annals of Ulster* claiming his son and so many others 'of Argyll, and of Kintyre, and of the Hebrides and of the Norse of Dublin . . . slain with him', while the continuation of the *Annals of Tigernach* confirms Somerled and his son 'killed by the men of Scotland, and with them the Norse of Dublin were slaughtered'.

The monastic chroniclers of Man and Melrose are in agreement with the Irish annalists, adding in their own evidence of the location at Renfrew and references to divine retribution; this last perhaps lending credibility to their ambitious claims for 'a handful of men' and 'a few people of that district' having defeated a huge invasion force and slain its notorious leader, 'with his son and others beyond counting'. There are, in fact, aspects of both those chronicle entries which might be read to suggest their authors' having themselves been informed by another source: the aforementioned *Carmen de Morte Sumerledi*, an account of 'how by very few was slain Somerled Sit-by-the-king' composed in Latin verse by one William, apparently a Glasgow cleric who dedicates his testimony to Glasgow's patron saint 'Kentigern's honour and glory'.

While the precise chronology of the progress of William's narrative is less than clear, its opening passage apparently referring to Somerled's rising of 1153 is followed by an enthusiastic description of ravages inflicted by the rebels and a statement of 'the people of Glasgow wounded fled from the sword-strokes' which would seem to be a specific reference to events of 1164. William goes on to tell of the (fully historical) bishop Herbert and his prayers to Kentigern which inspire him to lend his episcopal presence to those resisting the invaders.

'Although Somerled and a thousand enemies were ready for battle against a hundred of the innocents,' writes William, 'yet they came on to make an attack upon the ranks of the treacherous men of Argyll', and his following few lines of rhymed references to 'heather and furze bushes . . . burnt thyme and branches . . . shadows of thyme and smoke' having 'caused panic' imply the attack made under cover of smoke-clouds from burning foliage.

> And in the first cleft of battle the baleful leader fell. Wounded by a spear thrown, slain by the sword, Somerled died. And the raging wave swallowed his son, and the wounded of many thousand fugitives, because when this fierce leader was struck down, the wicked took flight and very many were slaughtered, both at sea and on land. When they wished to board their ships among the blood-tinged waves, they were drowned in troops, one after another, in the water. Rout and slaughter were made of thousands of the traitors; while none of their assailants was wounded or killed.
>
> Thus the enemy ranks were deluded and repelled, and the whole kingdom with loud voices praised Kentigern. A priest cut off the head of the unfortunate Somerled and gave it into the bishop's hands.

'This, which he saw and heard, William has composed.' If so – and there seems no reason to doubt William's word – then his account must be accepted (with due allowance made for his religious fervour and interpretation) as first-hand, and thus quite decisive, evidence for the circumstances and character of Somerled's death.

The quite different version of events preserved in the two Clan Donald histories acknowledges Somerled's having been killed in the course of his invasion of the Clyde, but has no recollection of any battle being fought and so explains his violent death as the work of an assassin. The MacMhuirich version – following directly on from its account of the battle in Morvern – deals with some twenty or more years of Somerled's career in just two sentences:

> He spent part of his time in war and part in peace, until he marched with his army to the vicinity of Glasgow, when he was slain by his page, who took his head to the king in the year of our Lord 1180 [sic]. His own people assert that it was not to make war against the king that he went on that expedition, but to obtain peace, for he did more in subduing the king's enemies than any war he waged against him.

If the MacMhuirich account implies some allusion to a source in older tradition, the narrative detail embroidering the corresponding passage from the Sleat historian would suggest his evidence as hardly better than apocryphal anecdote.

> The messenger returned with this answer [from Somerled and as quoted above] to the king, whose party was not altogether bent upon joining battle with Sommerled, neither did the king look much after his ruin, but, as most kings are commonly led by their councillors, the king himself being young, they contrived Sommerled's death in another manner. There was a nephew of Sommerled's, Maurice MacNeill, his sister's son, who was bribed to destroy him. Sommerled lay encamped at the confluence of the river Pasley into Clyde. His nephew taking a little boat, went over the river, and having got private audience with him, being suspected by none, stabbed him, and made his escape.
>
> The rest of Sommerled's men hearing the death and tragedy of their leader and master, betook themselves to their galleys. The king coming to view the corpse, one of his followers, with his foot, did hit it. Maurice being present, said, that though he had done the first thing most villainously and against his conscience, that he was unworthy and base to do so; and withal drew his long scian [corrupt form of the Gaelic *sgian*, 'knife'], stabbed him, and escaped by swimming over to the other side of the river, receiving

> his remission from the king thereafter, with the lands which were formerly promised him.

Despite its being taken seriously by some number of more recent writers – influenced, perhaps, by Donald Gregory's full endorsement in his *History of the West Highlands* of 1836 – the claim for Somerled's death by assassination is found in no source older than the two Clan Donald histories. Not one of the earlier accounts – those preserved in annals and chronicles of the twelfth and thirteenth centuries and those of later Scottish historians, from Fordun in the fourteenth century to Buchanan some two hundred years after him – has any doubt as to his having been killed in battle. Even when allowance is made for the almost unanimous hostility of those sources towards Somerled, the historical value of their evidence cannot be denied, so the contradictory claim for his assassination, which does not make its first appearance until more than five hundred years after the event and so cannot be considered authentically historical, must be recognised as a fiction and one devised within Clan Donald tradition at some time before the later seventeenth century.

When death in battle in defence of what is claimed as a just cause could hardly be thought shameful or ignoble, even when facing an enemy said to have been inferior in numbers, some explanation must be found for the invention of the assassination story by the seannachies and the one historian who appears to have given the matter any serious thought is R. Andrew McDonald. He points to the rise of the Campbells in seventeenth-century Argyll and to evidence for their presentation of Somerled as 'a grand rebel' conspiring against his king representing 'yet another example of MacDonald treason. The view expressed by the MacDonald historians may have been designed to counter such claims . . . attempting to justify Somerled's rebellion and, by implication, to clear the name of his MacDonald descendants'.[19] If such was the intention of the seannachies' reworking the circumstances of Somerled's demise, something of their version may well have been inspired by another assassination of not so very distant memory: that of Angus Og, rebel son of the last Lord of the Isles, who had been murdered by his Irish harper at Inverness in 1490.

It is, perhaps, no less than might be expected of a MacMhuirich, or of the Sleat historian, that he should come to the defence of Somerled's good name at what can be seen now as a critical point in the history of the Clan Donald. Their histories, after all, were being set down not so many years before 1692, when troops led by a Campbell of Glenlyon were to earn an enduring notoriety in Highland tradition when they carried out their orders 'to fall upon the rebels, the MacDonalds of Glencoe, and to put all to the sword under seventy'.

As to the death of Somerled, however, history must rely upon the testimony of the most closely contemporary sources: that he was killed in battle at Renfrew, that his son – assuredly the illegitimate Gillecolm – was killed there with him, and that those of his forces who escaped the ensuing slaughter were driven back to their ships.

To which might be added just one more reference which bears with some precision on the location of the battle when it records a local tradition at least as old as the eighteenth century, claiming it to have been fought around the rise of ground between Renfrew and Paisley called the Knock. That traditional – if not, indeed, plausibly historical – association was drawn to the attention of Thomas Pennant when he visited Renfrew in 1772 and noted by him in the published account of his *Tour in Scotland*.

> On the road see mount or tumulus, with a foss round the base, and a single stone erected on the top. Near this place was defeated and slain Sumerled, Thane of Argyle, who in 1164, with a great army of banditti, collected from Ireland and other parts, landed in the bay of St Laurence [at Greenock], and led them in rebellion against Malcolm III [sic].

'That this mount was raised in memory of so signal an event', concludes Pennant, 'is not improbable.'

There is little more that can be said of Somerled's last battle that does not rest largely upon speculation. If his 'immense army' was indeed routed 'by very few' – as William's poem claims it to have been – it is more than probable that those numerically inferior forces were mailed and mounted knights supported by men-at-arms; and in a contest between such forces it is fully possible to imagine the greater rebel host

– which William himself estimates in terms of 'thousands' – thrown into rout following the death of their leader.

William's own reference to Somerled having been brought down 'in the first cleft of battle . . . by a spear thrown' calls to mind the similar situation at Clontarf on Good Friday in the year 1014, where a Scandinavian coalition had been assembled – from Orkney, Caithness, the Hebrides and even Iceland – to join the Dublin Norse and their Leinster allies' resistance to the expansive ambitions of Brian Boru. The warlord at the head of the Norsemen on that occasion was Sigurd the Stout, the jarl of Orkney said by the sagas to have fought under a raven banner woven by a sorceress to bring victory to him, but death to any warrior who carried it into battle.

In the blood-fray at Clontarf – according to the most detailed account of events preserved in *Njal's Saga* – one after another of Sigurd's banner-bearers fell until he himself seized up the raven-flag and was slain by a thrown spear. The Norse line of battle collapsed around his fallen body. There is nowhere any reference to magic banners at Renfrew – although that story would have been known to many who fought for Somerled, some of whom would have claimed ancestors who had been at Clontarf on that day – but there is every reason to believe the sight of Somerled brought down by a spear and slain by a sword would have thrown his Gaelic-Norse battle-host into the same disarray as had followed the death of Sigurd just a hundred and fifty years before. Pursuit of an enemy in chaotic flight would have lent itself well to the fighting skills of Norman knights on horseback and resulted in such a rout along Clydebank as is described by William's eye-witness account and confirmed by so many other sources.

As to any further detail of Somerled's own fate, there are the two references to his decapitation, and while their occurrence in sources so disparate as the *Carmen de Morte Sumerledi* and the MacMhuirich *History* would almost seem to lend credibility, the idea cannot shed the overtones of association with one of the more sinister ritual features of pagan Celtic warfare.

A further – and very much less unsavoury – possibility was suggested to Colin MacDonald by the charter evidence for Ranald mac Somerled's endowment of Paisley abbey when he wondered 'why Ranald chose a religious house in Paisley as recipient of his benefactions and whether it was because of some association . . . which the monks of Paisley may have had with his father Somerled who met his death not many miles from Paisley'.[20] The abbey represented the principal monastic foundation of Walter the Steward and, while it is not thought to have been established until 1169, its founding community of Cluniac monks had already been brought to Renfrew from Wenlock in Shropshire around 1163. It is fully possible, then, that some office or service for the fallen Somerled had been undertaken by the monks who were later to become the Paisley community. If, for example, they had allowed his body temporary sanctuary in their chapel at Renfrew, it was a gesture which was remembered long afterwards and generously acknowledged by his son Ranald.

In that same context, it is just as likely that the Sleat historian could have been preserving an authentic record of a similarly conciliatory gesture on the part of Malcolm IV in his statement that 'the king sent a boat with the corpse of Sommerled to Icollumkill at his own charges'.

6

'ICOLLUMKILL'

THE HOUSE OF SOMERLED & THE CHURCH ON IONA

The claim set down in the Sleat *History of the MacDonalds* for the king's having 'sent a boat with the corpse of Sommerled to Icollumkill' – which must be taken to mean his having been laid to rest on Iona – represents the earliest surviving record of any location for his place of burial.

Unusually for him, the Sleat historian goes on to offer at least a clue as to his source of information when he adds that 'this is the report of twenty writers in Icollumkill, before Hector Boetius and Buchanan were born'. Boece and Buchanan – of whom he goes on to say (and with some justice) that they 'never spoke a favourable word of the Highlanders, much less of the Islanders and Macdonalds' – were writing at the beginning and the end of the sixteenth century respectively, so his 'report of twenty writers in Icollumkill' must be taken to indicate evidence from the fifteenth century or earlier. The Sleat historian uses a curious form of words, however, which has been taken to suggest 'that he had access to, or was owner of a now lost chronicle from Iona',[1] and not unreasonably so, unless some further consideration might point rather more closely to the character and origin, if not to the actual identity, of his source.

When Dean Donald Monro visited Iona in 1549, he was shown 'three Tombs of stanes formit like little chapellis', wherein 'according to our Scottis and Irish Chronicles' lay the remains of forty-eight Scottish, four Irish and eight Norwegian kings. While there is no reason to doubt Monro's description of these tombs, it is hardly likely that the claim for the numbers of kings buried therein was derived from his own researches in the chronicles to which he refers. It is very much more likely that Dean Monro learned of it from the churchmen on Iona who would have assuredly welcomed so prestigious a visitor with an informative tour of the holy island and its antiquities. Modern investigation of the monastic site has produced convincing evidence, from the thirteenth and fifteenth centuries especially, for the development of later medieval Iona as a major centre of pilgrimage. Archaeologist Peter Yeoman explains how 'the paved Street of the Dead [along which royal funerals were said to have progressed] was resurfaced and enlarged . . . and geophysical surveying of the area to the south of the abbey [where lay the tombs of the kings] has revealed a complex pattern of paths and ditches, all of which would have been part of a system designed to control pilgrim traffic'.[2]

The attraction and entertainment of pilgrimage was evidently becoming an increasingly important aspect of the life and economy of the Benedictine monastery on Iona from the thirteenth century onwards, and sites associated with the tradition of royal burial there would seem to have been prominent among its features of interest. Those engaged in guiding the pilgrims' progress around the tombs of the kings – and probably, by the later fourteenth century, of west Highland chieftains also – would doubtless have been well-schooled as to the impressive numbers and the more celebrated names of notables believed to lie in that sacred earth. Their information would have been researched for just that purpose from 'our Scottis and Irish Chronicles' in the monastery library and, no less probably, prepared for their use in the form of a written script. If some numbers of such documents had been set down over two or three hundred years – many of them, perhaps, attributed to the work of respected scribes or learned abbots of the time – it would be reasonable to suggest a compilation from the more impressive examples, claiming the authority of as many as a score of monastic scholars and composed in Gaelic or Latin or both, having been set down before the end of the fifteenth century. Some such document, perhaps preserved in the library or among the papers of one of the Clan Donald kindreds, would seem to offer the most likely form of the 'report of twenty writers in Icollumkill' claimed by the Sleat historian as his evidence for Somerled's burial on Iona.

His placing of such emphasis on the authority of his information might be taken to imply the Sleat historian's having intended to counter claims, already known to him in the later seventeenth century, for Somerled's remains lying elsewhere. Indeed, clan historians of some two hundred years later were pointing with full confidence to a quite different location for Somerled's tomb and one which was by then firmly established in MacDonald tradition on the evidence of the first volume of *The Clan Donald* published in 1896:

> The tradition of the family has always been that Saddel [Saddell on Kintyre], where Somerled had commanded the erection of a monastery which was afterwards completed by his son Reginald [Ranald], was the last resting-place of the great Celtic hero.

A similar claim had been made more than fifty years earlier in 1843 when the Reverend John Macfarlane wrote the history of his parish of Saddell and Skipness for publication in the *New Statistical Account*:

> His body was, according to the best and most authentic traditions, conveyed to Saddell, and there buried by Reginald his eldest [sic] son.

The Reverend Macfarlane identifies no further detail of these 'best and most authentic traditions', but his following reference to Somerled's assassination by 'Maurice McNeil' points conclusively to the Sleat historian as the ultimate source of at least some of his information. The Sleat *History of the MacDonalds*, however, had not yet appeared in print by 1843 so the minister had either obtained privileged access to the manuscript (at that time in the possession of Donald Gregory) or – and much more probably – had read of the Sleat historian's version of the assassination story in Gregory's *History of the West Highlands* first published in 1836.

It might be not entirely coincidental, then, that Gregory's *History* contains the earliest reference (or, at least, the earliest that I have found) to the location of Somerled's burial at Saddell when it follows a quotation from the Sleat historian's account of the boat sent 'with the corpse of Sommerled to Icollumkill' with the statement that 'modern inquiries rather lead to the conclusion that he was interred at the Church at Sadale in Kintyre, where Reginald, his son, afterwards founded a monastery'.[3]

Gregory supplies no information as to the form or identity of these 'modern inquiries', so the most generous assessment of his conclusion can only assume their having drawn on some source of local tradition from Kintyre. It is curious, then, that the Reverend George Macleish, who contributed the history of his parish of Saddell and Skipness to the 'Old' *Statistical Account* of 1799, made no reference to any such local tradition. He did, however, recognise Somerled's initiative in the foundation of the monastery.

> The abbey of Saddel, a monastery of the Cistercian order, was begun by Somerled, Lord of Kintyre and the Isles . . . and finished by his son Reginald.

The Reverend Macleish's statement does have genuinely historical substance when it is supported by evidence found in two sources of greater antiquity, both of them Cistercian in origin. It was, in fact, a Cistercian historian writing in the early seventeenth century who set down the earliest surviving record to link the foundation of Saddell with the name of Somerled (albeit in a garbled Latin form) when he stated that 'Lord Sorlius Maderdi, ruler of Kintyre, founded there the monastery of Sandal'.[4]

Very much older supporting evidence is preserved in a manuscript in the British Library, written in the mid-thirteenth century and almost certainly in the mother house of the order at Cîteaux, which supplies a list of all Cistercian houses at that time under their dates of foundation. Saddell abbey appears to be entered twice – as 'Sconedale' under the year 1160 and 'Saundell in Cantire' under 'circa 1163' – the first entry presumably signifying a grant of land for the building of a monastery and the second possibly marking the start of work on its construction. The year 1160, of course, lies well within Somerled's lifetime – and, indeed, at the high point of his ascendancy – so a grant of land within his territory of Kintyre at that date would attribute to him the initial foundation of Saddell abbey.

A similar association would be implied by the entry under 1163 if that year could be taken as precisely accurate, but the fact of its being entered only as an approximate date would allow it to be read as 1164 or later, and thus suggest his son Ranald as responsible for the building at Saddell. Such a reading would take reasonable account of all the Cistercian evidence and still correspond to that of the 1799 *Statistical Account*, as it would also to the evidence preserved in a papal mandate of 1393 which shows the fourteenth-century monks of Saddell having recognised Ranald mac Somerled as the founder of their church.[5]

However convincing the evidence for Somerled's initiative in that foundation, it does not necessarily follow that he was buried there, especially when all that is known of the progress of the monastery building indicates its not having been completed, if indeed it was even properly under way, when he was killed in 1164. The architectural evidence of the surviving ruins at Saddell certainly dates its earliest building work to the second half of the twelfth century,[6] but other evidence suggests that the monastery may not even have been completed before Ranald's death. It is certainly not included in the list of Scottish abbeys compiled between 1205 and 1211 which is preserved in the famous *Mappa Mundi*, so the Sleat historian may well be correct in his claim for Ranald's son, Donald of Islay (who lived until c.1247), having 'built the Monastery of Sadell in Kintyre, dedicated to the honour of the Virgin Mary', if 'built' can be taken to mean 'completed'.

Set within the time-frame indicated by that evidence, the land granted for the building of Saddell abbey would seem not yet to have offered any sort of fitting place of burial for a king of Argyll and the Isles at the time of Somerled's death. It is still possible, even without the benefit of any detail of Donald Gregory's 'modern inquiries', to conjecture that Somerled's dust might lie in its earth today if he had been originally buried elsewhere and only later 'conveyed' (to borrow the Reverend Macfarlane's term) to Saddell. It may have been that he had expressed a wish to be laid to rest in the church he intended to found and in a place for which he had some special regard, although there is nowhere any evidence to that effect and it is rather more likely that his grant of land for a monastery there was intended as a gesture underlining his claim on the mainland territory of Kintyre. If indeed Somerled's remains were removed from their original place of burial – presumably by his son Ranald, but no less possibly by his grandson Donald – the most likely purpose in so doing would have been to confer prestige on the monastic foundation they had at long last brought to completion.

Although working from very much the same evidence, those few modern historians who have given scholarly consideration to the whereabouts of Somerled's tomb have settled upon Iona almost as enthusiastically as their nineteenth-century counterparts endorsed Saddell – and the more recent opinion does have a great deal to be said for it. If there is any substance of truth to the Sleat historian's claim for Somerled's corpse sent for burial on the authority of the king – and especially to his implication of that gesture as one of conciliatory grace – then Iona would have been its most obvious and most honourable destination. It would, indeed, have been even more so in the light of the fully credible claim made by the MacMhuirich *History of the MacDonalds* for Iona's having been the traditional place of interment for a 'king of the Fionngall', by which must be meant the Hebridean Norse chieftains to whose title of *ri' Innsegall* Somerled had won wide recognition as successor. If his remains were, in fact, 'conveyed to Saddell' for reburial at some later time, then it is almost certain that they were brought there from 'Icollumkill'.

Piety is not the most prominent of the many qualities attributed to Somerled by even the most enthusiastic of those writers, ancient or modern, who have set down an account of him. It is perfectly possible to explain his initiative in the foundation of Saddell abbey, for example, exclusively in terms of political interest, but what is known of the activities of his sons and daughter would certainly not suggest their having been raised in an irreligious family.

On the one occasion when he appears as an adult in the historical record, the eldest son Dugall is found at Durham cathedral receiving 'the [presumably honorary] brotherhood of our church at the feet of Saint Cuthbert'. His brother Ranald – effectively Somerled's successor when he could style himself king of the Isles as well as lord of Argyll and Kintyre – is well-recorded as a benefactor of the church, in the building of Saddell and generous endowment (with privileged lay membership) of Paisley abbey, as also in the establishment of the Benedictine abbey on Iona with its associated nunnery, of which his sister Bethoc appears to have been the founding prioress.

It is impossible to know whether these ecclesiastical interests of Somerled's children were principally derived from their mother rather than their father, but the *Chronicle of Man* makes no reference to her religious inclinations and had they been especially noteworthy it surely would have done so. As to Somerled himself – towards whom that same chronicle had every reason to bear hostility – the 'account of a miracle of Saint Maughold' which is interpolated into its entry of the raid on Man in 1158 bears undeniable testimony to his respect for the sanctity of the saint, when Somerled objects to the proposal of an attack on Maughold's church 'saying that he could never allow Saint Maughold's peace to be violated'. While the story itself can hardly be considered historical, the inclusion by the chronicler of that specific reference to Somerled can be taken as genuine evidence for some recollection of his respect for holy places preserved in the monastic tradition of Rushen.

Whatever might be the true value of any such hint at the religious aspect of his character, there is evidence of real substance for Somerled's having had an especial regard for the church on Iona – an interest apparently passed to his children and from them down the generations to the Lords of the Isles – and the most decisive documentary item of that evidence is entered in the *Annals of Ulster* at 1164:

> Representatives of the community of Iona – that is the *sagart mor* ['great priest'] Augustine; the lector Dubsidhe; the *disertach* [hermit] who was the son of Gilladubh; the head of the culdees who was the son of Forcellach; and other notables of the community with them, came to ask of the *co-arb* ['successor'] of Columcille, namely Flaithbertach Ua-Brolchan [abbot of Derry], that he accept the abbacy of Iona, on the advice of Somerled and the men of Argyll and of the Innsegall. But the *co-arb* of Patrick [the archbishop of Armagh] and the king of Ireland, [Muirchertach] Ua-Lochlainn, and the nobility of the Cenel Eogain [the king's kindred] prevented him [from accepting].

An unusually lengthy entry by the Ulster annalist, but one worthwhile quoting in full, not only because it is the last notice of Somerled to appear anywhere in the sources prior to his invasion of the Clyde and death at Renfrew in the same year, but because it represents the only surviving record of the church on Iona in Somerled's lifetime.

There had been no other reference bearing on Iona anywhere in the sources since the entry – by the same annalist at the year 1099 – of the obituary of its abbot Duncan, who would certainly have been in office when Magnus Bareleg's fleet came west-over-sea in the previous year. Magnus' *Saga* tells how he descended on the Hebrides, raging with fire and sword from Lewis down to Mull until he 'came with his forces to the holy island and gave peace and safety to all men there', a statement which bears its own clear testimony to the Norse attitude to Iona prevailing in the last years of the eleventh century. The time when this most holy island of the western sea had offered irresistible prey to viking raiders, from Ireland as well as the Scandinavian homelands, lay long in the past and not only by reason of the Norwegian king Olaf Tryggvasson's imposition of Christianity – at sword-point where necessary – upon his kingdom and its Atlantic dominions following his own baptism into the faith (in the Isles of Scilly according to the saga accounts) in the year 995.

There was, as it happened, a very much later Norse raid on Iona in the summer of 1210, when chieftains impoverished by their involvement on both sides of the civil wars in Norway planned to restore their fortunes with the profits of a viking expedition to the Hebrides. On their return 'they were severely rebuked by the bishops for their piracy', according to one of the saga accounts, which also demonstrates the most extraordinary failure of memory in its reference to their having 'plundered the holy island, which the Norse have always held sacred'.[7] Such an esteem for Iona so well established four full centuries after the first 'devastation of I-Columcille' by the northmen owes at least as much, and assuredly a great deal more, to cultural interchange between Norse and Gael, particularly in the orbit of the Hebrides, than it does to any evangelical policy on the part of a Christian convert in the kingship of Norway at the end of the tenth century.

Despite the absence of Iona from the historical record throughout almost all of Somerled's lifetime, there is a sufficient weight of evidence (some of which will have further bearing here) for its recognition by the Norse as the pre-eminent holy island of the western sea long before he was born. What can be said with confidence of the church on Iona in Somerled's time – if only on the evidence of the annal entry quoted above – is that it had successfully resisted the sweeping ecclesiastical reforms which ran in tandem with the feudalisation of Scotland through the twelfth century. The titles and personal names of those notables of its community who made up the deputation to Derry in 1164 supplies impressive evidence for the church on Iona having maintained its traditional Irish character in resistance to the reforms of liturgy and organisation which had been sponsored by the house of Canmore since the first initiatives in that direction taken by Malcolm Canmore's sainted queen Margaret.

Among thc principal targets of the new reforms were the culdees (from the Irish *céli dé* or 'companions of God'), who had, in fact, disappeared from monasteries in Ireland but were still to be found in Scotland, where they had fallen away from their originally strict observances and thus given due cause for their replacement by the canons regular of the new monastic orders. The presence of the 'head of the culdees', as also of the *disertach* (literally 'desert man', the Irish term for a hermit or anchorite), in the deputation from Iona, then, can be taken as evidence for ecclesiastical reform having not yet made impact on that most traditional of monastic communities. The fact of its being led by one styled 'the great priest' shows there to have been no abbot in office on Iona, although it is unknown for how long that had been so; but their appeal for a new incumbent having been made to an Irish rather than to a Scottish or northern English church – and, still more significantly, to the abbot of Derry, who represented the head of the Columban *paruchia* in Ireland – cannot be read as other than a gesture of defiance to the tide of change which had swept away the old traditions of the church on mainland Scotland. That same attitude would seem to have been shared by Somerled 'and the men of Argyll and of the Isles' upon whose advice the Iona mission was acting.

All of which casts some doubt on the accuracy of the claim made by Orderic Vitalis for the extent of Queen Margaret's influence:

> Among the other good things which the noble lady did, the faithful queen rebuilt the monastery on Iona which . . . Columba, the servant of Christ, had built, but which had been destroyed in the time of wars and by great age. And she gave to the monks revenue suitable for the Lord's work [when she] restored it.

For all that chronicler's unreliability, there are far too many lengthy gaps in the historical record of Iona from the ninth to the eleventh centuries to reject Orderic's evidence out of hand, and – as the historian Alan Macquarrie has written – 'perhaps it is to St Margaret's credit that there was a flourishing monastic community at Iona in the mid-twelfth century'. The evidence of the Ulster annalist's entry, however, offers no remaining trace of her reforming influence, so the more convincing probability is the one which Dr Macquarrie suggests in his following paragraph: 'Perhaps the revival of Iona as a monastic centre was due in part to Somerled's influence and was part of a general Gaelic resurgence in Argyll and the Isles in the twelfth century'.[8]

If, indeed, Somerled did have such an influence on Iona's adherence (or, perhaps even, its return) to the older Irish tradition, then there is some irony in the establishment there of the new monastic orders having been accomplished by his children, and principally – on the evidence of the MacMhuirich *History of the MacDonalds* – by his son Ranald.

> Three monasteries were erected by him, that is a monastery of the Black Monks [Benedictines] in Iona, in honour of God and Columcille; a monastery of Black Nuns [Augustinians] in the same place, and a monastery of Gray Friars at Saddell.

The date usually assigned to Ranald's Benedictine foundation on Iona is 'c.1200', although some authorities have preferred a more precise date of 1203, largely on the coincidence of two items of evidence, the first of them a letter of Pope Innocent III (preserved in the Vatican library) dated 9th December 1203 and the other an entry placed at the following year in the *Annals of Ulster*. The Pope's letter addressed to Celestine, Benedictine abbot of Iona, confirms several land grants to the new foundation and places its community under papal protection, which was evidently not to deter the active hostility of Irish churchmen entered in the *Annals of Ulster* at 1204.

> A monastery was made by Cellach in the middle of the sheepfold of Iona, without any right and in violation of the community of Iona, and did great damage to the town. But the clergy of Ireland [the bishops of Tyrone and Tirconnel and the abbots of Armagh and Derry are named by the annalist among the 'great number of the clergy of the North'] . . . came together and destroyed the monastery according to the law of the church. The above named Amalgaid [Ua-Fergail, abbot of Derry] took the abbacy of Iona, by the preference of the Gall and the Gael.

The annal entry might, perhaps, be brought into a more realistic perspective when its fiercely partisan viewpoint is qualified by some cautious attempt at interpretation.

The name *Cellach* represents the Irish form of Celestine and must identify the Benedictine abbot named in Pope Innocent's letter as the man responsible for the 'monastery . . . made in the middle of the sheepfold', by which is probably meant an alternative monastic site, seemingly located nearer to the township on Iona, intended for the use of the culdees and others opposed to the new order who would not have been happily accommodated within the Benedictine abbey. For all that he was a direct descendant of Columba's brother and thus represented a traditionally eminent candidate for the abbacy of Iona, there is no further record of Amalgaid in that office so his appointment cannot have amounted to much more than a gesture of protest, especially when it is so unlikely that an abbot of Derry would have been able to take up residence on the island.

Neither is there indication of the Irish incursion having made any sort of lasting impact on the new Benedictine foundation, so it can be fairly assumed that the culdees and their kind either left the island or, as elsewhere in Scotland, opted to become canons under the new order on Iona. As to the annalist's claim for the 'preference of the Gall and the Gael', it can be safely dismissed as an archaistic rhetorical flourish, when – as John Dunbar and Ian Fisher observe in the most recent RCAHMS account of Iona – 'clearly all three main branches of Somerled's descendants approved the foundation [because] its original endowments included lands throughout the regions that they controlled, in the islands of Canna, Coll, Muck, Colonsay and Islay as well as in the mainland district of Lorn'.[9]

While Ranald is the only son of Somerled whose name is specifically associated with the Benedictine foundation, the inclusion of lands of Lorn among its earliest endowments points quite decisively to the involvement in some wise of his elder brother Dugall. The Isle of Iona itself, lying just off the Ross of Mull, would have lain also within Dugall's territory, so the absence of his name in any connection with the new foundation there is probably most simply explained by the aforementioned MacMhuirich bias in favour of the Clan Donald branch of the house of Somerled. Dugall's involvement must be reckoned as more than strong probability, and would be shown to extend some way beyond the endowment of land grants, if it can be linked with what is known of his visit to Durham in 1175.

There is no doubt as to the Benedictine order having been established on Iona by the early thirteenth century, but neither is there any firm evidence (or, at least, none that I have found) as to which monastery supplied its founding community. Durham, however, must be recognised as one of the most likely candidates, when its new cathedral represented the preeminent Benedictine house of northern England in the twelfth century. Its influence certainly extended not only into Scotland,[10] but even as far north as the Norse jarldom of Orkney where masons from Durham had been at work building the cathedral dedicated to Saint Magnus at Kirkwall more than twenty years before Dugall came to pay homage at the shrine of Cuthbert. As the successor foundation to the monastery on Lindisfarne, which had been first founded from Iona in the seventh century, the church of Durham had a connection of great antiquity with its original mother house and so would have offered the obvious source of a core community for the new foundation planned there by the sons of Somerled.

Historians have never found any fully satisfactory explanation for Dugall's unexpected appearance at Durham, but he is known to have been accompanied by his chaplain and to have entered into some form of brotherhood of the community of Cuthbert 'at the feet of' the saint where he offered two gold rings and promised further tribute each year 'for as long as he lived'. All of which would bear close comparison to what might be expected of one who had come there to request a body of clergy for a newly reformed foundation on the most holy island of his own province at the distant edge of the western sea.

It does not, of course, follow that Iona's Benedictines did come from Durham, although it must remain a possibility, and such an involvement of Dugall with the initiative for that foundation really rests on little more than my speculation. The association of his sister Bethoc with Iona, by contrast, is supported by a convincing range of evidence, and not only from the Clan Donald historians although it is the Sleat *History of the MacDonalds* which identifies her (in the anglicised nameform) as 'Beatrix who was a prioress of Icollumkill' which would correspond to her description as 'a religious woman and a Black Nun' in the MacMhuirich *History.*

It is that latter source which also preserves the earliest surviving claim for Bethoc having founded the *Teampall Trionaid* ('Chapel of the Holy Trinity') at Carinish on North Uist,[11] and yet while it confirms her having been a nun of the same order as the Augustinian canonesses of Ranald's foundation on Iona, it makes no reference to her having held office there. All the more valuable then is the transcription made by Martin Martin – on his visit to Iona not so many years after the Clan Donald histories were written – of as much as was still legible of an inscription carved in stone almost five hundred years before.

Behag Nijn Sorle vic . . . ll . . . vrid Priorissa
(Bethoc, daughter of Somerled mac Gillebride, Prioress)

There is no tombstone recorded on Iona in modern times which bears any visible remnant of the text recorded by Martin Martin, so Bethoc's grave-marker – if, indeed, such it was – must be accounted long since lost. There is, however, one other item with very credible bearing upon her life in religion which has survived and is preserved today in the National Library of Scotland. Known as the 'Iona Psalter', it is a manuscript of late twelfth- or early thirteenth-century date, certainly written for a nun in a Scottish Augustinian house, and for one with a special interest in saints of Iona on the evidence of the feast days of Columba, Baithene (his successor), Adamnan, and Oran entered in its calendar. Most impressive of all is what appears to be a personal name entered in the margin of one folio: *Beota*, more than probably a Latin form of Bethoc and suggesting this to have been the personal psalter of Bethoc, daughter of Somerled and founding prioress of the nunnery on Iona.

Of the substantial ruins of that nunnery still to be seen today, the cloister and south range of buildings are of later medieval construction, but the church itself is of the first quarter of the thirteenth century and thus dates from the time of Ranald's original foundation. It is still, however, not the oldest surviving of the monastic buildings on Iona because that distinction belongs to the chapel dedicated to Saint Oran (Gael. *Odhran*) which stands to the south of the abbey in the ancient burial ground known by the Gaelic name of the *Reilig Odhrain.*[12]

This 'St Oran's Chapel' was once attributed to Margaret's rebuilding and thus dated to the later eleventh century, but the most recently published RCAHMS survey places it almost a hundred years later with the suggestion that it 'was probably erected as a family burial chapel by Somerled or his son . . .'

> Its rectangular plan, with a single doorway in the west wall, is characteristically Irish, while the chevron and beak-head ornament of the doorway also resemble Irish work of the third quarter of the twelfth century.[13]

When the last fourteen years of Somerled's lifetime lay within the third quarter of the twelfth century and if the 'characteristically Irish' architecture and decoration might be taken to suggest his own rather than his son's commission, it would not be wildly ambitious, perhaps, to recognise this chapel as the most tangible item of the legacy of Somerled mac Gillebride.

What can be said with every confidence, especially now that the Sleat historian's claim has become so well accepted in scholarly circles, is that the Oran Chapel would have been Somerled's place of burial on Iona. It was certainly used as a burial-place for his descendants, even down to the fifteenth century when the tomb recess in its south wall is thought to have been erected by John, the last Lord of the Isles. If it was intended for his own burial, it was not to be so because John died in poverty in Dundee in 1503, ten years after his forfeiture of the Lordship to James IV, and was buried – at his own request – in Paisley Abbey. Neither, in fact, had his father Alexander, the third Lord, been buried on Iona, but instead at Fortrose (and probably as a gesture in support of the Lordship's claim to Ross), thus breaking with a tradition which had been maintained – at least according to the Clan Donald historians – in the house of Somerled over some two hundred and fifty years.

While the precision of its dating is invariably in error, there is no reason to doubt the other detail preserved in the MacMhuirich *History* when it says of Ranald mac Somerled that 'after having received a cross from Jerusalem,[14] partaken of the Body of Christ, and received unction, he died and was buried in the Reilig Odhrain in the year of our Lord 1207'.[15] The same source preserves no similar detail for Ranald's son Donald, but the Sleat historian is able to confirm that 'he died at Shippinage [Skipness castle, Kintyre] . . . and was buried at Icollumkill'. Neither does the MacMhuirich historian identify any place of burial for Donald's son Angus Mor (d. 1292), but the Sleat historian is again able to supply rather more detail: 'He died at Kilcummin [Kilchoman] in Islay . . . and, with the accustomed solemnity of his predecessors, was buried at Icollumkill'. Even if it was not Angus Mor himself who introduced the MacMhuirich bardic family into the service of the Clan Donald, they were certainly associated with that kindred in the time of his second son (and successor) Angus Og, and so the entry of his obituary in the MacMhuirich *History* can be taken to preserve a first-hand record: 'This Angus Og died in Islay, and his body was interred in Iona in the year of our Lord 1306'.[16]

It was this Angus Og also who is to be recognised as the immediate forebear of the Lords of the Isles, because his son John was the first of the house of Somerled to be formally styled *dominus Insularum*, an eminence which would seem to be reflected in the detailed account of his last rites and funerary offices set down in the MacMhuirich *History*.

> He died in his own castle of Ardtornish [on Morvern], while monks and priests were over his body, he having received the body of Christ and having been anointed, his fair body was brought to I-Columcille, and the abbot and monks and vicars came to meet him as it was the custom to meet the body of the king of Fionngall, and his service and waking were honourably performed during eight days and eight nights, and he was laid in the grave with his father in Teampull Odhrain in the year of our Lord 1380 [1387].

So too, on the quite precise evidence of the same source, was his son and successor Donald of Harlaw, the second Lord of the Isles but the last to be buried on Iona, when he 'died in Islay, and his full noble body was interred on the south side of the Teampull Odhrain'. The record preserved by Clan Donald historians of the burial on Iona of six consecutive generations of his descendant successors – specifically in the Oran Chapel in the last two instances and possibly in earlier ones also – bears its own testimony to the enduring significance of 'Icollumkill' for the house of Somerled. So too does the fact of that custom having continued through the fourteenth and fifteenth centuries when a chapel and burial ground formed part of the Finlaggan complex on Islay, which represented the official power base of the Lordship from the time of John, the first Lord of the Isles.

That significance of Iona, and of the Reilig Odhrain in particular, was reflected by Dean Donald Monro, writing less than sixty years after the forfeiture of the Lordship, in his recognition of 'this Sanctuarie [as] the sepulture of the best men of all the Isles, and als[o] of our Kingis as we have said; because it wes the maist honorable and ancient place that west in Scotland in those dayis, as we reid'. It is curious, though – in view of Monro's implied association of 'the sepulture of the best men of all the Isles' with the tombs of the kings of Scots – that the Clan Donald seannachies make no similar reference to the tradition of Scottish royal burial on Iona. Instead, the MacMhuirich account of the funeral of the first Lord of the Isles indicates its following the custom of burial of 'the king of Fionngall', by which can only be meant those Norse chieftains styled – as, of course, was Somerled himself – *rí Innsegall* or 'king of the Hebrides'.

It must be said that there is no remotely contemporary documentary evidence for such a Norse tradition of burial on Iona, and that is hardly surprising in view of the sparse and fragmentary character of the historical record of the monastery through the three centuries following the transfer of its abbot to Kells. There is, of course, the evidence of the saga sources to confirm the establishment of a formal Norse respect for the sanctity of Iona by the time of Magnus Bareleg's expedition through the Hebrides in 1098, and even to suggest the adoption of Columba as an honorary Norse saint by the mid-point of the thirteenth century.[17] As to Norse burials on the island, the archaeologist Anna Ritchie points to some impressive evidence cut into stone: 'Three gravestones carved to suit Norse taste have survived [on Iona], all dating to the late tenth or early eleventh century. One is made of a grey shaly sandstone best matched in the Isle of Man, and the style of decoration also suggests that it was imported, ready-made, from the Isle of Man. This was an upright grave-marker, as was the larger fragment . . . of black shale, probably from the island of Lismore. The third fragment is half a recumbent graveslab . . . Along its border runs a runic inscription, which reads "Kali the son of Olvir laid this stone over his brother Fugl".'[18] Such gravestones might very well represent evidence of Norse burials from the kingdom of Man and the Isles, but one or more of those fragments of that period might otherwise be linked to Olaf Sitricsson, the Norse king of Dublin and York (sometimes called Olaf *Cuaran* or 'sandal') who entered monastic retirement on Iona and died there – according to his obituary in the *Annals of Tigernach* – in the year 980.

All of which supplies a plausible context, if not specific evidence, for the burial on Iona of at least some Norse kings or chieftains of the Isles. There is, however, just one entry in the *Chronicle of Man* which might be read as an echo of such a custom, and that is the obituary of Godred Olafsson, who had returned from Norway soon after the death of his old enemy Somerled in 1164 and reigned for another twenty-three years in kingship over Man and what remained of his former dominion in the Isles.

> In the same year [of 1087], on the fourth day before the Ides of November [10th November], Godred, king of the Isles, died in the Island of Saint Patrick in Man. At the beginning of the following summer, his body was removed to the island called Iona.

It is possible also that some blurred recollection of burial of Norse kings of the Isles on Iona lies at the root of the claim recorded by Dean Monro (and also by Martin Martin) for eight 'Kingis of Norway' entombed in the Reilig Odhrain.[19]

There may very well, then, have been some genuinely historical basis for the funeral rites of a fourteenth-century Lord of the Isles – and, presumably also, of his forebears, even back to the time of Somerled himself – having followed the same custom of burial associated with the old Norse kings of the Innsegall. Of more strategic importance here, though, is the evidence for a seventeenth-century MacMhuirich seannachie having believed it to have been so, because that belief bears its own clear testimony to the enduring Norse element in the cultural milieu of the house of Somerled.

Even though the Clan Donald historians seem to take no account of the custom of Scottish royal burial on Iona, there is the possibility of an association of Somerled himself with the burial there of one king of Scots and it hinges on the evidence for the curious posthumous history of Domnall Ban, brother and successor to Malcolm Canmore.

It should first be said that modern scholarly opinion has grown sceptical about the claim for Iona as the burial-place of kings of Scots, and there is certainly no evidence to support Dean Monro's total of forty-eight Scottish kings entombed there.[20] The earliest evidence for Scottish royal burial on Iona is found in just five of the annotated regnal lists – collectively known as the *Chronicle of the Kings* and preserved in manuscripts of the thirteenth century and later date – and it indicates the custom to have begun with Kenneth mac Alpin in 858 and to have been continued with almost all of his successor kings down to the end of the eleventh century.

The one royal burial on Iona of immediate interest here, however, is that of Domnall Ban, who had emerged out of the Gaelic west in 1093 to claim the succession on the death of his brother, reclaimed it after being driven out by his nephew Duncan and reigned again until finally deposed by another nephew Edgar in 1097. Just two manuscripts of the *Chronicle of the Kings*, both of them dated to the mid-thirteenth century, preserve an account of his fate thereafter.

> Donald was captured by Edgar son of Malcolm [Canmore], was blinded and died at Rescobie. He was buried at Dunkeld; and his bones were removed thence to Iona.

Even though the *Chronicle* supplies the most comprehensive account, evidence from other sources makes clear that it has greatly compressed the time-scale of the events it describes. The continuation of the *Annals of Tigernach* enters the blinding of Domnall at 1099, some two years after he was driven from the kingship. Although a much less reliable source than the immediately contemporary Irish annalist, Orderic Vitalis' indication of Domnall's having been killed by Alexander at the time of his succession to the kingship in 1107 is still no less than credible.[21] The later medieval Scottish chronicler Andrew of Wyntoun offers a more lurid account in which Domnall murders the young son of David I in revenge for his own mutilation and suffers death by starvation in consequence, which would date his demise still later (although probably not as late as the year 1130 indicated by Wyntoun).

Whatever the precise date and detail of his death, there seems no reason to doubt his burial at Dunkeld, formerly the royal church of the Mac Alpin dynasty. At some point thereafter, then, Domnall's 'bones were removed . . . to Iona' where no king of Scots (other than possibly the short-lived Duncan II) had been buried since Lulach, Macbeth's stepson and successor, slain by Malcolm Canmore in 1058. Malcolm's own final place of burial was beside his queen Margaret in the church of their foundation at Dunfermline,[22] where their sons Edgar, Alexander and David were also buried, as was Malcolm IV on his death in 1165. As the royal church of the house of Canmore and the chosen place of sepulchre for its kings, Dunfermline abbey had long since superseded Iona in that eminence by the time of Domnall Ban's translation from Dunkeld.

All of which raises the questions of when, why, and – most importantly here – by whom the remains of Domnall Ban should have been taken up from Dunkeld and re-interred on Iona. As to the date, all that can be said is that Domnall was put to death some years after he was driven from the kingship, if not in 1107 as Orderic claims then in the earliest decades of the twelfth century, and buried at Dunkeld; and yet by the time of writing of the version of the *Chronicle of the Kings* quoted above – thought to have been between 1249 and 1255 and thus not so very remote from the events described – his bones had been (presumably long since) 'removed to Iona'.

Whatever the respect for his royal lineage implied by burial at Dunkeld – and some there surely must have been – Domnall Ban in his last years could only have presented the most pathetic, even sinister and certainly anachronistic, figure to his nephews and their court circles. From the viewpoint of the Gaelic outlands, however – and, perhaps especially, from Argyll and the Isles – he would have been accorded the stature of a rightful king driven out by the new and hostile feudal order. Through the decades following his death, and thus through the period of the Mac Heth risings and of Somerled's emergence as the foremost champion of Gaelic Scotland, Domnall Ban would have come to represent something akin to a martyr in Gaeldom's cause. While there is no firm evidence to involve Somerled's father and grandfather with Domnall Ban's succession and restoration of the 1090s – unless the references to him by the Sleat historian might be read as such – the historical context would infer some such involvement as all but inevitable. When so strong a likelihood is taken together with the evidence for Somerled's interest in Iona and its traditions and for the island's having been brought into his territory by the high point of his ascendancy, a period which lies so strategically within the time-frame for Domnall's translation from Dunkeld, then something more than pure coincidence points to Somerled as the most likely, if not the only, figure of stature in a position and of an inclination to arrange that reburial, possibly even under the terms of his *concordia* with Malcolm IV in 1160.

Whether or not he was, in fact, responsible for the last interment of a king of Scots on 'Icollumkill', there can be no doubt that the restoration of Iona as a major medieval ecclesiastical centre was due in very great part to its patronage by his house, and ultimately to the personal regard of Somerled himself. Indeed, it might be said that the enduring stature of Iona as the great shrine of the Gael can be recognised even today as one of the long shadows cast by Somerled over the history of Gaelic Scotland.

7

GÀIDHEALTACHD

THE LONG SHADOWS OF SOMHAIRLE MOR

Very few – if, indeed, any at all – of the significant figures from Scotland's past have been presented by historians, ancient and modern, lay and learned, in quite such a variety of guises as has Somerled of Argyll.

The Irish annalists, who must be counted among the very earliest sources for his history, apparently recognised in him a provincial king of the traditional Irish type, as is most clearly indicated by the immediately contemporary continuator of the *Annals of Tigernach* when he styles Somerled *ri' Indsi gall & Cind tire*. The Manx chroniclers seem to have taken a quite similar view of the most formidable rival to their own royal house, but to the closely contemporary Scottish chroniclers, whatever legitimate status they might have intended by the style of *regulus*, he was undoubtedly a rebel first and last. Their opinion more than probably reflected that of the Anglo-Norman court of the Canmore kings and was certainly shared also by the immediately contemporary *Carmen de Morte Sumerledi*. Indeed, much the same view of Somerled has been taken by Scottish historians ever since, certainly by Fordun and his successors, and by the majority of modern academics who seem to see him as almost an anachronism when they have occasion to consider him at all, and invariably as the personification of 'reactionary' and 'conservative' opposition to the 'modernising' policies of the twelfth-century Scottish crown.

The first appearance of a more than generous appreciation is found, of course, in the Clan Donald histories set down in the seventeenth century, although with a claim on source material of greater antiquity preserved in the oral tradition by generations of seannachies for whom his primary importance was as the forebear of their patron kindred, and ultimately of the Lords of the Isles. While the genealogical account preserved in the MacMhuirich *History* has been shown to be of genuinely historical substance, almost all of the other evidence for

Somerled's career supplied by that source, and by the other *History* attributed to 'Hugh MacDonald' of Sleat, is unquestionably derived from or distorted by 'traditions' of rather later origin than the twelfth century. In fact, neither of the two Clan Donald histories can be said to represent remotely contemporary evidence for Somerled, when the Sleat historian draws so heavily on clan traditions of much later origin and the MacMhuirichs – whose *History* might be considered the more distinguished of the two if it is read as the legacy of the hereditary bards to the principal descendant line of the house of Somerled – did not enter the service of that kindred until the century after the death of its founding dynast.

The dubious historicity of so much of this testimony offered by the Clan Donald seannachies has only rarely deterred less scholarly modern writers on the subject from retailing it as real history, and they may well have been encouraged so to do by the respected nineteenth-century historians who would seem to have derived inspiration from those same sources for their presentation of Somerled as 'the great Celtic hero'. It was this view which overtook and eventually superseded the counter-claim – a view which gained currency in the wake of Professor Munch's edition of the *Chronicle of Man*, first published in 1860 and republished with an English translation fourteen years later – for Somerled's direct Norse (even, by implication, Orkney Norse) descent.

Even though it is probably true to say that the Irish annalists saw him much as he saw himself, none of the later recognitions by historians down the centuries would seem to offer anything like a fully-rounded portrait of the historical Somerled. Each one of them, though, does have its own bearing on what I have come to recognise as the wider historical significance of this man remembered in the language of his own culture as *Somhairle Mor* ('the great Somerled'), that of a figure of singular prominence standing at a strategic juncture in the history of Gaelic Scotland where he casts long shadows both before and behind him.

While there is no shortage of evidence to support the recognition of Somerled as a rebel, the immediate importance of that view here lies in his association in that role with the western and northern outlands which can only have appeared from the perspective of the Canmore courts as reservoirs of hostility and the persistent threat of rebellion in arms. Such a perception would have been understandably coloured by experience of the Moray and Mac Heth risings, but can also be seen as a response to the change in cultural character of the former heartland of the kingdom of the Scots, a transformation brought about by three centuries of its absorption of the Norse impact.

The Gaelic west over which Somerled attained his lordship by the mid-twelfth century – and, indeed, out of which Domnall Ban had emerged to claim the kingship of Scots some sixty years earlier – no longer represented the same people and culture which Kenneth mac Alpin had left behind him when he transferred his power base to Tayside in the 840s. Through the intervening centuries, the west Highland coastland and the Hebrides had come to form a single cultural zone with Dublin and Man, and a part of the wider Scandinavian world which extended from Norway to Normandy, from the Norse trading towns of Ireland to the North Atlantic settlements of Iceland and beyond. Even by the time of Domnall Ban, the Isles, and much of their neighbouring mainland coastline also, had come under the successive rule of jarls of Orkney, kings of Dublin and kings of Man.

It was clearly that context which encouraged the proposal of a Scandinavian origin for Somerled, a claim which has been shown to be without true genealogical substance when it hinges upon a misconstrued lineage constructed on the basis of a misplaced annal entry. Even though now discredited, this 'Somerled as Viking' school of thought might have at least some virtue in pointing up the Norse connections largely obscured by the ascendancy of the counter-claim for 'Somerled as Celtic hero'. The Norse element of his own descent, which is indicated by his *Gall-Gaedhil* lineage and further confirmed by his given name, well corresponds to his own and his family's wider Norse kinship by marriage, when his father's sister is said to have been married to Harald Gilli, king of Norway, his own wife known to have been a daughter of Olaf, king of Man, and her mother very probably a daughter of Hakon, jarl of Orkney. Another Orkney link – and one further extended to the Celtic-Norse aristocracy of Caithness – is found in the next generation when Gormflaith, the daughter of Somerled's sister and Malcolm mac Heth, became the wife of Jarl Harald Maddadsson.

None of which can be said to offer any remotely plausible context for the MacMhuirich historian's claim that 'he cleared the western side of Scotland of the *Lochlannach*'.[1] Somerled would probably, if not almost certainly, have come into conflict with Hebridean Norse rivals during his rise to power in Argyll, which might possibly have supplied some genuinely historical kernel for the traditional tale of his famous battle in Morvern, and the evidence for his war on the Norse kingdom of Man is beyond doubt. Neither of those examples, however, can be realistically recognised as anything other than politically-based conflict, because – as R. Andrew McDonald points out – 'it makes little sense to suppose that Somerled entertained racial hostility towards his neighbours and kinsmen'.[2] The idea of 'Somerled as Celtic hero' is thus rendered as meaningless as that of 'Somerled as Viking' is inaccurate, and all the more so when the term 'Celtic' has no strictly meaningful application to Somerled and his kind, or indeed to any other of Scotland's peoples or cultures after the end of the eleventh century. The Celtic character of the Gaelic ascendancy of the Mac Alpin courts had been already diminished in the reign of Malcolm Canmore – on the evidence of Domnall Ban's succession when his supporters 'drove out all the English who were with King Malcolm before' – and, after the short 'Celtic twilight' of Domnall's reign, is nowhere apparent in the Anglo-Norman orbit of the sons of Malcolm who became established as Scotland's royal house through the twelfth century. So too had the Celtic character of the Gaelic north – as represented by the culture of the house of Moray in the time of Macbeth – been diffused by its contact, hostile and otherwise, with the Orkney Norse mainland possessions beyond Strath Oykel. The Norse impact on the Gaelic west had been still more decisive, when the Hebrides had been formally passed to Norwegian sovereignty by the end of the eleventh century and the neighbouring mainland, especially in the further north-west, related very much more closely to the realm of the Isles than to the emerging feudal kingdom of the central mainland. 'Celtic Scotland', then, must be said to have lain entirely in the past by Somerled's lifetime.

It is the cultural implication of that situation, however, which bears most specifically on another claim made for Somerled, and one which might be read as a more realistic extension of the 'Celtic hero' school of thought when it proposes his enduring achievement having been a

Gaelic 'revival' in the west Highlands and the Hebrides. While it is patently absurd to suggest his having expelled the Norse from Scotland's western seaboard after three hundred and fifty years of interbreeding and integration between northman and native, the proposal of Somerled's having replaced Norse with Gaelic as the language and culture of the ruling kindred of the west Highlands and the Isles might seem to be reflected in the tenaciously Gaelic cultural character which so distinguished his descendants' Lordship of the Isles, were it not for the doubt cast upon it by the probability that Gaelic was already established as the vernacular tongue of the kings and the kingdom of Man and the Isles some decades before Somerled was born. Such serious doubt, in fact, that the authors of one of the most recent of the few scholarly papers focussing upon him are quite insistent that 'any idea of Somerled's "Gaelic revival" must be seriously questioned',[3] and while they themselves do not pursue the question on that occasion, their remark is especially useful here in its implications for Somerled's place in the history of Gaelic Scotland.

Personal names regularly serve the historian as a useful index of cultural character, and the comparison of the names of Somerled's descendants – and indeed of his immediate forebears – with those of their contemporaries of the ruling kindred of Man would initially suggest a dramatic divergence in language. The given names borne by all the descendants of Godred Crovan through five generations to the end of the Norse sovereignty over Man and the Isles are distinctly Norse in character.[4] Those of Somerled's grandfather (who would have been Godred Crovan's immediate contemporary) and of his father are characteristically *Gall-Gaedhil*, while those of at least some of his sons and most of his grandsons are unmistakably Gaelic. The inference, then, would seem to be one of Somerled's having 'revived' Gaelic as the dominant language and culture of the kindred which was to assume full lordship of the Isles when the kingdom passed from Norwegian to Scottish possession in 1266.

Closer investigation, however, does not lead to precisely the same conclusion. While Gaelic names are borne by most of his grandsons, especially those of what was to become the Clan Donald line of descent, the names of his sons are predominantly Norse or Gaelicised Norse in character, assuredly reflecting the influence of their mother Ragnhild.

Olaf, for example, was the name of her father, while Ranald (which occurs in the Latinised form of *Reginaldus* in the immediately contemporary sources) represents a Gaelicised form of the Norse *Ragnall*, the same name given to his cousin, the son and successor of Godred of Man. Dugall, the given name of his eldest son and the ancestor of the MacDougall lords of Lorn, is certainly of Irish Gaelic origin, but post-Scandinavian impact in date if it represents a personal name deriving from the Irish term *Dubh-gaill* distinguishing the Danes from the Norse or *Finn-gaill*.[5] The name of Somerled's natural son apparently bore some form of the Gille- prefix and so would have been of the same *Gall-Gaedhil* character as those of his father and grandfather; which leaves only Angus, his third son by Ragnhild, with a name of genuinely 'Celtic' origin when it represents the Scottish form of the very old Irish *Oengus*.

The names of his grandsons include examples of Norse and Gaelicised Norse etymology, but are nonetheless more decidedly Scottish Gaelic in character,[6] a pattern which would correspond to the Gaelic culture of the house of Somerled as clearly as it contrasts with the invariably Norse nomenclature of the kings of Man descended from Godred Crovan through the same number of generations. Those names, however, cannot be taken as decisive evidence for the house of Crovan having been as characteristically Norse in language and culture as the house of Somerled was Gaelic. They might equally well be seen as following a family tradition, and one also reflected in the Norse names given to two of the four sons borne to Somerled by Ragnhild. That tradition may well have assumed a more political significance for the kings of Man in Somerled's time if – as the Manx specialist Basil Megaw suggests – 'the "Norwegian dimension" must have seemed an indispensable political shield against the increasingly powerful neighbours which threatened Man and the Isles through the twelfth and thirteenth centuries'.[7]

As he goes on to suggest in the same influential paper, the language spoken by the ruling kindred of Man is more accurately indicated in the Gaelic epithets borne by its kings than by their Norse names. The first and most significant illustration of that proposal would be Godred Crovan himself, whose Norse given name is followed by the unmistakably Gaelic *Crobh-bhán* ('the white-handed'). When the Irish sources call him by a quite different epithet (*Méarach* from *méar* or 'finger'), the origin of his 'Crovan' tag can only lie in the Gaelic of the Isles, and especially so in view of his father Harald – and inevitably, then, Godred himself originally – having been of Islay. Thus when a Norse-descended Hebridean became the founding dynast of the ruling kindred of Man in the last quarter of the eleventh century, there is hardly reason to doubt the language and culture of his royal house having been already established as the language and culture of the Isles. While drawing upon a vastly wider range of evidence than has been mentioned here, Basil Megaw reaches much the same conclusion when he writes that 'we now see that even our "Scandinavian" kings [of Man and the Isles] were characteristically Gaelic speakers'.[8]

All of which does indeed 'seriously question' the claim for Somerled's 'Gaelic revival'. While there is good reason to credit his descendants with maintaining the Gaelic character of their domain through the later medieval centuries, there would seem to be no decisive evidence for Somerled himself having restored that language and culture to the government, and still less to the people, of either the west Highlands or the Hebrides. Indeed, there is no clear evidence for such a revival having been necessary in the southern Hebrides and Argyll where the Norse land-takers appear to have adopted the Gaelic host culture. In the Outer Hebrides, however, and especially on the northernmost island of Lewis, there is no indication of Gaelic having been established as the dominant tongue at the time of the arrival of the northmen. It would appear, in fact, to have only thoroughly penetrated the Hebrides north of Skye some time after the Norse settlement, although probably before the later eleventh century and as a part of the process of its having become the vernacular of the Norse kingdom of the Isles.

The core territory of Scotland's *Gàidhealtachd* – in the geographical sense of 'the domain of the Gaelic-speaking peoples' – is firmly located today in the west Highlands and the Hebrides where the Western Isles especially, and the Isle of Lewis in particular, represent its capital stronghold. Some thousand years ago, however, very much the same could have been said of that region, and with just the same local emphases, in terms of Norse settlement in Scotland. The Gaelic language became established, then, in what is now recognised as its heartland while that territory lay within Norwegian possession, and that seeming paradox bears its own testimony to the true character of the cultural roots of modern Gaelic Scotland.

Scottish and Irish Gaelic are both descended – as, of course, is the Manx form also – from the *Goidelic* of Celtic Ireland, but Scottish Gaelic and Manx were recognised by the eminent authority Kenneth H. Jackson as 'very much more simplified and corrupted than the Gaelic of Ireland'. While the great territorial extent of that Scottish form might be attributed as much to its having overlain the older Pictish and Britonic on the eastern Scottish mainland as to its interaction with Norse in the west and north, Professor Jackson had no doubt as to the prominence of Scandinavian influence on the language. 'One of the chief differences between Scottish Gaelic and Irish is the much greater Norse element in Gaelic vocabulary in Scotland'. He notices also 'some impressive evidence to suggest that Norse language had a quite direct effect on the pronunciation of Scottish Gaelic such as it never had on Irish'.[9]

The source of those differences between languages of a common 'Q-Celtic' origin can only lie in the difference between the nature and extent of Norse settlement in Scotland and that of Ireland where the Scandinavian population was much less numerous, probably more transient, and largely contained within its own enclaves around trading towns such as Dublin and Limerick. Even though there is no documentary evidence for the vernacular Gaelic of the west Highlands and Hebrides in Somerled's time,[10] it would follow that the Norse elements preserved in modern Scottish Gaelic might have been still more prominent when it first emerged as the language of the Celtic-Scandinavian cultural province from which today's *Gàidhealtachd* is directly descended.

The concept of culture – in the sociological rather than the 'artistic' sense of the term – extends far beyond its defining bedrock of language to encompass a whole spectrum of skills and technologies, beliefs and symbols, perspectives and horizons, and it is in that sense that the culture of Somerled's world and time is most fully described as a Norse-Gaelic fusion. So too, it is in that context that his wider significance is brought properly into focus, because he cannot be recognised either as a Norseman or as a Celt, and certainly not as a Celtic revivalist driving the *Lochlannach* and their language back into the sea – but he can be recognised as the one historical figure who reflects in his every aspect the same fusion of Norse and Gael which binds the deeper cultural roots of modern Gaelic Scotland.

If the foregoing pages have achieved any semblance of a portrait of Somerled mac Gillebride, I would hope that they have been able to indicate the occurrence of that Norse-Gaelic fusion at almost every point in his life and his legend: from his name-form conjoining a Norse given name with a typically *Gall-Gaedhil* patronymic to his burial on the holy island of the patron saint of the Gael, but according to the custom of Norse kings of the Isles.

As to the long shadows of *Somhairle Mor*, they do seem to lie across the greater extent of the history of the Gael in Scotland. The parent tongue of Scottish Gaelic must have made its first firm footholds along the western seaboard of north Britain with the Irish settlements established there at least as early as the fourth century AD, but recorded only in the sources of Irish tradition. One such settlement is indicated by the legend of Colla Uais, who is said to have held 'great lands on the mainland and in the isles' of Alba almost two hundred years before the royal house of Dalriada crossed from Antrim to Argyll and who is claimed by the genealogists as the ultimate ancestor of Somerled and the Clan Donald. When Kenneth mac Alpin, who was afterwards to accomplish the Gaelicisation of the Pictish kingdom of Fortriu, first rose to ascendancy in Dalriada in the second quarter of the eighth century, his ally is identified by the annalist as having been Somerled's direct ancestor, Gothfrith mac Fergus. The shadow of Somerled does, of course, lie most distinctly over the later medieval history of Gaelic Scotland in the person of his descendant Lords of the Isles. There is, then, some irony attendant upon the sombre occasion at Dunstaffnage in 1493 when John, fourth and last of the Clan Donald Lords, formally surrendered his Lordship to James IV, who was not only a Stewart but also the last of Scotland's kings known to have spoken the Gaelic.

Perhaps the darkest of the shadows is that cast by Somerled's fatal invasion of the Clyde when it targeted Renfrew as the focus of the expanding Stewart lordship's threat to the west. Professor Barrow's authoritative analysis of the 'well-nigh monopolistic power' wielded by the Campbells in Argyll from the late fifteenth to the eighteenth century proposes its having been 'due in large measure to the fact that the

Campbells of Lorne fell heir to the complex of lordships built up by the Stewarts between 1200 and c.1370, and that in turn was based on the Clyde lordship created for the first of the Stewarts by David I and Malcolm IV'.[11] Long shadows indeed when they can raise up the prospect of so very different a subsequent course of history had Somerled's great host of west Highlanders, Islesmen and Dublin Norse not failed in the venture of 1164.

Alexander Carmichael's monumental *Carmina Gadelica* collection of Gaelic incantations makes reference to Somerled in two variations of verses addressed to an apple tree. Lines from one of them – a song made for 'Mackay of the Rhinns of Islay' – seem to me to offer an apt form of coda:

Craobh nan ubhal, gu robh Dia leat,
Gu robh gealach, gu robh grian leat,
Gu robh gaoth an ear 's an iar leat,
Gu robh Dùile mór nan sian leat,
Gu robh gach nì thàna riamh leat,
Gu robh Somhairle Mór 's a chliar leat.

O apple tree, may God be with thee,
May moon and sun be with thee,
May east and west winds be with thee,
May the great Creator of the elements be with thee,
May everything that ever existed be with thee,
May great Somerled and his band [of bards] be with thee.[12]

NOTES & REFERENCES

Chapter 1: *Gall-Gaedhil*:

CELTIC SCOTLAND & THE NORSE IMPACT

1. *Annals of Ulster* @ 793=4 (*ESSH*, i. p.255). The Irish annals were compiled at various times between the eleventh and seventeenth centuries. While some do include contemporary entries, their record of earlier times was transcribed from older sources which are only rarely identified and must be assumed to have been long since lost. Their original dating systems are variously complex and known to be sometimes in error, so all year dates assigned to annal entries here represent what is recognised as the true historical date of the event entered by the annalist.
2. 'Fergus Mor mac Erc, with the people of Dalriada, held part of Britain; and there he died.' *Annals of Tigernach* @ c. 501 (*ESSH*, i. p.1). Fergus is accorded a reign of three years by almost all of the later medieval lists of kings of Dalriada (*ESSH*, i. p.cxxix).
3. Bede, *Historia Ecclesiastica*, I. i. (*SAEC*, p.4). The late fourteenth-century Irish sources are the *Book of Ballymote* and the *Lebor Brecc* ('The Speckled Book').
4. The *Book of Leinster* and Rawlinson MS. B502; also included in the MacMhuirich *History of the MacDonalds* from the *Book of Clanranald* (see Ch. 2, pp. 26–30 below).
5. The two forms are recognised as P-Celtic and Q-Celtic by reason of the consonant sounding 'p' in the former occurring as 'q' (or 'k') in the latter. The most convenient illustration is found in the respective terms for 'son of', which occur as *mac* in the Goidelic and as *map* in the Brythonic form (from which the *ap-* prefix of many Welsh surnames).
6. Watson, *The History of the Celtic Placenames of Scotland* (1986), pp.120–1.
7. Obituary of Kenneth mac Alpin, *Annals of Ulster* @ 858 (*ESSH*, i. p.287).
8. Principally *Annals of Ulster, Annals of Innisfallen* and *Annals of the Four Masters* @ 795 (*ESSH*, i. pp.255–6).
9. *Dublin Annals of Innisfallen* @ 807; see also *Annals of Ulster* @ 802, 804, 806, 807 (*ESSH*, i. pp.258–9).
10. Crawford, *Scandinavian Scotland* (1987), p.46.
11. The earlier *-stadr* suffix is found as *-shader* on Lewis, while the slightly later

-bolstadr suffix is more widely distributed throughout the full extent of the Hebrides, occurring as *-bost* on Lewis and as *-bus* or *-bols* on Islay.

12. The names of almost all of the principal islands themselves are descended from Norse forms of what are known to have been earlier Celtic names. Jura and Staffa (from the Norse *dyr-ey* or 'deer isle' and *stafr-ey* or 'basalt isle' respectively) are the outstanding exceptions when the names of Skye, Rum, Eigg, Coll, Tiree, Mull and Islay are all recognisably derived from Celtic forms by which they were known at the end of the seventh century. Harris (Gaelic: *Na h-Earra*) has been identified as deriving from the Norse *haerri*, 'the higher land' (i.e. the higher southern extent of lower-lying Lewis), but no entirely convincing Norse origin has yet been proposed for Lewis or the Uists, so leaving open the possibility of *Ljódhus* and *Ívist* having been Norse approximations of older Pictish or even pre-Celtic names.
13. Oftedal, 'Norse Place-names in Celtic Scotland', in Ó Cuív (ed.), *The Impact of the Scandinavian Invasions on the Celtic-speaking Peoples c.*800–1100 AD (1975), p.44.
14. Alcock, 'Excavations at Dunollie Castle, Oban', *PSAS* 117 (1987), pp.129–30.
15. Jackson, 'The Celtic Languages during the Viking Period', in Ó Cuív (ed.), *The Impact of the Scandinavian Invasions on the Celtic-speaking Peoples c.*800–1100 AD (1975), p.6.
16. Brown, 'The Norse in Argyll', in Ritchie, G. (ed.), *The Archaeology of Argyll* (1997), p.230.
17. The *Annals of the Four Masters* – compiled in the 1630s from earlier annals and from tradition by four of the greatest Irish scholars of their time – do represent a very late source and one sometimes considered less than authoritative, especially on the grounds of its notoriously wayward chronology. As the sole annal source for Gothfrith mac Fergus, their evidence for his historicity might be called into question but has been vigorously and convincingly defended by David Sellar in his paper 'The Origins and Ancestry of Somerled', *SHR* 45 (1966), pp.134–7.
18. A. & A. Macdonald, *The Clan Donald* (1896–1904), vol. iii p.178.
19. Smyth, *Warlords and Holy Men* (1989), p.192. It should be said that Professor Smyth discusses a wider range of evidence for Norse relations with Kenneth and his successors which is not strictly pertinent here.
20. Smyth, 'Ketil Flatnose', in Williams, Smyth & Kirby (ed.), *A Biographical Dictionary of Dark Age Britain* (1991), p.168. Professor Smyth's detailed account of Ketil is published in his *Scandinavian Kings in the British Isles* (1977), pp.118–126.
21. *Cogadh Gaedhel re Gallaibh* ('The Wars of the Irish with the Gall', Munster, 12th century); *Dublin Annals of Innisfallen* @ 1014 (*ESSH*, i. pp.536–7).

22. The epithet 'Crovan' is thought to be a corruption of the Gaelic *crobh-bhán* ('the white-handed' or 'of the white hand'), but its precise meaning as applied to Godred is unclear.
23. The *Chronicle of Man* actually reads 'of Ysland', but Islay is generally thought to have been meant because the same source states that Godred died on Islay where his burial place is marked – according to local tradition – by the standing stone called *Carragh Bhan* near Kintra.
24. Magnus' epithet is explained by his *Saga* when it says of him that 'he had much those fashions and manner of dress that were usual in the western lands; and so had many of his men. They went bare-legged in the street and had short tunics and also over-cloaks. Then men called him Magnus Bareleg' (*ESSH*, ii. p.118). The 'manner of dress' is alike to that worn by immediately contemporary Scots warriors described in accounts of the First Crusade and would seem to represent an early medieval form of the later Highlander's linen shirt (Gael. *léine*) and belted plaid (Gael. *breacan an fhéilidh*).
25. Duncan & Brown, 'Argyll and the Isles in the earlier Middle Ages', *PSAS* 90 (1956–7), p.194.
26. Lamont, *The Early History of Islay* (1970), p.15.

Chapter 2: '*Gillebride's son*': THE EMERGENCE OF SOMERLED

1. Dean Donald Monro's *Description of the Western Isles* of 1549 calls Somerled *Somerle* in his genealogy of the Clan Donald Lords of the Isles. The modern Gaelic *Somhairle* (anglicised as Sorley) is popularly believed to be the Gaelic form of the name Samuel, its Norse origin apparently having long since passed from local memory.
2. The reference is found in the Poppleton manuscript of the *Chronicle of the Kings* and in its passage bearing on Indulf, son of Constantine II and king of Scots 954–962, a period when the Scandinavian influence on the mac Alpin court is very evident, not least in Indulf's own name deriving from the Norse *Hildulfr* (*ESSH*, i. pp.468–9).
3. Fellows-Jensen, 'Some Orkney Personal Names' in Bate, Jesch & Morris (ed.), *The Viking Age in Caithness, Orkney and the North Atlantic* (1995), p.400.
4. The *Orkneyinga Saga* claims Somerled having been slain in battle with Svein Asleifsson. Further to which see Chapter 5, pp. 105–7 below.
5. Chadwick, 'The Vikings and the Western World' in Ó Cuív (ed.), *The Impact of the Scandinavian Invasions on the Celtic-speaking Peoples c.*800–1100 AD (1975), p.32.
6. Smyth, *Scandinavian York and Dublin* (1987), p.310.

7. Saint Brigid (Scottish Gael. *Bride*) of Kildare, d. c.525 and Saint Adamnan (Irish. *Adomnán*) of Iona, d.704. The Gaelic forms of the names appear in various spellings in the different sources, e.g. *Giolla Bhride* and *Giolla Oghamhnan* in the *Books of Clanranald, Gilla Brighdi* in the *Annals of Tigernach* and *Gille-Adhamhnain* in the *Annals of Ulster*.
8. Henderson, *The Norse Influence on Celtic Scotland* (1910), p.58.
9. The most fully extended form of the traditional descent of Somerled from Colla Uais is tabulated in the Genealogical Chart I 'The Traditional Descent of Somerled', p.162 below.
10. Author unknown, *Historical and Genealogical Account of the Clan or Family Macdonald* (1819), pp.2–3.
11. Munch, *The Chronicle of Man and the Sudreys* (1860), pp.74–5.
12. Sellar, 'The Origins and Ancestry of Somerled', *SHR* 45 (1966), pp.123–42.
13. Sellar, 'Origins and Ancestry', *SHR* 45 (1966), p.141.
14. Some decades after the forfeiture of the Lordship of the Isles to the Scottish crown in 1493, the MacMhuirichs moved from their lands in Kintyre to the Western Isles where they attached themselves to the MacDonalds of Clanranald, hence the title of the *Books of Clanranald*.
15. MacBain & Kennedy (ed.), *Reliquae Celticae* (1894), ii. pp.139–40. NB. 'MacVurich' is, of course, a phonetic anglicisation of the Gaelic *MacMhuirich*.
16. Dr Bannerman also identifies an Aodh of the Beatons of North Uist as likely to have been the father of Christopher Beaton who wrote the greatest part of the 'Black' *Book of Clanranald* and, pointing to the seventeenth-century custom of persons in the service of a noble family adopting their employer's surname, makes the suggestion that 'since Hugh is the English equivalent of the Gaelic *Aodh*, it is possible that Aodh Beaton and Hugh MacDonald are one and the same person.' Bannerman, *The Beatons* (1986), pp.16–19.
17. By the nineteenth century, the term 'Danes' had long been indiscriminately applied to medieval Scandinavians in much the same way as the term 'Vikings' is used nowadays. While Alexander Cameron's translation of the MacMhuirich *History* which accompanies the Gaelic text in the *Reliquae Celticae* edition of 1894 accurately renders *Finngallach* as 'Norse', it consistently mistranslates *Lochlannach* as 'Danes' even when the context would suggest its indicating the Hebridean or Manx Norse.
18. Sellar, 'Origins and Ancestry', *SHR* 45 (1966), p.129–30.
19. Gillebride's Gaelic soubriquet is generally referred to as being of some antiquity, although the earliest references which I have been able to trace are those found in A. & A. Macdonald, *The Clan Donald* (1896–1904), i. p.37; iii. p.179.
20. The text of the Sleat *History of the Macdonalds* used here is that published

in The Iona Club's *Collectanea de Rebus Albanicis* (1847) and I have followed that edition in reproducing the eccentricities and inconsistencies of the original.

21. MacDonald, 'The Vikings in Gaelic Oral Tradition' in Fenton & Palsson (ed.), *The Northern and Western Isles in the Viking World* (1984), p.273. John MacInnes' paper on 'Clan Sagas and Historical Legends' offers another sidelight on the Morvern battle tradition: 'According to the version I have known since childhood, Somerled asked the MacInneses for their support, which they gave; according to Clan Donald sources, the MacInneses asked Somerled to lead them.' *TGSI* 57 (1991), p.381.
22. Thomson, 'The MacMhuirich Bardic Family', *TGSI* 43 (1966), p.284.
23. Munch, *Chronicle of Man* (1860), pp.53–4.
24. Duncan, *Scotland: The Making of the Kingdom* (1978), p.166.

Chapter 3: '*In wicked rebellion against his natural lord*': GAELDOM'S CHALLENGE TO THE CANMORE KINGS

1. A. A. M. Duncan and A. L. Brown suggest that 'the grant by David I to Dunfermline Abbey of "the half part of my tenth from Argyll and Kintyre in that year namely when I myself shall have received cain [tribute] thence" may represent a division of the revenues of Argyll between the king and Somerled'. 'Argyll and the Isles', *PSAS* 90 (1956–7), p.195.
2. Descent from a Norse-Celtic family, probably intermarried with native Galloway elements, is proposed by the historian Richard Oram as 'the most viable option' for Fergus' origins and ancestry. 'Certainly, the traditional outlook of the Galwegians, away from Scotland towards the powers of the Irish Sea and Hebrides, suggests that it was from those areas that Fergus' predecessors were drawn.' 'Fergus, Galloway and the Scots' in Oram & Stell (ed.), *Galloway: Land and Lordship* (1991), p.122.
3. Brooke, *Wild Men and Holy Places* (1994), p.79.
4. Duncan & Brown, 'Argyll and the Isles', *PSAS* 90 (1956–7), p.195–6. Interestingly though, and as John MacInnes points out, '*Am Mormhaire* (The Mormaer) is the normal and still current style of MacDonald of Sleat.' 'Gaelic Poetry and Historical Tradition' in L. Maclean (ed.), *The Middle Ages in the Highlands* (1981), p.147.
5. 'Canmore' apparently derives from the Gaelic *ceann mor.* Thus, when such Gaelic epithets usually describe physical appearance, Malcolm Canmore might be taken to mean 'Malcolm of the great head', but the historian Michael Lynch has suggested the term is 'better translated from the Gaelic as Chief rather than great head [and] was probably part of a reconstruction of the image of kingship'. *Scotland: A New History* (1992), p.74. If he is correct, then the name can be taken as a propagandistic

attempt to devise a pseudo-Gaelic praise-name for a king who was probably not remembered with the greatest esteem by the Gael.

6. R. L. G. Ritchie, *The Normans in Scotland* (1954), p.5.
7. Edward, the first-born son of Malcolm and Margaret, had been killed with his father in 1093. Edgar, the second son, was thus the eldest surviving in 1097 when he seized the kingship and put to death his next eldest brother, Edmund, who had conspired with his uncle Domnall against Duncan. The fourth son, Etheldred, became earl of Fife and abbot of Dunkeld, while the two youngest followed Edgar into the kingship, Alexander in 1107 and David in 1124. See Genealogical Chart III 'The House of Canmore', p.164 below.
8. Donaldson, *A Northern Commonwealth* (1990), p.62.
9. Robert de Torigni (properly Thorigny, his family home in Normandy) was a Benedictine monk appointed in 1154 to be prior of the monastery of Mont Saint Michel, a major centre of northern pilgrimage, where he was usefully placed to gather information from the regular flow of visiting churchmen, kings and nobles.
10. See Genealogical Chart IV 'The House of Moray', p.165 below.
11. Cowan, 'The Historical Macbeth', in Sellar (ed.), *Moray: Province and People* (1993), p.141 making reference to Mackay, *The Book of Mackay* (1906), p.21.
12. A. McDonald, 'Monk, Bishop, Imposter, Pretender: The Place of Wimund in 12th century Scotland', *TGSI* 58 (1992–4), p.258.
13. McDonald, 'Monk, Bishop, Imposter, Pretender', *TGSI* 58 (1992–4), p.261.
14. John of Hexham (*SAEC*, pp.230–1). The Hexham chroniclers' interest in David I and his son Henry assuredly owes something to their gift to the monastery of property in Carlisle.
15. Malcolm IV was described by the early sixteenth-century historian Hector Boece as 'ane prettie pleasand page' and is sometimes called 'Malcolm the Maiden', although by no source earlier than the fifteenth century when the epithet is clearly a reference to chastity (Malcolm neither having married or fathered offspring) rather than to youthful appearance.
16. R. L. G. Ritchie, *The Normans in Scotland* (1954), p.346. Malcolm IV is the first king of Scots whose coronation is located at Scone by a contemporary source (John of Hexham; *SAEC*, p.232).
17. It should be mentioned that a curious, but closely contemporary, account of Somerled's invasion of 1164 (*Carmen de Morte Sumerledi*) apparently refers to his earlier rebellion of 1153 in its opening paragraph describing his warriors as *Galienses, Argaidenses, freti vi Albanica*, translated as 'Hebrideans and Argylesmen, supported by a force of Scots' by A. O. Anderson

who suggests that 'perhaps the men of *Innse gall* are meant' by the term *Galienses.* (*ESSH* ii, p.256).

18. The insistence on the jealousy of nobles at Malcolm's court having provoked contention between Somerled and the crown occurs again in the Sleat *History* in the context of the events of 1164, and the demand that Somerled 'give up his right to Argyle or abandon the Isles' is not only closely similar to the one made of him by the king in the crisis of that year but would not have been strictly applicable before Somerled's settlement with the king of Man in 1156. The Sleat historian is known to have been capable of reworking historical detail to slight those he saw as hostile to his favoured Clan Donald kindreds, so it would not have been unthinkable for him to have re-styled an historical earl of Menteith 'Thane of Angus' for just such a purpose, quite possibly one related to yet another battle – well-known to him and not dissimilar in some respects to this one – fought by Somerled's descendant Donald, the second Lord of the Isles, at Harlaw in 1411 where an Angus contingent was included in the opposing forces under the Earl of Mar and a Sheriff of Angus was numbered among the slain.
19. R. A. McDonald, *The Kingdom of the Isles* (1997), p.53.
20. Cowan, 'The Historical Macbeth' in Sellar (ed.), *Moray: Province and People* (1993), p.132.

Chapter 4: '*The ruin of the kingdom of the Isles*': SOMERLED'S WAR ON THE KINGDOM OF MAN

1. The *Chronicle of Man* (or, more properly, the *Chronicle of the Kings of Man and the Isles*) supplies a history of the kingdom from 1066 to 1316, preceded by earlier entries thought to be derived from the *Chronicle of Melrose.* It survives in only one manuscript, of which the main part is in a hand of the later thirteenth century, set down by monks of Rushen working either in that monastery itself or in the scriptorium of its mother house at Furness in Cumbria. It should be noted, though, that its chronology is notoriously erroneous and that dates applied here to its entries represent, wherever possible, the true historical date of the event recorded.
2. Professor Munch points out that Ingibjorg was born after her father's full establishment as jarl of Orkney, probably between 1105 and 1110 and so her relationship with Olaf cannot be realistically dated much earlier than 1125, thus rather later than his marriage to Affrica and possibly even after her death. Munch, *Chronicle of Man* (1860), p.74.
3. The year 1152 is indicated for Godred's departure for Norway and the invasion by the Haraldssons placed 'in the same year', but the assassination of Olaf is placed – with the obituaries of David I and Saint Bernard of

Clairvaux – in the following year of 1153, where it is specifically dated to 'the day of the apostles Saints Peter and Paul' (29th June); which indicates a rather longer interval – and rather more opportunities for hostility – between the arrival of the invaders and the death of Olaf than the *Chronicle* either suggests or describes.

4. The *Chronicle* first indicates a date of 1154 for Godred's succession (which would correspond to his reign-length of 'thirty-three years' and his obituary under the year 1187), but afterwards assigns events of 'the third year of his reign' to the year preceding 1156, which would assume his reign having been dated from the death of his father. These and other chronological discrepancies are best explained as a result of the *Chronicle* having been (or been compiled from) the work of different scribes working to different systems of calculation.
5. Duffy, 'Irishmen and Islesmen in the kingdoms of Dublin and Man', *Ériu* 43 (1992), p.127.
6. As Vaughan Young helpfully explains in his concise history of the kingdom of the Isles: 'After the battle of Sky Hill [in 1079], Godred Crovan gave the south of the Isle of Man to those of his Hebridean forces who wished to settle . . . and gave the north of the Isle of Man to the surviving Manxmen. It is of interest to note that even in the seventeenth century, the people in the south spoke the Hebridean dialect of Gaelic while those in the north spoke the Ulster dialect of Gaelic.' Young, *The Lewis and Skye Groups of the Hebrides under the Norse* (1996), p.6.
7. R. A. McDonald, *The Kingdom of the Isles* (1997), p.56.
8. Cheape, 'Recounting Tradition: A Critical View of Medieval Reportage' in Fenton & Palsson (ed.), *The Northern and Western Isles in the Viking Age* (1984), p.218.
9. *Carmen de Morte Sumerledi*, see Note 17 to Chapter 3, above.
10. The MacDonalds of Clanranald and of Sleat were both ultimately branches of descent from John of Islay, the first Lord of the Isles: the Clanranald kindred from Ranald, John's son by his first wife Amy MacRuairi, and the MacDonalds of Sleat from Hugh, second son of John's grandson Alexander, third Lord of the Isles. See Genealogical Chart II 'The Clan Donald', p.163 below.
11. Both the *Annals of Ulster* and the *Carmen de Morte Sumerledi* record a son of Somerled to have been killed with his father in 1164, but neither of those sources names the son slain. An interpolated episode in the *Chronicle of Man* under the year 1158 mentions 'one of the more powerful chieftains called Gilcolm' being involved in Somerled's raid on Man in that year. Although the story is hardly historical in character, it is possible this Gilcolm was the same natural son similarly named by other sources,

which would suggest his having been sufficiently mature by 1158 to lead his own personal warband in alliance with his father.

12. The death of Ranald is dated to 1207 by the MacMhuirich *History of the MacDonalds*, but its dating for the period is less than reliable when it places the death of Somerled (who is known to have been killed in 1164) in 1180. Historians have suggested dates ranging from 1192 to as late as 1227 for Ranald's true obituary. If true, the statement in the Sleat *History of the MacDonalds* that he 'died in the fifty-fourth year of his age' would suggest an earlier rather than a later date within that range.
13. C. M. MacDonald, *The History of Argyll* (1950), p.85.
14. *Liber Vitae* of the Church of Durham (*SAEC*, p.264).
15. Reginald of Durham, *Libellus de admirandi beati Cuthberti virtutibus* (ed. Raine, 1835), p.251.
16. 'Said to have been Paul Balkanson, Norwegian Lord of Skye', according to a note in A. & A. Macdonald, *The Clan Donald* (1896). Although not impossible, the identification is unlikely when the historical Paul Balkisson of Skye – described by the *Chronicle of Man* as 'powerful in the whole kingdom of the Isles' – was still active in 1225 and is noticed again, with his son Balki, in 1230 by *Hakon Hakonsson's Saga*. Even if not the same man, the 'Paul' who is noticed by the *Chronicle* entry under 1155 may very well have been his kinsman.
17. Duncan, *Scotland: The Making of the Kingdom* (1978), p.86.
18. Rixson, *The West Highland Galley* (1998), pp.122–3.
19. *Registrum Monasterii de Passelet* [Register of Paisley Abbey], Maitland Club (1832), p.149.
20. By Duncan & Brown, 'Argyll and the Isles', *PSAS* 90 (1956–7), p.198. A still earlier date of 1180 is proposed by A. & A. Macdonald in *The Clan Donald* (1896).
21. Clark, *The Lord of the Isles Voyage* (1993), p.27.
22. Crawford, *Scandinavian Scotland* (1987), p.26.
23. The entry at 1156 in the *Annals of the Four Masters* records 'great snow and intense frost in the winter of this year'. Such conditions, explains Wallace Clark, 'can beget calms and clear nights in which a fleet could manoeuvre and men with the moon up could see to fight. The full moon that year was on 12th January. That or a couple of days later is the most probable date for the battle, six days after the traditional one. Epiphany would have been the nearest reference date in pre-calendar days.' *The Lord of the Isles Voyage* (1993), p.22.
24. The Orkney fleet – for comparison – has been estimated at approximately seventeen ships. Rixson, *The West Highland Galley* (1997), pp.58–9.
25. Brøgger & Shetelig, *The Viking Ships* (1971), p.172.
26. Gregory, *History of the West Highlands and Isles* (1836), 1881 edn., p.14.

27. Lamont, *Early History of Islay* (1970), p.17.
28. Maughold's feast is entered under 27th April in the eighth-century *Martyrology of Oengus*, where he is acclaimed as 'the great bishop MacCaille'. His legend tells of his having been 'a pirate in Ireland, who was told by [Saint] Patrick to put to sea in a coracle without oars as a penance for his misdeeds. He landed on the Isle of Man where, after suitable reparation, he was made bishop.' Farmer, *Oxford Dictionary of Saints* (1987), p.273.

Chapter 5: '*As good a right to the lands . . .*':

INVASION OF THE CLYDE & DEATH AT RENFREW

1. Those two titles correspond impressively to the entry of Somerled's obituary at 1164 in the continuation of the *Annals of Tigernach* where he is styled *ri Indsi Gall & Cind tire*, 'king of the Hebrides and Kintyre', especially when 'Kintyre' is known to have been used elsewhere in the Irish sources to mean 'Argyll'.
2. Earl Ferteth's father was the 'Malisse, earl of Strathearn' said by Ailred of Rievaulx to have spoken scathingly before the Battle of the Standard of the king's reliance upon the 'Gauls' (i.e. the Norman knights) in the Scots forces, remarks which suggested to R. A. McDonald and S. A. McLean 'that anti-Norman sentiments were shared by father and son'. 'Somerled of Argyll: A New look at Old Problems', *SHR* 71 (1992), p.21.
3. While historians are not in full agreement on this question, the majority do share G. W. S. Barrow's view that 'it can hardly be doubted that Fergus, lord of Galloway, was one of the confederacy; and though record never styles him "earl", a chronicle might do so.' Barrow (ed.), *Regesta Regum Scottorum* I, p.12.
4. The full Latin text (with notes) of the charter granting lands 'in the district of Elgin' to Berowald the Fleming 'for the service of one knight in Elgin castle' is included in Barrow (ed.), *Regesta Regum Scottorum* I, pp.219–20.
5. Barrow, 'The Date of the Peace between Somerled of Argyll and Malcolm IV', *SHR* 73 (1994), p.223.
6. A letter assigned to a date between November 1160 and September 1162 in which the king commands 'Malcolm, earl of Ross' to protect and maintain the monks of Dunfermline. 'These were presumably the monks of the Benedictine priory of Urquhart', explains A. O. Anderson. 'It may therefore be deduced that Malcolm's earldom extended to the Spey.' (*ESSH* ii, p.233). When the *Orkneyinga Saga* mentions Malcolm mac Heth – by reason of his daughter *Hvarflod* (Gael. *Gormflaith*) having become the second wife of the Orkney jarl Harald Maddadsson – it calls him 'Malcolm, earl of Moray'.
7. The text actually reads 'Sicebi the king', which is recognisable as a garbled

form of the early Middle English *Sitte-bi* and thus in modern English 'Sit-by-the-king'. (*ESSH* ii, p.256).

8. 'It would hardly be surprising', in the view of R. A. McDonald, 'if the army had contained men from Galloway, Moray, or even the Orkneys, as well.' *The Kingdom of the Isles* (1997), p.67. Despite the absence of supporting evidence, the suggestion is, nonetheless, plausible.
9. Sawyer, *Kings and Vikings* (1982), p.99.
10. In 1165, Henry II hired 'ships from Dublin and from other towns in Ireland' for an expedition to Wales, according to the Welsh *Brut Tywyssogion* ('Chronicle of the Princes'). The Dublin Norse were apparently willing to oblige, but could supply so few ships to Henry at Chester that he abandoned the enterprise; which arouses the suspicion that the Dublin fleet had been greatly depleted in 'the slaughter of the *Gall* of Dublin' on the Clyde in the previous year.
11. Dendochronological analysis of the Skuldelev ships found in Roskilde Fjord has shown the largest of them – the oak-built longship known as 'Skuldelev 2' – 'which was built around AD 1060–70, was . . . in fact Irish and was probably built in the Dublin region'. Bonde, 'Found in Denmark . . .', *Archaeology Ireland* 45 (1998), p.27.
12. C. M. MacDonald, *The History of Argyll* (1950), p.79.
13. R. A. McDonald, *The Kingdom of the Isles* (1997), pp.62, 65–6.
14. The 'tradition' claiming Banquo, a thane of Lochaber descended from ancient kings of Scots, as the ancestor of the house of Stewart is a fiction which made its first appearance in Hector Boece's Latin *History and Chronicles* of 1527 and entered into wider circulation by way of Shakespeare's *Macbeth*. There is no genuinely historical evidence for any such Banquo.
15. Robert II – son of Walter, the sixth Steward and his wife Marjorie, daughter of the Bruce – succeeded to the throne as the only surviving grandson of Robert (I) the Bruce.
16. Barrow, *The Anglo-Norman Era in Scottish History* (1980), p.64.
17. R. A. McDonald, *The Kingdom of the Isles* (1997), p.65.
18. Cheape, 'Recounting Tradition', in Fenton & Palsson (ed.), *The Northern and Western Isles in the Viking Age* (1984), p.219.
19. R. A. McDonald, 'The Death and Burial of Somerled', *West Highland Notes and Queries* (1991), pp.7–8.
20. C. M. MacDonald, *The History of Argyll* (1950), p.93.

Chapter 6: '*Icollumkill*':

THE HOUSE OF SOMERLED & THE CHURCH ON IONA

1. R. A. McDonald, 'The Death and Burial of Somerled', *West Highland Notes and Queries* (1991), p.8.

2. Yeoman, *Pilgrimage in Medieval Scotland* (1999), p.82. The same author's suggestion that by the early fifteenth century 'most of the Iona pilgrims would have been Gaels from Ireland and from the west highlands and islands' (p.85) would also have some bearing here.
3. Gregory, *History of the West Highlands and Isles* (1836), 1881 edn., p.16.
4. Crisostomo Henriquez, *Monologium Cistertiense*, published in Antwerp, 1630.
5. This mandate of Pope Clement VII, dated 27th June 1393 and confirming old land grants to Saddell, quotes a submission from the monastery referring to its foundation by 'Reginaldus'.
6. A. L. Brown has pointed to the probability that Saddell's architectural 'inspiration and craftsmen came from Ireland', which would correspond to the evidence – found in a papal bull of Clement VII – for its having been a daughter house of the important Irish Cistercian foundation of Mellifont near Drogheda, County Louth. 'The Cistercian Abbey of Saddell, Kintyre', *Innes Review* (1969), p.132.
7. *Ingi Bardsson's Saga (ESSH*, ii p.378–82). One of those raiders named by the saga was 'Uspak the Hebridean', who is believed to have been a son of Dugall mac Somerled resident in Norway. This same Uspak adopted the name of Hakon and returned in 1230 with a Norse fleet as the Norwegian king Hakon Hakonsson's candidate for kingship of the Isles. The expedition was aborted when Uspak-Hakon was killed whilst attacking Rothesay castle on Bute. It is perhaps just possible that the fractious situation developing in the Isles at the time, and inevitably involving the descendants of Somerled, might have prompted Donald of Islay to remove his grandfather's remains from Iona to the greater safety of Saddell on Kintyre.
8. Macquarrie, *Iona through the ages* (1983), p.14.
9. Dunbar & Fisher, *Iona: A Guide to the Monuments* (1995), p.18.
10. A prior of Durham wrote the closely contemporary *Life of Saint Margaret*, and her principal foundation of Dunfermline abbey was in great part the work of Durham craftsmen.
11. 'It is she that erected the *teampall* [at] Chairinis in Uist.' The Sleat historian also supplies an item of probable bearing in his statement that Donald, son of Ranald, granted 'the Island Heisker to the nuns of Iona.' 'Island Heisker' (now Heisgeir) indicates the very fertile Monach island group lying off the North Uist coastline neighbouring Carinish. 'Donald, son of Ranald', was, of course, Bethoc's nephew.
12. While there was an historical Saint Odhran – whose feast is entered in the Irish calendars under 27th October, whose obituary by the Four Masters at the year 548, and whose association with the west of Scotland is attested by numerous place-name dedications – his association with Iona is more

securely rooted in tradition than in history. The name of the *Reilig Odhrain*, 'Odhran's burial ground', would seem to derive from the legend of his ritual burial alive by Columba at the foundation of the monastery on Iona, a story first found in the *Betha Coluim Cille*, the Irish life of the saint composed at Derry in the twelfth century.

13. Dunbar & Fisher, *Iona* (1995), pp.13–14.
14. The claim for Ranald's having 'received a cross from Jerusalem' has been taken by some historians to suggest the possibility of his having gone on crusade. The context of the MacMhuirich reference, however, does seem to imply his receipt of 'a cross from Jerusalem' at the time of his death, perhaps as a nominal form of the absolution granted to those who went on crusade or even as a literal reference to an actual relic or token.
15. See Note 12 to Chapter 4 above. Dates from the MacMhuirich *History* quoted here are corrected either in parentheses – e.g. '1380 [1392]' – or in an explanatory note.
16. Angus could not possibly have died in 1306 when he served Robert the Bruce with such distinction at Bannockburn eight years later. Although nowhere reliably recorded, but often placed around the time of the Bruce's death in 1329, Angus' death has been most recently dated to 1318 by R. A. McDonald in *The Kingdom of the Isles* (1997), pp.186–7.
17. *Hakon Hakonsson's Saga* includes an account of the expedition of 1249 by which the Scots king Alexander II set out to claim the Hebrides for the Scottish crown. When his fleet lay in Kerrera Sound the king dreamed of three men appearing to him: one in regal garb, a second tall, slender and youthful, the third nobly dressed and apparently tonsured in the old Irish manner, 'very bald in front . . . by far the largest in build and the most frowning of them all'. This third man bade him turn back from 'plundering in the Hebrides' and said he would brook no refusal. When the king spoke of the dream, his men pleaded with him to turn back but he refused them, and was soon afterwards taken ill and died, so the expedition was abandoned. 'The Hebrideans say that these men appearing to the king while he slept were Saint Olaf, king of Norway; Saint Magnus, jarl of Orkney; and Saint Columba.'
18. A. Ritchie, *Iona* (1997), p.97. The Norwegian scholar Aslak Liestøl points to names in the *Orkneyinga Saga* which might possibly link 'Kali Olvisson' and 'his brother Fugl' with Norse kindreds on Lewis and in Sutherland. 'Runes' in Fenton & Palsson (ed.), *The Northern and Western Isles* (1984), pp.230–1.
19. Olaf Cuaran, Godred of Man and Uspak-Hakon (who was taken to Iona for burial, according to the *Chronicle of Man*, after his death on Bute in 1230) are the only candidates on record who might be in any way qualified for inclusion in Monro's 'Tomb of the Kingis of Norway'.

20. There is no remotely contemporary evidence for any king of Scots (i.e. of Scotic Dalriada) buried on Iona before Kenneth mac Alpin, but the *Chronicle of the Kings* may reflect a belief held in ninth-century tradition when it says of Kenneth that he 'was buried in the island of Iona where the three sons of Erc were buried'. While Fergus mac Erc, founding dynast of the kingdom of Dalriada in Argyll, is considered to be genuinely historical, his two 'brothers' Oengus and Loarn are not, so the 'three sons of Erc' can be taken to be an example of the same formulaic triad found elsewhere in Irish tradition.
21. 'Alexander his [Edgar's] brother slew Donald [Ban] and received the kingdom. And thus as the avenger and successor of his brother, Alexander [I] reigned for several years.' Orderic Vitalis, *Historia Ecclesiastica.* (*SAEC*, p.128). The full range of evidence bearing on the mutilation and death of Domnall Ban is surveyed by A. O. Anderson (*ESSH*, ii p.119).
22. Malcolm Canmore was first buried at Tynemouth after his death at Alnwick in 1093 and his remains brought to Dunfermline by his son Alexander some time after 1107. It should, perhaps, be mentioned that the terms of the agreement of 1098 with Magnus Bareleg placed the Isle of Iona (at least technically) within Norwegian territory.

Chapter 7: *Gàidhealtachd*:

THE LONG SHADOWS OF SOMHAIRLE MOR

1. Donald A. MacDonald's illuminating study of 'The Vikings in Oral Tradition' shows how the *Lochlannach* appearing in Gaelic stories and ballads have 'little to do with the reality of the Scandinavian countries or the Norse invaders. In the ballads Lochlann is a mysterious and magical place across the sea inhabited by larger-than-human characters and by monsters.' Fenton & Palsson (ed.), *The Northern and Western Isles* (1984), p.267.
2. R. A. McDonald, *The Kingdom of the Isles* (1997), p.57.
3. R. A. McDonald & S. A. McLean, 'Somerled of Argyll', *SHR* 71 (1992), p.15.
4. See Genealogical Chart V 'The House of Man', p.166 below.
5. The Irish terms *Finn-Gaill* indicating the Norse and *Dubh-Gaill* indicating the Danes are most usually translated as the 'White Foreigners' and 'Black Foreigners' respectively, but A. P. Smyth has convincingly proposed their more accurate translation as the 'Old Foreigners' and the 'New Foreigners' in his paper 'The Black Foreigners of York and the White Foreigners of Dublin', *Saga Book* 19 (1975–6), pp.101–17.
6. See Genealogical Chart II 'The Clan Donald and related kindreds', p.163 below.

7. Megaw, 'Norseman and Native in the Kingdom of the Isles: A Re-assessment of the Manx Evidence', *Scottish Studies* 20 (1976), p.16.
8. Megaw, 'Norseman and Native in the Kingdom of the Isles', *Scottish Studies* 20 (1976), p.29. There is good reason to believe at least one of the kings of Man having also spoken Norse when the Godred who was driven out by Somerled spent some six years of exile in Norway.
9. Jackson, 'The Celtic Languages during the Viking Period' in Ó Cuív (ed.), *The Impact of the Scandinavian Invasions on the Celtic-speaking Peoples c.*800–1100 AD (1975), p.9. Professor Jackson's comment on pronunciation has particular bearing on spoken Gaelic on Lewis where I have regularly recognised the distinctly Norse form in which local place-names of Norse origin are pronounced by at least one of my native Gaelic-speaking neighbours who I'm sure has no recollection of ever learning or speaking any Norwegian.
10. It should be mentioned that the famous 'Gaelic Notes' of land grants and a foundation legend preserved in the *Book of Deer* were added into that ninth-century liturgical manuscript at some point in the reign of David I and thus within Somerled's lifetime. Professor Jackson's authoritative study of the text explains that their language is not 'in any sense what we mean by Scottish Gaelic – other than that they are Scottish and Gaelic'. The principal difference between the Gaelic of Deer (at that time a Cistercian house in north-east Aberdeenshire) and late Middle Irish are 'the numerous incorrect, and occasionally fantastic, spellings. But these are due to the carelessness and ignorance of the scribes of that remote monastery, and not to any genuine linguistic differentiation already occurring as between Scotland and Ireland.' Jackson, *The Gaelic Notes in the Book of Deer* (1972), p.150.
11. Barrow, *The Anglo-Norman Era in Scottish History* (1980), p.70.
12. Carmichael, *Carmina Gadelica* (1928), V, pp.6–7. The adjustment to the translation indicated by the parentheses in the last line is my own suggestion.

GENEALOGIES

I The Traditional Descent of Somerled

II The Clan Donald and related kindreds

III The House of Canmore

IV The House of Moray

V The House of Man

- I -

THE TRADITIONAL DESCENT OF SOMERLED
from Conn of the Hundred Battles and Colla Uais

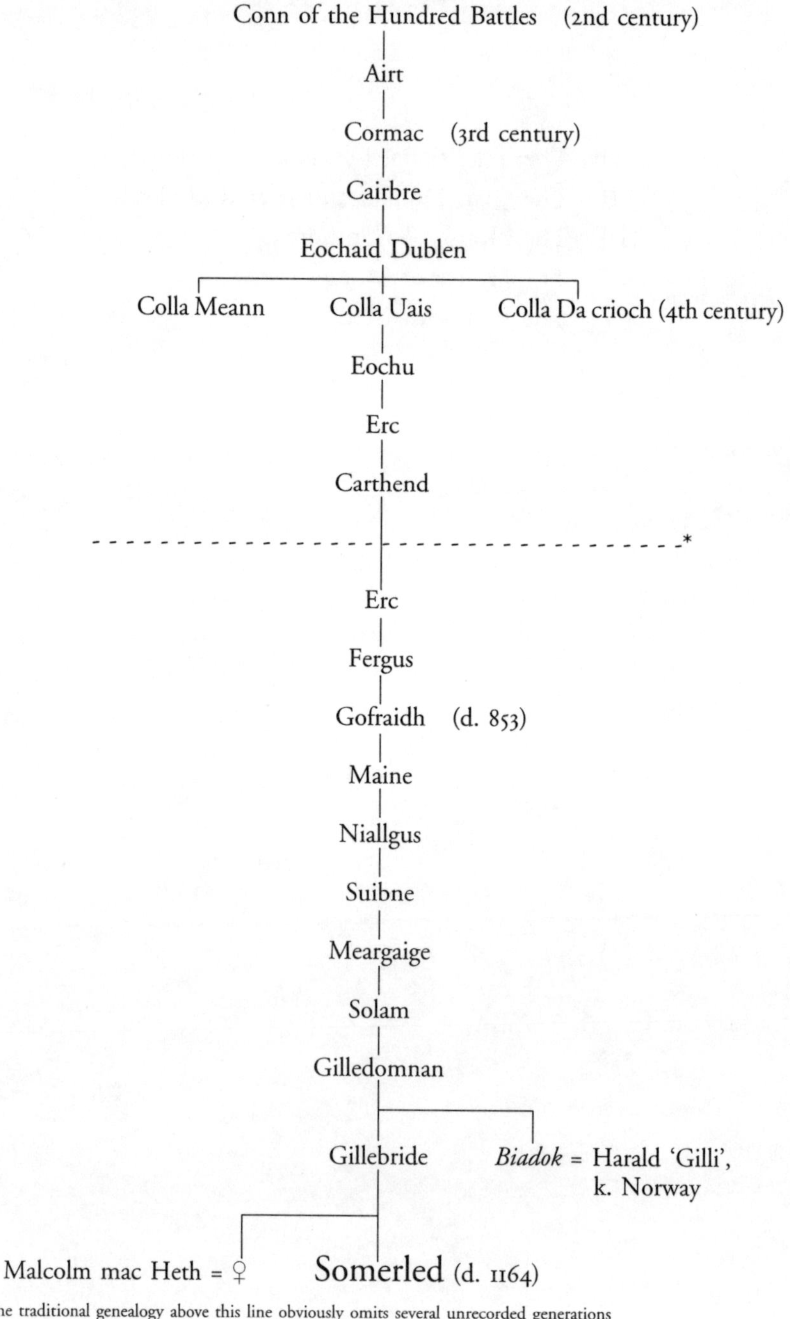

*The traditional genealogy above this line obviously omits several unrecorded generations

- II -
THE DESCENT OF THE CLAN DONALD
and its related kindreds from Somerled

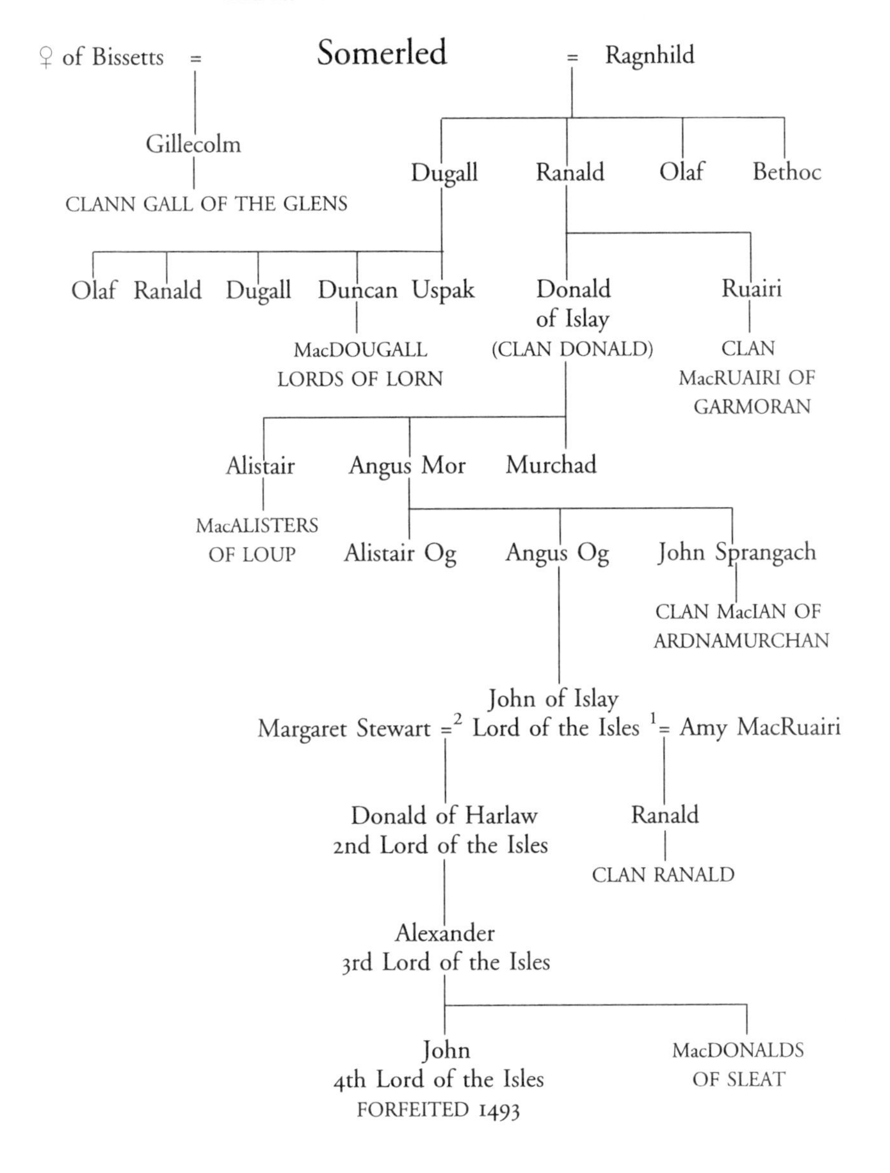

- III -
THE HOUSE OF CANMORE
Descent of the Kings of Scots – 1058–1214

(DATES OF REIGN INDICATED IN PARENTHESES)

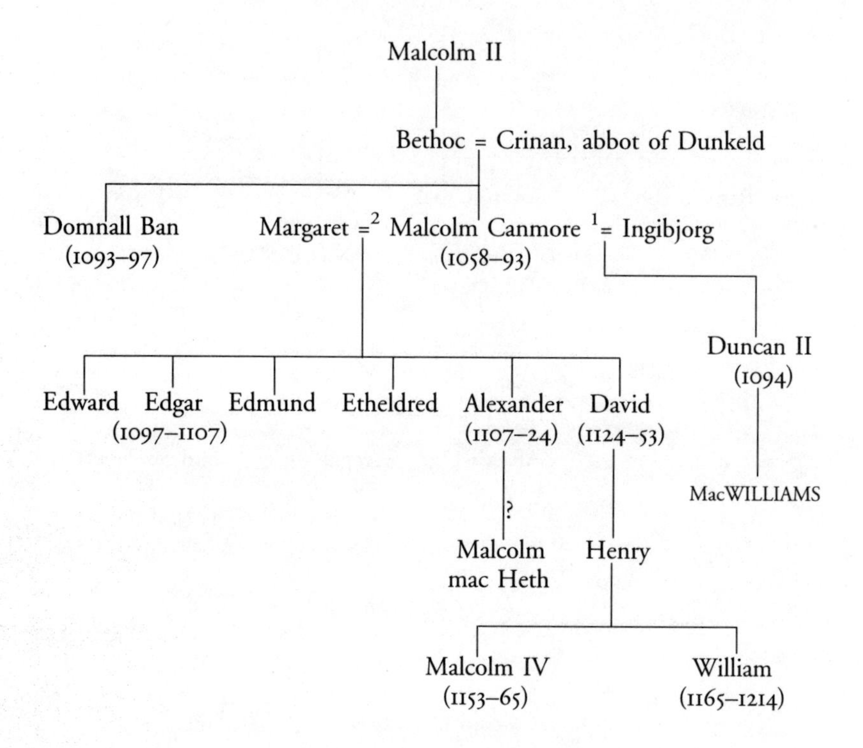

- IV -
THE HOUSE OF MORAY
Descent of the Moray claim to the kingship of Scots

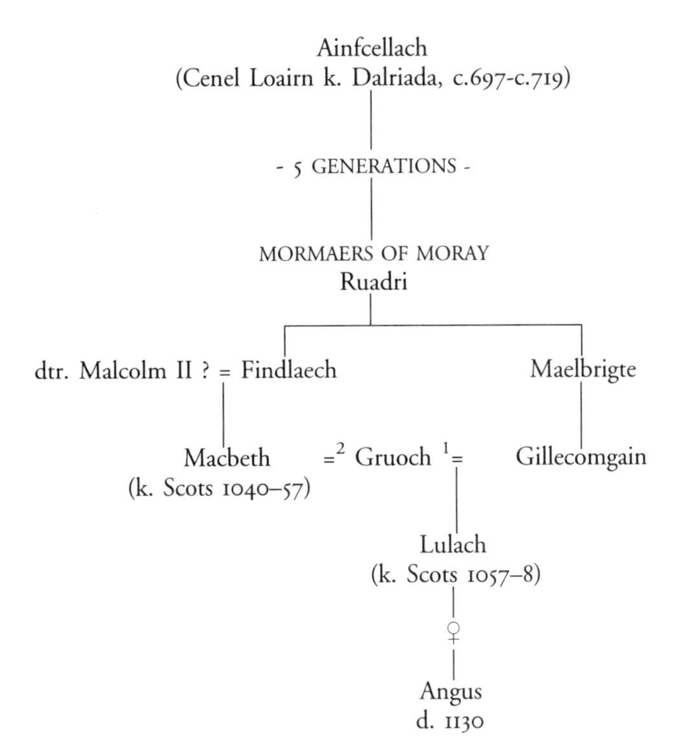

- V -
THE HOUSE OF MAN
Descent of the kings of Man from Godred Crovan

(DATES OF REIGNS POST-1187 INDICATED IN PARENTHESES)

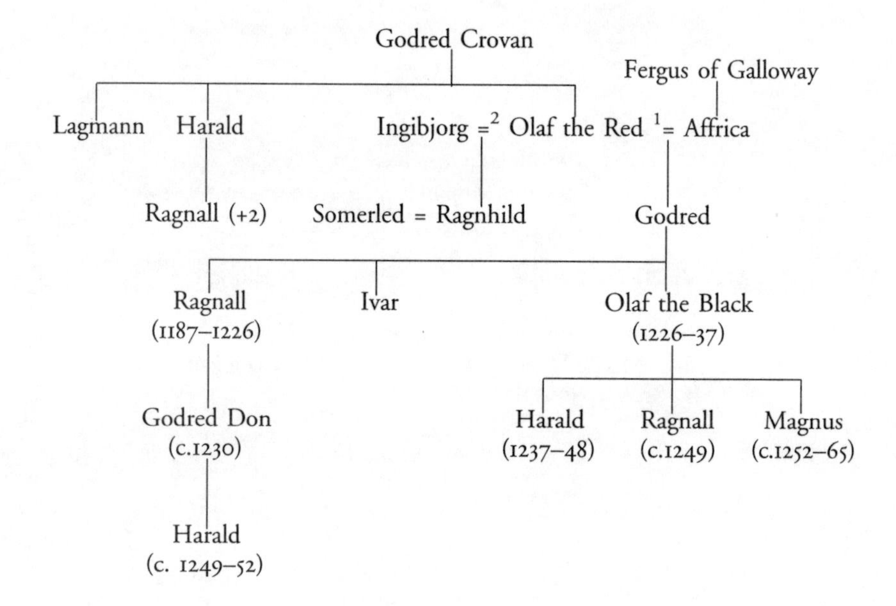

BIBLIOGRAPHY

Ailred of Rievaulx *De Standardo* ('Of [the battle of] the Standard') see Anderson, *SAEC*, pp.191–207.

Alcock, L. & E. A. 'Excavations at Dunollie Castle, Oban' *PSAS* 117, 1987

Anderson, A. O. (ed./trs.) *Scottish Annals from English Chroniclers AD* 500 to 1286 London, 1908; rev. Stamford, 1991

—— ,*Early Sources of Scottish History AD* 500 to 1286 Edinburgh, 1922; rev. Stamford, 1990

—— , *The Chronicle of Melrose* London, 1936

Anderson, M. O. (ed.) *The Chronicle of Holyrood, A Scottish Chronicle known as* Edinburgh, 1938

—— ,*Kings and Kingship in Early Scotland* Edinburgh, 1973

Anglo-Saxon Chronicle see under Garmonsway; Thorpe

Annals of Clonmacnoise see under Murphy

—— *of the Four Masters* see under O'Donovan

—— *of Tigernach* see under Stokes

—— *of Ulster* see under Hennessy & MacCarthy

Armit, I. *The Archaeology of Skye and the Western Isles* Edinburgh, 1996

Author unknown *Historical and Genealogical Account of the Clan or Family of Macdonald* Edinburgh, 1819

Baldwin, J. R. (ed.) *Caithness: A Cultural Crossroads* Edinburgh, 1982

Bannerman, J. *Studies in the History of Dalriada* Edinburgh, 1974

—— , *The Beatons: a medical kindred in the classical Gaelic tradition* Edinburgh, 1986

see also under Steer

Barrow, G. W. S. (ed.) *Regesta Regum Scottorum I: The Acts of Malcolm IV* Edinburgh, 1960

—— , *The Anglo-Norman Era in Scottish History* Oxford, 1980

—— , *Kingship and Unity: Scotland* AD 1000–1306 rev. Edinburgh, 1989

—— , 'The Date of the Peace between Malcolm IV and Somerled of Argyll' *SHR* 73, 1994

Batey, C. E., Jesch, J. & Morris, C. D. (ed.) *The Viking Age in Caithness, Orkney and the North Atlantic* Edinburgh, 1993; rep. 1995

Batho, E. C. & Husbands, H. W. (ed./trs.) *Hector Boece: The Chronicle of Scotland* Edinburgh, 1941

Bloomfield, M. W. & Dunn, C. W. *The Role of the Poet in Early Societies* Cambridge, 1989

Bonde, N. 'Found in Denmark, but where do they come from? . . . Viking ships found in Roskilde fjord' *Archaeology Ireland* 45, 1998

Bremner, R. L. *The Norsemen in Alban* Glasgow, 1923

Broderick, G. (ed./trs.) *Chronicle of the Kings of Man and the Isles* Edinburgh, 1973

Brøgger, A. W. *Ancient Emigrants: A History of the Norse Settlements of Scotland* Oxford, 1929

—— & Shetelig, H. *The Viking Ships: Their Ancestry and Evolution* London, 1971

Brown, A. L. 'The Cistercian Abbey of Saddell, Kintyre' *Innes Review* 20, no.2, 1969

see also under Duncan

Brooke, D. *Wild Men and Holy Places: St Ninian, Whithorn and the Medieval realm of Galloway* Edinburgh, 1994; rep. 1998

Carmen de Morte Sumerledi see Anderson, *ESSH* ii, pp.256–8

Carmichael, A. (ed./trs.) *Carmina Gadelica* Edinburgh, 1928

Christiansen, R. Th. *The Vikings and Viking Wars in Irish and Gaelic Tradition* Oslo, 1931

Chronicle of Holyrood see under Anderson, M. O.; Stevenson

—— *of Man* see under Broderick; Munch

—— *of Melrose* see under Anderson, A. O.; Stevenson

Clanranald, Books of see under MacBain & Kennedy; see also Skene, (*Celtic Scotland*, vol. iii)

Clark, W. *The Lord of the Isles Voyage* Naas, Co. Kildare, 1993

Crawford, B. E. *Scandinavian Scotland* Leicester, 1987

Donaldson, G. *A Northern Commonwealth: Scotland & Norway* Edinburgh, 1990

Duffy, S. 'Irishmen and Islesmen in the Kingdoms of Dublin and Man, 1052–1171' *Ériu* 43, 1992.

Duncan, A. A. M. *Scotland: The Making of the Kingdom* rev. Edinburgh, 1978

—— & Brown, A. L. 'Argyll and the Isles in the earlier Middle Ages' *PSAS* 90, 1956–7

Farmer, D. H. *The Oxford Dictionary of Saints* Oxford, 1987

Fenton, A. & Palsson, H. (ed.) *The Northern and Western Isles in the Viking World* Edinburgh, 1984

Fisher, I. & Dunbar, J. G. *Iona: A Guide to the Monuments* rev. Edinburgh, 1995

Foote, P. G. & Wilson, D. M. *The Viking Achievement* London & New York, 1990

Fordun, John of see under Skene

Garmonsway, G. N. (ed./trs.) *The Anglo-Saxon Chronicle* rev. London, 1973
Graham-Campbell, J. *The Viking World* London, 1980
—— ,(ed.) *A Cultural Atlas of the Viking World* Oxford, 1994
Grant, I. F. *The Lordship of the Isles* rep. Edinburgh, 1982
Gregory, D. *The History of the West Highlands and Isles of Scotland* London & Glasgow, 1881
Henderson, G. *The Norse Influence on Celtic Scotland* Glasgow, 1910
Hennessy, W. M. & McCarthy, B. (ed./trs.) *The Annals of Ulster* Dublin, 1887–91
Iona Club, The (ed.) 'Fragment of a Manuscript History of the MacDonalds', *Collectanea de Rebus Albanicis* Edinburgh, 1847
Jackson, K. H. *Language and History in Early Britain* Edinburgh, 1953
—— , *The Gaelic Notes in the Book of Deer* Cambridge, 1972
Johnsen, A. O. 'Payments from the Hebrides and the Isle of Man to the crown of Norway, 1153–1263' *SHR* 48, 1969
Jones, G. *The Norse Atlantic Saga* Oxford, 1986
Lamont, W. D. *The Early History of Islay* Dundee, rep. 1970
Lynch, M. *Scotland: A New History* London, rev. 1992
Logan, F. D. *The Vikings in History* London, 1991
MacAulay, J. *Birlinn: Longships of the Hebrides* Cambridge, 1996
Macbain, A. & Kennedy, J. (ed.), Cameron, A. (trs.) 'The History of the MacDonalds' from the *Books of Clanranald, Reliquae Celticae* vol. ii Inverness, 1892–4
Macdonald, A. & Macdonald, A. *The Clan Donald* Inverness, 1896–1904
MacDonald, C. M. *History of Argyll* Glasgow, 1950
MacDonald of Sleat, Hugh see under lona Club; Macphail
McDonald, A. 'Monk, Bishop, Imposter, Pretender: The Place of Wimund in Twelfth-Century Scotland' *TGSI* 58, 1994
McDonald, R. A. 'The death and burial of Somerled of Argyll' *West Highland Notes & Queries*, 2nd series 8, 1991
—— ,'Images of Hebridean Lordship in the 12th and early 13th centuries: The Seal of Ranald MacSorley' *SHR* 34, 1995
—— , *The Kingdom of the Isles: Scotland's Western Seaboard, c.*1100-c.1336 East Linton, 1997
—— & McLean, S. A. 'Somerled of Argyll: A New Look at Old Problems' *SHR* 71, 1992
Maceacharna, D. *The Lands of the Lordship* Port Charlotte, 1976
Maclnnes, J. 'West Highland Seapower in the Middle Ages' *TGSI* 48, 1974
Maclnnes, J. 'Clan Sagas and Historical Legends' *TGSI* 57, 1990–2
Mackay, A. *The Book of Mackay* Edinburgh, 1906
McKerral, A. 'A Chronology of the Abbey and Castle of Saddell, Kintyre' *PSAS* 86, 1951–2

MacKillop, J. *Fionn mac Cumhaill: Celtic Myth in English Literature* Syracuse, 1986
Maclean, L. (ed.) *The Middle Ages in the Highlands* Inverness, 1981
McNeill, P. & Nicholson, R. (ed.) *Historical Atlas of Scotland, c.*400-c.1600 St Andrews, 1975
Macquarrie, A. *Iona through the Ages* Coll, 1983
——, *Scotland and the Crusades* 1095–1560 Edinburgh, 1985
Macphail, J. R. N. (ed.) 'History of the MacDonalds', attrib. Hugh MacDonald of Sleat, *Highland Papers* vol. i Edinburgh, 1914
Magnussen, M. & Palsson, H. (ed./trs.) *Njal's Saga* Harmondsworth, 1960
——, *King Harald's Saga* Harmondsworth, 1966
Marcus, G. J. *The Conquest of the North Atlantic* Woodbridge, 1980
Marsden, J. *The Fury of the Northmen: saints, shrines and sea-raiders in the viking age* London, 1993
——, 'Magnus Bareleg on Iona' *Medieval World* 8, 1993
——, *The Tombs of the Kings: An Iona Book of the Dead* Felinfach, 1994
——, *Alba of the Ravens: In search of the Celtic Kingdom of the Scots* London, 1997
Martin, M. *A Description of the Western Islands of Scotland* 1716; rep. 1981
Megaw, B. 'Norseman and Native in the Kingdom of the Isles: A Reassessment of the Manx Evidence' *Scottish Studies* 20, 1976
Metcalfe, D. *A History of the County of Renfrew* Paisley, 1905
Monro, D. see under Munro, R. W.
Munch, P. A. (ed.) *The Chronicle of Man and the Sudreys* Christiana, 1860
Munro, R. W. (ed.) *Monro's Western Isles of Scotland and Genealogies of the Clans,* 1549 Inverness, 1961
—— J. & R. W. (ed.) *The Acts of the Lords of the Isles* 1336–1493 Edinburgh, 1986
Newburgh, William of see under Stevenson
'New Statistical Account' *The Statistical Account of Argyleshire* Edinburgh & London, 1845
Ó Corráin, D. *Ireland before the Normans* Dublin, 1972
Ó Cuív, B. (ed.) *The Impact of the Scandinavian Invasions on the Celtic-speaking Peoples c.*800–1100 Dublin, 1975
O'Donovan, J. (ed./trs) *Annals of the Kingdom of Ireland by the Four Masters* Dublin, 1948–51
Oftedal, M. 'On the frequency of Norse loan-words in Scottish Gaelic' *Scottish Gaelic Studies* 9, 1961–2
Ó hÓgain, D. *Myth, Legend & Romance: An Encyclopedia of the Irish Folk Tradition* New York, 1991
'Old Statistical Account' see under Withrington & Grant
Oram, R. O. & Stell, G. P. (ed.) *Galloway: Land and Lordship* Edinburgh, 1991

O'Rahilly, T. F. *Early Irish History and Mythology* Dublin, 1946
Palsson, H. & Edwards, P. (ed./trs.) *Orkneyinga Saga: The History of the Earls of Orkney* London, 1978
—— , *Eyrbyggja Saga* rev. London, 1989
Pennant, T. *A Tour in Scotland and Voyage to the Hebrides* Chester, 1774
Raine, J. (ed.) Reginald of Durham: *Libellus de admirandis beati Cuthberti virtutibus* Durham, 1835
RCAHMS *Argyll: An Inventory of the Monuments* vol. 4 Iona Edinburgh, 1982 vol. 5 Islay, Jura, Colonsay & Oronsay Edinburgh, 1984
Ritchie, A. *Iona* London, 1997
Ritchie, G. (ed.) *The Archaeology of Argyll* Edinburgh, 1997
Ritchie, R. L. G. *The Normans in Scotland* Edinburgh, 1954
Rixson, D. *The West Highland Galley* Edinburgh, 1998
Sawyer, P. H. *Kings and Vikings* London & New York, 1982
Sellar, W. D. H. 'The Origins and Ancestry of Somerled' *SHR* 45, 1966
—— , 'Family Origins in Cowal and Knapdale' *Scottish Studies* 15, 1971
—— , 'Marriage, Divorce and Concubinage in Gaelic Scotland' *TGSI* 51, 1978–80
—— , (ed.) *Moray: Province and People* Edinburgh, 1993
Skene, W. F. (ed./trs.) *John of Fordun's Chronicle of the Scottish Nation* Edinburgh, 1871–2; rep. Felinfach, 1993
—— , *Celtic Scotland: A History of Ancient Alban* Edinburgh, 1886–90
Smyth, A. P. 'The Black Foreigners of York and the White Foreigners of Dublin' *Saga Book of the Viking Society* 19, 1975–6
—— , *Scandinavian Kings in the British Isles* 850–880 Oxford, 1977
—— , *Warlords and Holy Men: Scotland* AD 80–1000 Sevenoaks, 1984; rep. Edinburgh, 1989
—— ,*Scandinavian York and Dublin* Dublin, 1987
see also under Williams, A. et al
Steer, K. A. & Bannerman, J. W. M. *Late Medieval Monumental Sculpture in the West Highlands* RCAHMS, Edinburgh, 1977
Stell, G. *Dunstaffnage and the castles of Argyll* Edinburgh, 1994
Stevenson, J. (ed./trs.) *Contemporary Chronicles of the Middle Ages* 1853–8; rep. Felinfach, 1988
—— , *Mediæval Chronicles of Scotland: The Chronicles of Melrose & Holyrood* 1853–8; rep. Felinfach, 1988
—— , *Florence of Worcester: History of the Kings of England* 1853–8; rep. Felinfach, 1988
—— , *The Chronicles of Robert de Monte* [a.k.a. 'de Torigni'] 1856; rep. Felinfach, 1991
—— , *The History of William of Newburgh* 1856; rep. Felinfach, 1996
Stokes, W. (ed./trs.) *The Annals of Tigernach* Paris, 1895–6; rep. Felinfach, 1993

Stratford, N. *The Lewis Chessmen and the enigma of the hoard* London, 1997

Taylor, A. B. (ed./trs.) *Orkneyinga Saga* Edinburgh, 1938

Thomson, D. S. 'The MacMhuirich Bardic Family' *TGSI* 43, 1963

—— , *An Introduction to Gaelic Poetry* Edinburgh, 1989

Thorpe, B. (ed./trs.) *The Anglo-Saxon Chronicle* Rolls Series, 1861

Todd, J. H. (ed./trs.) *Cogadh Gaedhel re Gallaibh* (The War of the Gaedhil with the Gaill) Rolls Series, 1867

Torigni, Robert de see under Stevenson

Trenholme, E. C. *The Story of Iona* Edinburgh, 1909

Vigfussen, G. (ed.) & Dasent, G. W. (trs.) *Icelandic Sagas relating to the Northmen in Britain* Rolls Series, 1887–94

Watson, W. J. (ed./trs.) *The History of the Celtic Placenames of Scotland* Edinburgh, 1926; rep. Dublin, 1986

—— , *Scottish Verse from the Book of the Dean of Lismore* Edinburgh, 1936

Whittington, G. & Whyte, I. D. (ed.) *An Historical Geography of Scotland* London, 1983

Williams, A., Smyth, A. P., & Kirby, D. P. *A Biographical Dictionary of Dark Age Britain* London, 1991

Williams, R. *The Lords of the Isles: The Clan Donald and the early Kingdom of the Scots* London, 1984

Withrington, D. J. & Grant, I. R. (ed.) *The Statistical Account of Scotland* (originally published 1791–9) Wakefield, 1983

Worcester, Florent of see under Stevenson

Yeoman, P. *Pilgrimage in Medieval Scotland* London, 1999

Young, G. V. C. *The Lewis and Skye Groups of the Hebrides under the Norse* Peel, 1996

—— , *The Hebridean Birlinn, Nyvaig and Lymphad* Peel, 1997

INDEX

ab.	abbot of	g/f.	grandfather of
a/bp.	archbishop of	k.	king of
bp.	bishop of	qu.	queen to
dtr.	daughter of	s.	son of
f.	father of	wf.	wife to
n. ref. p.	note number referring to page number in main text		

Abernethy 52
Acharacle 38
Adamnan (*Adomnán*), St 26, 127, 148
Affrica (*Aufreka*), dtr. Fergus of Galloway 69, 151, 166
Ailred of Rievaulx 44, 57–8, 61, 154
Airgialla see under Oriel
Alcock, L. & E. 146(n.7 ref. p.12)
Alexander I, k. Scots 52, 54, 55, 57, 58–9, 132–3, 150, 164
Alexander II, k. Scots 157
Alnwick 52, 158
Anderson, A. O. 150–1, 158
Anglo-Saxon Chronicle 23, 53, 56
Angus, s. Somerled 74, 77, 87, 140, 163
Angus Mor, s. Donald of Islay 83, 129, 163
Angus Og, s. Angus Mor 41, 76, 89, 129, 163
Angus Og, s. John, last Lord of the Isles 110
Angus of Moray 55–6, 58, 59, 60, 165
annals, Irish 1, 6–8, 135, 136, 145
Annals of Clonmacnoise 72
Annals of the Four Masters 14–17, 27–8, 40, 72, 145, 146, 153, 156
Annals of Inisfallen 145
Dublin Annals of Inisfallen 145, 146
Annals of Tigernach 19, 131, 145; continuation of 27, 99, 107, 132, 135, 148, 154
Annals of Ulster 17, 18, 27, 56, 72, 99, 100, 107, 121–2, 124, 145(n.1 ref. p.1), 148, 152
Antrim 1, 2
Applecross 6
Ardgour 34
Ardnamurchan 35, 43, 87
Ardtornish 89, 129
Argyll ix, 1–4, 12, 15, 16, 31, 42, 47, 88–9, 104, 154 et passim; *RCAHMS Inventory of* 89
Arran, Isle of 78, 87
Aud 'the Deep-Minded', dtr. Ketil Flatnose 18

Ballymote, Book of 26, 145(n.3 ref. p.2)
Bannerman, John 31, 150
Banquo 155
Barbour, John (*The Bruce*) 21
Barra, Isle of 78
Barrow, Geoffrey 96, 103, 143–4, 154
Beatons, the 31; Christopher 148
Bede 2, 27
Benedict of Peterborough (*Chronicle*) 78
Berowald the Fleming 96
Bethoc, dtr. Somerled 33, 74–5, 120, 126–7, 163
'Biadok' (Bethoc?), dtr. Gilledomnan 33, 137, 162
birlinn see under galleys
Bissets of Antrim, 'a woman of' 75, 76
Bjorn Cripplehand 20

Boece (*Boetius*), Hector 115, 155
Brigid, St 26, 148
Britons, Britonic language 3–4, 5, 17, 142, 145
Brøgger, A. W. 85
Brooke, Daphne 48
Brown, A. L. 156; see also under Duncan, A. A. M.
Brown, Marilyn 146(n.16 ref. p.14)
Bruce dynasty 103; see also under Robert (I) the Bruce and Robert de Brus
Brut Tywyssogion (Welsh 'Chronicle of the Princes') 155
Buchanan, George 101, 110, 115
Bute, Isle of 78, 87, 157; Rothesay 156
Byland, monastery of 59, 60

Cairbre Riada 2, 27
Caithness 19, 34, 47, 50, 105, 106, 137
Cameron, Alasdair 38
Cameron, Alexander (*Book of Clanranald*) 148
Campbell, the Clan 110–11, 143–4
Canmore, house of 52–3, 55, 63–4, 94, 97–8, 135, 138, 164 et passim
Canna, Isle of 125
Cape Wrath 1
Carham, battle of 50
Carlisle 57, 62, 94
Carmen de Morte Sumerledi 97, 107–8, 111–2, 135, 150–1, 152
Carmichael, Alexander (*Carmina Gadelica*) 144
Carswell, John, bp. Argyll 39
Castle Sween 88
Celestine, ab. Iona 124–5
Cellach, ab. Iona 7
Celts, Celtic languages and culture 3–5, 145; 'Celtic Scotland' 5, 7, 138
Cenel Gabrain 3, 11, 51
Cenel Loairn 3, 11–12, 51, 56
Cenel Oengusa 3
Chadwick, Nora 25
Cheape, Hugh 73, 104
Chester 94
Chronicle of Holyrood 42, 47, 48–9, 63, 64, 66, 67, 93–7, 101, 105
Chronicle of the Kings, Scottish 50, 54, 132–3, 147(n.2 ref. p.23)
Chronicle of Lanercost 86
Chronicle of Man 19–20, 41, 43, 69–73, 74–5, 79–80, 82, 83, 85–6, 89–92, 93, 98, 99, 101–2, 105, 107, 120–1, 131, 135, 136, 147, 151–2, 157
Chronicle of Melrose 19, 49, 57, 66, 93–5, 98, 101, 105, 107, 151
Cistercian sources (for Saddell abbey) 118
Clan Donald 27, 40–1, 75–6, 111, 143, 163 et passim (see also under Lords of the Isles); tradition 16, 25, 27, 74–6, 77, 110, 130–2, 135–6 et passim (see also under A. & A. Macdonald, MacMhuirich and Sleat *History of the MacDonalds*)
Clanranald, Macdonalds of 148, 152; *Books of* 29–30, 148 (see also under MacMhuirich)
Clark, Wallace 84, 153
Clement VII, Pope 156(n.5 ref. p.118)
Clontarf, battle of 19, 23, 112
Cnut, k. England and Denmark 52
Cogadh Gaedhel re Gallaibh ('Wars of the Irish with the Foreigners') 146(n.21 ref. p.19)
Coll, Isle of 78, 125, 146
Collas, the Three 2, 27; Colla Uais 2, 27, 28–9, 30, 143; Colla Da crioch 30
Colonsay, Isle of 78, 125
Columba, St 6, 125, 127, 130, 157
Conn of the Hundred Battles (*Conn Céadcathach*) 27
Cowal 2
Cowan, Edward 59, 66
Crawford, Barbara 8, 84
Crinan, ab. Dunkeld 54
Crusades 40, 147, 157
Cumbria 19, 94
Cuthbert, St 77–8, 120, 126

Dalriada 1–2, 3, 7, 11–13, 16, 17, 50, 51, 144 et passim
Danelaw, English 24, 25
Danes, Denmark 18, 31–2, 35–6, 140, 148, 155, 158 et passim
David I, k. Scots 44–5, 47–9, 51, 52, 55–9, 60–1, 62–4, 69, 102–4, 133, 144, 150, 164 et passim

Deer, Book of 159
Derry 15, 29, 157; abbots of 121(Flaithbertach), 124–5 (Amalgaid)
Diarmait, s. Maelnambo, k. Leinster 19
Diarmait, s. Murchada, k. Leinster 100
Domesday Book 24
Domnall, s. Alpin, k. Scots 16
Domnall, s. Malcolm mac Heth 66–7, 97
Domnall, s. Tagd, k. Man 20
Domnall Ban, k. Scots 31–3, 51, 52, 53–5, 61, 121–4, 137, 138, 164
Donald Dubh 101
Donald of Islay, s. Ranald 75, 119, 128, 156, 163
Donaldson, Gordon 55
Down 21–2
Dublin, Norse kingdom of, Dublin Norse 8, 10, 18–19, 20, 25–6, 70–3, 99–101, 155 et passim
Duffy, Seán 72
Dugall, s. Somerled 38, 72–9, 87, 120, 125, 140, 163
Dumbarton 4, 5, 34
Dunadd 12
Dunbar 50
Dunbar, John & Fisher, Ian 125, 157(n.13 ref. p.128)
Duncan, k. Scots 32, 50–1
Duncan II, k. Scots 32, 52–4, 132, 133, 164
Duncan, A. A. M. 44–5, 80
——— & Brown, A. L. 48, 147(n.25 ref. p.21), 149(n.1 ref. p.47), 153(n.20 ref. p.83)
Dunfermline abbey 47, 133, 149, 154, 156
Dunkeld 54, 132–4
Dunollie 12, 89
Dunstaffnage 89, 143
Dunyveg 89
Durham 50–1, 77–8, 120, 126; Reginald of 153(n.15 ref. p.78)
Durrow 7

Edgar, k. England 19
Edgar, k. Scots 52, 54, 132, 133, 150, 164
Edmund, s. Malcolm Canmore 52, 150, 164
Edward, s. Malcolm Canmore 52, 150, 164
Edward the Confessor, k. England 52
Eigg, Isle of 82, 146
Elgin 51, 56, 96
Eoganan, s. Oengus, k. Fortriu 17
Epiphany battle 79–80, 83–6, 99–100
Espec, Walter 57–8
Etheldred, s. Malcolm Canmore 52, 150, 164
Eyrbyggja Saga 18

Faereyinga Saga 85
Farmer, D. H. 154
Fellows-Jensen, Gillian 147(n.3 ref. p.24)
Fergus of Galloway 43, 48, 69, 94, 95–6, 149
Fergus Mor, k. Dalriada 2–3, 27, 145, 158
Fermanagh 30, 34
Ferteth, earl of Strathearn 95, 154
feudalisation of Scotland see under Norman and Anglo-Norman impact
Fingal, s. Godred Sitricsson, k. Man 20
Finlaggan 89, 129–30
Finn MacCool (*Fionn mac Cumhaill*) 38–9
Florent of Worcester (*Chronicle*) 53–4
Fordun, John of (*Chronicle*) 54–5, 89, 101, 110, 135
Forfar 66
Forres 56
Fortriu, kingdom of 5, 11, 17, 143
Furness, monastery of 60, 61, 151

Gabran, s. Domangart, k. Dalriada 3
Gaels, Gaelic language and culture 3–4, 11–13, 80, 137–42, 159; Gaelic Scotland 136, 141–3; et passim
Gall-Gaedhil 14, 16, 18, 21, 26, 29, 50, 55, 104, 139–40, 143 et passim
galleys, Highland 13–14, 80–3, 99–101 et passim
Galloway 19, 47, 49, 70–1, 95–6, 104; see also under Fergus of

'Gilchrist, thane of Angus' 65, 151
Gilchrist, earl of Menteith 65–6, 151
Gilla-, *Gille-*, *Giolla-* name-form 26, 106–7, 139–40
Gilla-Odran 105–7
Gillebride, s. Gilledomnan, f. Somerled 23–4, 26, 28, 30–7, 133, 148, 162
Gillecolm (or 'Gillies'), s. Somerled 74–6, 90, 98–9, 111, 140, 152–3, 163
Gillecomgain, mormaer of Moray 56, 165
Gilledomnan, g/f. Somerled 26, 28, 32–4, 133, 162
Gilli, 'Jarl' 19, 28
Glencoe 111
Godred, s. Sitric, k. Man 20
Godred, s. Olaf, k. Man 70–3, 77, 79, 84–8, 89–90, 91–2, 131, 140, 151–2, 157, 166 et passim
Godred Crovan, k. Man 19–20, 41–2, 82, 139, 140–1, 147, 166
Gormflaith, dtr. Malcolm mac Heth 137, 154
Gothfrith, s. Fergus 14–18, 28–9, 143, 146, 162
Greenock 80
Gregory, Donald 31, 87, 110, 117, 119
Gudrod, s. Harald, k. Man 19

Hakon, s. Paul, jarl of Orkney 69–70, 137
Hakon Hakonsson's Saga 153, 157
Harald, s. Godred Crovan 20, 70, 166; sons of 70–1, 151–2
Harald the Black, f. Godred Crovan 19, 141
Harald Gilli, k. Norway 33, 137; *Harald Gilli's sons' Saga* 33
Harald Hardradi, k. Norway 19, 101
Harald Maddadsson, jarl of Orkney 137, 154
Harris 146
Hebrides ix, 1–2 et passim; Irish church in 6–7; island names 146; Norse raids on 1, 5–6, 9–10, 107; Norse settlement in 8–9, 10; in Norse world 8, 10–11; Norse place-names in 8–10; Norse kings of 18–21; Norse-Gaelic fusion in 12–14, 21 (see also under *Gall-Gaedhil*); Somerled's lordship in 73, 86–8, 91, 94, 100; in modern Gaelic Scotland 141–2; Inner ix, 1, 12, 14, 73, 94; Outer (Western Isles) ix, 1–2, 4, 8, 9, 10–11, 25, 100, 141–2 et passim
Henderson, George 148(n.8 ref. p.26)
Henry I, k. England 43
Henry II, k. England 78, 94–5
Henry, earl of Huntingdon, s. David I 78, 150, 164
Herbert, bp. Glasgow 108
Hexham chroniclers 63, 150; John of 150
Holyrood abbey 47, 49, 95

Iceland 7, 13, 23–4
Icelandic annals 91
Indulf, s. Constantine II, k. Scots 147
Inge, k. Norway 70, 91
Inge Bardsson's Saga 156(n.7 ref. p.122)
Ingemund, k. Isles 20
Ingibjorg, dtr. Hakon, qu.? Olaf of Man 69–70, 151
Ingibjorg, dtr. Thorfinn, qu. Malcolm Canmore 52
Innocent III, Pope 124
Innsegall see under Hebrides; Norse
Inverness 56, 110
Iona: stature of 6–7, 133; in Three Collas legend 2; entry in Durham ms. 78; impact of viking raids on 6–7, 12; burial of Somerled on 113, 115–7, 119–20, 128; burial of Lords of Isles on 128–30; Norse burials on 120, 130–1; Norse reverence for 20, 121–2; royal burials on 115–6, 131–2; translation of Domnall Ban to 54, 132–4; initiative to Derry 121–3; Benedictine foundation on 124–6; Augustinian nunnery on 124, 127; RCAHMS survey of 125, 128
Iona Psalter 127
Islay, Isle of 10, 20, 78, 80, 84, 87–8, 89, 125, 129, 146, 147; Lagavulin bay 89; Sound of 84

Jackson, Kenneth H. 13, 142, 159
James IV, k. Scots 75, 144
Jura, Isle of 41, 84, 87, 146

Kells, monastery of 7, 130
Kelso abbey 91
Kenneth, s. Alpin, k. Scots 5, 14–18, 50, 132, 137, 143, 145, 158
Kenneth Mac Heth 66
Kentigern, St 107–8
Ketil Flatnose 18
Kintyre 19, 21, 42, 47, 87, 99–100, 117–9, 148, 154 et passim; Tarbert 21
Krákumal 84

Lagmann, s. Godred Crovan 20–1, 70, 166
Lamont, W. D. 21, 89
Landnámabok 24
Laxdaela Saga 24
Lebor Brecc 145(n.3 ref. p.2)
Leinster, Book of 145(n.4 ref. p.2)
Lewis, Isle of 10, 11, 20, 78, 141, 146, 157, 159
Liestøl, Aslak 157
Limerick 8, 25
Lindisfarne, Northumberland 1, 126
Lismore, Isle of 130
Lords & Lordship of the Isles 37, 70, 75, 89, 121, 128–30, 135, 139, 143, 163 et passim; John of Islay, 1st Lord of the Isles 129–30, 163; Donald of Harlaw, 2nd Lord of the Isles 129, 153, 163; Alexander, 3rd Lord of the Isles 128, 163; John, last Lord of the Isles 101, 110, 128, 143, 163
Lorn 12, 38, 42, 44, 47, 87, 125 et passim
Lulach, k. Scots 51, 55–6, 133, 165
Lynch, Michael 149

Mac Alpin, house of 5, 50, 51 et passim
Macbeth, k. Scots 31–2, 43, 51, 55–6, 59, 165 *et passim*
Macdonald, Rev. A. & Rev. A. (*The Clan Donald*) 33, 84, 117, 146(n.18 ref. p.16), 148(n.19 ref. p.34), 153
MacDonald, Colin M. 77, 102, 122–3
MacDonald, Donald A. 38, 158
McDonald, Andrew 62, 63
McDonald, R. Andrew 65–6, 102, 110, 138, 152(n.7 ref. p.73), 155(n.1 ref. p.115), 157
——— & McLean, S. A. 154, 158(n.3 ref. p.139)
MacDougalls of Lorn 38, 75–6, 140, 163
Macfarlane, Rev. John (*New Statistical Account*) 117
Macguires of Fermanagh 30, 41
MacInnes, the Clan 37–8, 40, 149
MacInnes, John 149
Mackay, the Clan 59
Macleish, Rev. George (*Old Statistical Account*) 117–8
Macleod, Rev. John (*New Statistical Account*) 36–8, 39
Macleod, Rev. Norman (*Old Statistical Account*) 39
Macmahons of Monaghan 30, 41
MacMhuirich bardic kindred 29–30, 40–1, 129, 148; Muireadhach Albanach, ancestor of 40–1; Niall 29; their *History of the MacDonalds* 29–31, 33–5, 74–7, 108–10, 120, 124, 125, 126–7, 128–30, 135–6, 153
MacNeill, Maurice 109–10, 117
Macpherson, James (*Ossian*) 39
MacQuarrie, Alan 123–4
MacSween, the Clan 55
MacWilliams, the 66, 164
Maelsnechtai, mormaer of Moray 56
Magnus, s. Harald, k. Isles 19
Magnus, St, jarl of Orkney 157
Magnus Bareleg, k. Norway 20–2, 32, 43, 47, 101, 121, 130, 147, 158
Magnus Bareleg's Saga 20–1, 84, 121–2, 147
Malcolm II, k. Scots 50–1, 164
Malcolm III (Canmore), k. Scots 32, 51–4, 133, 149–50, 164 et passim
Malcolm IV ('the Maiden'), k. Scots 63–5, 91, 93, 94–8, 102, 104–5, 109–10, 113, 133, 134, 144, 150, 164
Malcolm mac Heth 42–3, 44, 56–9, 62–3, 66–7, 96–7, 137, 154, 162 et

passim; sons of 42, 63; see also Domnall Mac Heth, Kenneth Mac Heth
Man, Isle of 19, 34, 87 et passim; Somerled's raid on 89–91
Mappa Mundi 119
Margaret, St, qu. Malcolm Canmore 52–3, 123–4, 127, 133, 150, 164; *Life of* 156
Martin, Martin 31, 32, 127, 131
Martyrology of Oengus 154
Matilda, dtr. Henry I 44
Maughold (*Machutus*), St 90, 120–1
Megaw, Basil 140–1
Melrose, monastery of 49; Old Melrose 50
Monach Isles 156
Monro, Dean Donald 115, 130, 132, 147
Moray 12, 50, 55, 58–9, 138; ruling house of 42–3, 51, 55–6, 58, 138, 165
Morvern 12, 34–42
Muck, Isle of 125
Muirchertach, s. Lochlann, k. Ireland 71, 121
Mull, Isle of 20, 78, 87–8, 146
Munch, P. A. 27–8, 42, 136, 151
Munster 2, 18, 146

Nechtansmere, battle of 4
'New Statistical Account' (*Statistical Account of Argyleshire*) 36–9, 117
Njal's Saga 19, 28, 112
Norman and Anglo-Norman impact on Scotland 44, 49, 51–4, 57–8, 62, 94–5, 97, 102–4
Norse: viking raids 1, 5–8, 9, 10, 122; settlement 8–12, 141; place-names 8, 9–10, 12, 89; language and Gaelic 13, 80, 142; political impact 5, 10, 17; cultural interchange with Gael 11, 12–13, 14, 50; in Gaelic tradition 33, 38–9, 137–8, 158; kingship of the Isles 18–21, 94; reverence for and burials on Iona 120–2, 130–1, 157; ships, ship design, seafighting 13–14, 80–2, 85–6; et passim
Northumbria, Northumberland 4, 6, 51, 54, 94
Norway 9, 11, 70–1, 90–2 et passim

Oban 12, 89
Oftedal, Magda 146(n.13 ref. p.10)
Olaf, St 157
Olaf, k. Dublin 18
Olaf, s. Somerled 74–5, 77, 140, 163
Olaf the Black, k. Man 86
Olaf Cuaran, k. Dublin & York 131, 157
Olaf (*bitling*, 'the Red'), k. Man 20, 35, 43–4, 60, 61, 69–70, 74–7, 137, 151–2, 166 et passim
Olaf Tryggvasson, k. Norway 122
Old Statistical Account (*Statistical Account of Scotland*) 39, 118
Oram, Richard 149
Oran (*Odhran*), St 127, 156–7; *Reilig Odhrain* 128, 130–1, 157; St Oran's Chapel 127–9
Orderic Vitalis (*Chronicle*) 54, 56–7, 123, 132–3
Oriel (*Airgialla*) 14–16, 27, 29, 30
Orkney 1, 4, 5, 8, 11, 19, 20, 21, 23–4, 34, 126 et passim; Deerness 82; Kirkwall cathedral 126
Orkneyinga Saga 5, 9, 11, 19, 23, 24, 32, 40, 43, 69–70, 74, 82–3, 105–7, 147, 154, 157

Paisley abbey 83, 112–3, 120, 128
Paul (Balkisson?) 79, 153
Pennant, Thomas 111
Perth 94–7
Picts, Pictish language and culture 3–5, 11, 17, 142; see also under Fortriu
Prophecy of Berchan 16, 32–3

Ragnall, s. Godred, k. Man 140, 166
Ragnall, s. Gudrod, k. Isles 19
Ragnhild, dtr. Olaf of Man & wf. Somerled 43, 69–70, 74–5, 106, 140, 163, 166
Ranald, s. Somerled 74–7, 83, 87, 112–3, 117–20, 124–5, 127–8, 140, 153, 163
Rathlin ix, 6
Renfrew 98, 101–3, 105–7, 111–3, 143
Ritchie, Anna 130

Ritchie, R. Graeme 64, 150(n.6 ref. p.51)
Robert de Brus 57–8, 62
Robert (I) the Bruce, k. Scots 21, 76, 89, 155
Robert II, k. Scots 103, 155
Robert de Torigni 56–9, 150
Roxburgh 57, 61, 66, 91, 97
Rum, Isle of 146
Rushen, monastery of 60, 69, 121, 151

St Andrews 96
Saddell abbey 117–20, 124, 156
Santwat, battle of 72
Sawyer, Peter 100
Scone 64, 150
Sellar, David 28–9, 33, 146
Senchus fer nAlban 3
Shakespeare (*Macbeth*) 155
Shetland 1, 19
Sigurd the Stout, jarl of Orkney 19, 23, 28, 112
Siward, earl of Northumbria 51
Skipness castle 128
Sky Hill, battle of 20, 41–2, 152
Skye, Isle of ix, 1, 6, 20, 62, 78, 146
Sleat 78; MacDonalds of 31, 149, 152, 163; 'Hugh MacDonald' of 31, 148; *History of the MacDonalds* 31–3, 35–6, 39–43, 64–6, 75–7, 92, 98, 104–5, 109–11, 113, 115–7, 119–20, 126, 128–9, 133, 136, 148–9, 151, 153
Smyth, Alfred P. 17, 18, 25, 146, 158
Somerled: birth 22; name and parentage 23–6, 147; maternal descent 23–6; paternal descent 26–9; genealogies of 26–9, 162; claim for Norse descent 27–8; claim for descent from Gothfrith mac Fergus and Colla Uais 28–9; traditional sources for 29–30, 31; emergence and battle in Morvern 34–42; marriage to Ragnhild 43–4; offspring of 74–7; rise to lordship of Argyll 42–5; political status as *regulus* 47–8; involvement with Mac Heth rebellion 42–3, 63–7, 73; relations with David I 45–8, 149; ambitions on kingdom of the Isles 73–4; Epiphany battle 79–80, 83–6; division of the Isles with k. Man 86–8, 91–2; seapower and association with galleys 63, 81–3, 99–101; power base 88–9; raid on Man 89–91; relations with Malcolm IV 66, 93–4, 96–8; *concordia* with Malcolm IV 96, 134; invasion of the Clyde 25, 98–105, 143–4; death of 99, 105–12; place of burial 113, 115–20, 128, 156; foundation of Saddell 118, 120; piety and interest in Iona 120–1, 123–4, 127–8; translation of Domnall Ban to Iona 131–4; recognition by Irish sources 135–6; hostility of Scottish chroniclers 48–50, 97, 135–7; appreciation in Clan Donald tradition 135–6; claims for him as 'Viking' and 'Celtic hero' 136–8, 142; claim for his 'Gaelic revival' 138–142; significance in history of Gaelic Scotland 136, 142–4
Somerled, s. Jarl Sigurd 23, 28
'Somerled the Hold' 105–7
Staffa, Isle of 146
Stamford Bridge, battle of 19
Standard, battle of The 44–5, 47, 49, 57–8
Stephen, k. England 44, 57–8
Stewart, house of 102–4, 143–4
Stracathro, battle of 55–6
Strathclyde 4
Sutherland 47, 50, 157
Svein Asleifsson 9, 105–6

Thomson, Derick 41
Thorfinn, jarl of Orkney 19, 31–2
Thorfinn, s. Ottar 72–4, 79, 100
Tiree, Isle of 20, 78, 146
Torf-Einar, jarl of Orkney 40, 42
Toulouse, siege of 94–5

Ui Maic Uais 29, 30
Ui Neill 15
Uist 20, 78, 146; Carinish 127, 156
Uspak (Hakon), s. Dugall 156, 157, 163

Walter fitz-Alan the Steward 102–3, 113
Waterford 8
Watson, W. J. 145(n.6 ref. p.4)
Whithorn 66
William, 'Glasgow cleric' 107–8; see also *Carmen de morte Sumerledi*
William (I) the Conqueror, k. England 52, 53
William the Lion, k. Scots 78
William of Newburgh (*Chronicle*) 59–61
William (II) Rufus, k. England 53, 54
Wimund, bp. Man 59–62
Wyntoun, Andrew of (*Chronicle*) 132
Wyre, 'Cubbie Roo's Castle' on 88

Yeoman, Peter 116
York 25, 77–8; Thomas, a/bp. 61–2
Young, G. V. C. 152